AF658816

Theories and Techniques of
Marketing Management

Theories and Techniques of
Marketing Management

Vinod Patel

Oxford Book Company
Jaipur ▪ New Delhi

Published By

Oxford Book Company

Regd. Off. "Bony Residency", Gate No. 2
Opp. Tilak Public School, Vishweswariya Nagar,
Gopalpura Road, Jaipur - 302018, India
Ph: 0141 - 2761280, Telefax: 2761381
email - oxfordbookjpr@gmail.com
website - oxfordbookcompany.com

Delhi Office: 102, 1st Floor, Satyam House,
4327/3, Ansari Road, Darya Ganj,
New Delhi - 110002, India
Ph: 011-45652440

Distributed by

KEYA INTERNATIONAL PRESS LLP
E-mail: keyainternationalpressllp@gmail.com

Published in India, 2025

© All Rights Reserved

ISBN : 9788189473037

All Rights Reserved. No part of this publication may be reproduced, stored in a retrieval system, or transmitted, in any form or by any means, electronic, mechanical, photocopying, recording, scanning or otherwise, without the prior written permission of the copyright owner.

Typeset by Shivangi Computers, Jaipur

Printed and bound in India by Replika Press Pvt. Ltd.

PREFACE

Producers and consumers both undertake one or other kind of marketing activities to facilitate convenient transfer of goods and services. Marketing management involves planning, organising, directing and controlling of all marketing activities and has become very important for promotion of sales as well as consumers' satisfaction. Being an important operative function, it performs all managerial functions in the field of marketing. It is concerned with the direction of purposeful activities towards the achievement of marketing goals and looks after the production and sales of those goods and services which provide maximum satisfaction to the consumer. It increases the efficiency and effectiveness of marketing activities of organisation and implies coordination of several factors for mutual gain. Marketing management, as such, is the marketing concept in action.

The fully qualified marketing management team has a thorough understanding of the various activities that make up the marketing person's job, is aware of problems that marketing-people are likely to encounter, and is prepared to make practical suggestions for their solutions. Besides having practical experience, the marketing management should have a keen grasp of the theoretical aspects of marketing techniques. In addition, marketing management should have knowledge as to how the theories relate to field experience and work out in actual practice. The present book is an endeavour to bring before the readers various elements of marketing and marketing management, theories and techniques of marketing management combining both theoretical and practical aspects.

Vinod Patel

Contents

1

Marketing Management and Marketing Functions

Essentially, the marketing function is aimed at providing and distributing foods and services as required by the customers and in a manner which is at once efficient and economical.

The marketing functions may be classified as follows:

Marketing Functions

I- *Functions of Exchange*

1 Buying and Assembling

1 Selling and Dividing

II- *Functions of Physical Supply*

1 Transportation

1 Storage or Warehousing

III- *Facilitating Functions*

1 Marketing Research

1 Product Planning and Development

1 Standardisation and Grading

1 Packaging

1 Branding

1 Pricing

1 Promotion (advertising and sales promotion)

1 Financing

1 Risk-taking

Functions of Exchange

Exchange functions involve transfer of ownership. Ownership transfers occurs reportedly as physical products flow from producers to final buyers. Where physical products pass through different channels of distribution before reaching the final buyers, there may be more than one transfer of ownership. For example, when a manufacturer sells his output to wholesalers who, in turn resell it to retailers who, again in turn, resell it to consumers, the ownership in the product will be transferred thrice.

For affecting the transfer of ownership it is necessary that goods are both bought and sold. It is only the manufacturer who will only sell, though he is also engaged in buying raw material, stores, etc.

In the case of services, ownership transfer is not in the same sense as in the case of physical products. In this case the consumers obtain the right to consume or enjoy the services.

Buying and Assembling

Buying is the step in the process of making. A manufacturer has to buy his requirements of raw materials. The traders or the middlemen have to buy finished products from the manufactures. Efficient buying is essential for successful selling. It will enable the manufacturers or the traders to earn profits.

Buying refers to decision-making regarding:

(1) determination of business needs;

(2) the quantity to be purchased;

(3) the price;

(4) determining the time when goods will be needed; and

(5) determining the suppliers from whom purchases are to be made.

The goods may be purchased in any of the following ways, namely:

(1) by inspection;

(2) by samples or pattern; and

(3) by description of brand.

Buying by inspection involves inspection of the whole lot of goods proposed to be purchased. Buying by samples involves checking of a representative sample of goods before purchases. Buying by description is employed in the case of branded goods which have become popular through advertising. Purchase of goods mentioned in the catalogues and price list of the suppliers may also be referred to as purchasing by description.

There may be other kinds of buying such as:

(1) Forward buying which is made to accumulate goods in order to gain from price increases;

(2) contract buying under which goods are purchased from suppliers over a period of time under long term contracts; and

(3) concentrated buying which is resorted to when sources of supply are limited.

Assembling implies seeking out sources of supply; buying wisely to quality, quantity and variety, and making commodities available when and where they are wanted. The assembling function is performed in the case of goods which are purchased at different centres and which cannot be purchased by the manufacturers unless they are made available in large quantities. Thus, a manufacturer assembles raw materials to ensure smooth production while a trader assembles goods produced by a number of manufacturers.

Selling and Dividing

Marketing is basically concerned with bringing the buyers and the sellers together. It seeks to ensure that the right product is made available at the right place in the right quantity at the right place and at the right time to the consumer. This can be achieved only by performing the selling function.

Selling may be defined as affecting transfer of ownership in goods by the seller to the buyer in exchange for money. It may also be described as the dispersion function of marketing. It involves a process whereby the seller ascertains, activates and satisfies the needs or wants of the buyer to the mutual continuous benefits of both the buyer as well as the seller.

Functions of Physical Supply

Physical supply of marketing is concerned with imparting place and time utility to the goods. It consists in transfer of goods from one place to another and in storing the goods for use in the future.

Transport

Transport means conveyance, carriage and movement of materials and goods from one place to another. It plays an important role in marketing. It serves as a link between the producer and the consumer who may be separated by long distances. It helps in buying, assembling and selling of goods. It creates place utility by moving the materials and goods from the places where they are available in plenty, to places where they are in short supply. In the absence of quick and easy modes of transport, producers would not produce more than what the local markets could absorb, and the consumers would not be able to consume what is not produced locally.

Land, water and air transport are the various modes of transportation of goods and materials.

The decision as regards the choice of a particular mode of transport will have to be made keeping in view (1) the cost of transport; (2) speed; (3) flexibility; (4) reliability; and (5) availability of different modes of transport.

Warehousing

Warehousing refers to the holding and preservation of goods till the time they are sold and delivered to the customers.

In the present-day world, production of goods is largely in anticipation of demand. This necessitates a time-gap between production and consumption of goods. In the case of goods with seasonal production or demand, such time gap is inevitable.

Warehouses enable storage of goods till there is demand for them. They can also be used to store the raw materials in adequate quantity to carry on the production activity smoothly without any interruption. Other important functions of warehouses are creation of time utility, price stabilisation and safe custody of goods.

There are three types of warehouses, namely, private, public and bonded warehouses. Private warehouses are owned and operated by large manufacturers and traders. Public warehouses may be owned and operated by private individuals or groups thereof. They have to work under a licence in accordance with the prescribed rules and regulations. Any member of the public is free to make use of such warehouses, which provide excellent storage facilities at nominal cost.

Bonded warehouses are operated by the government mainly at ports. They are used to store dutiable goods, i.e., goods that are liable to customs duty. Duty on such goods does not become payable until they are removed from warehouse. The owner of the goods cannot interfere with them without the permission of the customs authorities.

Facilitating Functions

Facilitating functions are aimed at assisting the processes of exchange and physical supply of goods.

Marketing Research

Marketing research may be defined as the gathering, recording and analysis of all facts about any problem relating to the transfer and sale of goods and services from the producer to consumer.

Objectives

The objectives of marketing research are to determine:

(1) the degree up to which a product would be acceptable to consumers and the consumers' preference for any variation of the product;

(2) the reasons for particular consumer preferences;

(3) the time when the products are needed;

(4) the price which would be acceptable; and

(5) the most appropriate method of advertising.

Need for Marketing Research

As production is in advance of selling, marketing research assumes importance for the following reasons:

(1) The producer should aim at consumer satisfaction, in other words, he should market not what he is already producing, or what he considers to be convenient, efficient or attractive to market. Rather, he should market what his customers want.

(2) In order to avail the benefits of large-scale production, it is necessary to produce the goods in quantities that are most economical. Marketing research enables the enterprise to assess the extent of demand.

(3) Assessment of consumers' reaction to the product and his preference for any variation would enable advertising to be directed to exploit particular attitudes.

(4) Since production would involve sizeable expenditure, it is necessary for enterprise to estimate beforehand the quantity of goods that could be sold easily.

(5) Changes in the market as regards population, fashions social habits or attitudes, etc., may alter the demand for a product. It is necessary for the enterprise to assess the impact of these changes on the sales of its products.

(6) The enterprise must know the extent of competition prevailing in the market as regards the type of goods produced by it. This will enable it to make correct decision about the products to be marketed.

Types of Research

Marketing research will comprise product research, pricing research, distribution channel research, promotion research, etc. It may be undertaken by first defining the problem, collecting and analysing relevant information and data, identification and evaluation of alternative solution, and prescription of the solution which is the most favourable.

Both primary and secondary data are used in conducting market research. Primary data may be obtained from salesmen, dealers and customers. Secondary data may be obtained from various research publications and trade journals.

Research Techniques

The techniques employed for the purpose of carrying out the research may in the form of:

(1) *Quantitative surveys,* showing volumes of sales, indicating trends in various components of the market.

(2) *Attitude surveys,* involving use of appropriate methods to discover consumer attitudes by means of interviews, discussions, etc.

(3) *Test marketing,* involving a detailed examination of buying patterns in a limited area.

(4) *User tests,* showing first-hand reports from consumers after the use of a particular product.

(5) *Retail audits,* comprising surveys carried out at selected shops to ascertain the demand for competing products.

Uses of Marketing Research

Marketing research may be used for the following purposes:

(1) to ascertain the position of enterprise in the industry;

(2) to indicate the present and further trends of the industry;

(3) to help in development and introduction of new products;

(4) to improve sales of the existing products;

(5) to assess and improve the effectiveness of sales management; and

(6) to reduce the risks involved in marketing decision.

Products Planning and Management

Any product can be marketed successfully only when it possesses the characteristics which are in close conformity with the needs and desires of the buyers. This calls for frequent adaptation of the product to afford maximum satisfaction and utility to the present and prospective buyers.

It is the responsibility of the marketing department to design and develop the right type of products, including introduction of new products, improvement of the existing products, and dropping out products which have ceased to be popular with the consumers.

A company not engaged in appropriate product planning and development is bound, sooner rather than later, to face elimination for the market.

In the case of industries such as pharmaceuticals and electronics, there have been rapid changes over the past years and only companies which have kept themselves in step with changes have continued to survive and grow.

Standardisation and Grading

Standardisation is rightly a facilitating function of marketing because, it help in efficient performance of marketing functions, particularly those relating to buying and selling by sample and description. Standardisation means the production of such goods as will be uniformly of the same specification with regard to shape, size, colour, materials, performance, etc.

If a commodity is to be produced on a large scale by mass production methods, it will have to be standardised for the sake of availing economies of scale. The extent to which variety is required, is a limiting factor on the scale of production. However, standardisation is possible only if buyers are prepared to accept some restriction of choice.

Standardisation also helps in efficient and cost effective advertising.

Grading involves a division of products into classes made of units possessing similar characteristics of size and quality. Grading is not necessary in the case of most manufactured goods because they possess uniform characteristics. However, in the case of raw materials and other agricultural products, grading in accordance with fixed or varying standards of quality becomes necessary.

Grading enables the manufacturers to produce standardised goods. It removes the elements of uncertainty from buying. It facilitates the sale by sample and description. It enables the seller to obtain a better price for his goods.

Pricing

The price of a product relative to the quality, quantity and the package of the product will in a measure determine the consumers' attitude towards the enterprise. The level at which an enterprise sets its prices will affect both its sales and profitability. In some cases, it may be more profitable for an enterprise to concentrate on the more limited demand market. While the economic law of supply and demand, i.e., the lower the price the greater the demand, will apply in general to all pricing decisions, the demand for certain products displays greater sensitivity to price changes. Products with greater demand elasticity will have far less demand when the prices are increased. As against this, products with less demand elasticity will not be affected in the same proportion as increase in the price.

Pricing of products is also affected by considerations of availability of substitute products, durability and ability to postpone purchase, income, population and the prices of competing products.

While population and availability of disposable income with the people may influence the decision regarding the price determination, factors such as current fashion, individual tastes, prestige, imitation of others, convenience or security will also have an effect on price determination and buying behaviour of the people. In fact, certain products will sell more only if they are priced relatively high.

Among the many problems facing the setting up of the price of a product, the following bear special mention:

(1) The price of a new products is relatively more different to set as compared to the old and tried products.

(2) It is difficult to assess changes in the price of competitive products. Determination of the middle man's margin also poses problems.

(3) In case of two or more products having inter-related production cost, price setting for each create problems of allocations of costs.

(4) In any case the determination of the appropriate timings, frequency and amount of price changes is not an easy task.

Price determination in the case of products of an enterprise will also have to take into account the objectives, policies and constraints of the enterprise and the management. The areas which require decision-making in this respect may be as follows:

(1) Does the enterprise intend to project and image of quality producer of goods and services and identify this with price levels?

(2) Does the enterprise have short-term and long-term objectives in terms of overall profitability and the extent to which these objectives are to affect the pricing of products, regardless of whether they are new or well established?

(3) Does the enterprise intend to follow discriminatory pricing such that it wants to set it lower prices for the same goods is selected markets and a higher price in other?

(4) Does the company intend to retain its share in the existing market?

(5) Is the enterprise prepared to sacrifice short-term profits in favour of long-term objectives?

(6) Does the company propose to assume price leadership so as to gain from competitive price stability at a later stage?

(7) To what extent will the company co-exist with price-cutting measures adopted by its competitors?

Packaging

Packaging may be considered from three basic standpoints, namely,

(1) as productive device;

(2) as a product utility factor; and

(3) as a form of sales promotion.

A package on the shelf of a retail store and in the kitchen of a housewife is a form of an advertising. Where buying depends to a considerable extent on impulse, package shape or colour may be the major means of creating product preference. An ideal packing should have the following features:

(1) easy identification in all selling situations particularly vis-à-vis competitive products;

(2) effective appeal both in the shop and in the household;

(3) easy conversion of cartons or outer covers into display material;

(4) impact of product visibility, i.e., use of glass containers, visible packs, etc.;

(5) impact of colour; and

(6) the plus and minus points of returnable and non-returnable packaging.

Branding

Branding means giving a name to a product by which it should become known and be remembered by the consumers. The brand name distinguishes the products manufactured by one producer from those manufactured by others. Branded goods are also easy to be identified by the consumers.

Branding may be done in any of the following ways: (1) *symbols* and *marks* which may be used as brand names, such as, Wolf tools, Charminar cigarettes, etc.; (2) *special names,* which may be given for branded products such as Lux toilet soap, Maruti car, etc.; (3) *the name of the manufacturer,* which may be used as a brand name such as Tata textiles, Bata shoes, etc.

Branding results in several advantages to the manufacturers. For example, by repeating the brand name through advertise-ments in mass media, the products may carve a special place for themselves in the market. The brand name in course of time becomes its own advertising. In many cases brands are generally accepted as the very proof of quality of the products concerned. Branded goods may be sold straightaway to the consumers without availing the services of middlemen.

Channels of Distribution

The term channels of distribution refers to the systems of marketing institutions through which goods or services are transferred from the original producers to the ultimate users or consumers. Among the important institution which act as channels of distribution, the important ones are:

(1) retailers;

(2) wholesalers;

(3) agents and brokers; and

(4) facilitating institutions such as commodity exchanges, trade associations, freight carriers, and so on.

Decision-making as regards channels of distribution must ultimately be based on whether the producer wants to carry out the basic marketing processes himself or through the various channels. No doubt channels of distribution will mean increase in costs but it can be justified in terms of economic advantages such as increased profitability, market penetration, etc.

The choice of a particular channel will ordinarily be influenced by the following factors:

Product Factors

(1) **Unit Price:** A product which is priced too high will generally have short channel. Since demand for such a product will be limited, the producer can easily sell it directly to the consumers. As against this, a low-priced product with heavy demand will often have a long channel because of the producer's inability to deal directly with a number of consumers.

(2) **Weight and Size:** A product which is bulky or heavy in weight will generally have a short channel because of the high cost of transportation. As against, small or light-weight goods may often have a long channel.

(3) **Standardised or Job-based Production:** Where a product is manufactured according to standardised specifications, it will have a long channel because of universal demand. As against this, if a product is made to order in accordance with individual customer's taste and preference, it will possible a short channel because of the need of direct contact, as far as possible, between the buyer and the producer.

(4) **After-sales Service:** If the product requires servicing or other attention after its sale, it will have a short channel. If it can do without after-sale service, it may have a long channel.

(5) **Nature of Product:** A perishable product cannot have a long channel since time is of the essence of its saleability. A non-perishable product, on the other hand, can do with a long channel.

(6) **Seasonal Goods:** A product which has demand only in a particular season will often have a short channel because of the reluctance of middlemen to take the risk of blocking of capital. As against this, if a product is sold round the year may have a long channel.

Market Factors

(1) **Size of Market:** The larger the size of the market to be approached, the longer will be the channel. As against this, if a product is sold in a limited area, it will have a channel.

(2) **Nature of Consumers:** If a product is meant for personal use of the consumers, it may have a long channel. But if it is bought by industrial users who generally prefer to get their supplies directly from the producers, it will have a short channel.

(3) **Geographical Coverage:** In a densely populated area, the producer may profit more by dealing directly with consumers, thus shortening the channel. As against this, if the population is spread over a larger area in small pockets, there will have to be a long channel.

Consumer Factors

(1) **Number of Consumers:** The larger the number of customers, the longer will be the distribution channel and *vice versa.* The other influencing factors will be the concentration of dispersal of customers over the area.

(2) **Quantity of Goods to be Purchased:** Where a product is bought in large quantities, it may be beneficial for the producer to have direct dealings with consumers or have the distribution channel as short as possible. However, if the product is sold in small quantities, there may have to be a long channel.

(3) **Need for Credit:** Where goods are required to be sold on credit, the producer will need a long channel as it would facilitate recovery of dues. As against his, where goods are sold for cash, a short channel may also be helpful.

Middlemen Factors

(1) **Availability:** The length or shortness of the channel will often depend on the availability of middlemen and their willingness to act according to the producers' bidding.

(2) **Cost:** If the price of a product is likely to increase to an unreasonable extent due to intervention of middlemen, the channel ought to be kept short. As against this, if middlemen charge reasonably for the services rendered by them, the channel may be allowed to be long.

(3) **Contribution to Increased Sales:** The producer will require the services of middlemen only when he is convinced that by doing so, he would be able to sell more. If middlemen do not contribute to increased sales, the channel may be kept as short as possible.

Manufacturer Factors

(1) **Financial Soundness:** A financially sound producer can sell goods direct to big consumers and realise the sale proceeds at their convenience. But if the producer cannot afford to block his capital in this manner he will have to seek middleman so as to ensure so as to quick availability of funds.

(2) **Marketing Policies:** If a producer believes in establishing direct contact with his consumers, he will eliminate most of the middlemen such that the distribution attract only the customers belonging to the upper strata of society, he will have to bank on middlemen such that the channel will be long.

Advertising and Sales Promotion

Advertising is the non-personal communication directed at target audiences through various media in order to present and promote products, services and ideas. The cost of media space, time, advertisement production, is borne by the sponsor of sponsors.

Advertising should be distinguished from publicity by means of which an organisation derives benefits from favourable free showing, description and discussion of its products in a variety of media.

Retailers, wholesalers, trade shows, exhibitions, samples, special offers and demonstration are classified as sales promotion.

Advertising is an important element of marketing strategy - though it is difficult to measure its contribution to profits. However, the objectives of advertising will greatly contribute to assessment of an advertising campaign. The following may be stated to be the objectives of advertising:

(1) to ensure potential customers of a new product of services;

(2) to indicate new users of an existing product;

(3) to remind customers of existing products in order to maintain loyalty against competing pressures;

(4) to provide information about significant qualities of a product;

(5) to stimulate inquiries;

(6) to give reasons why middlemen should stock a product;

(7) to provide technical information about a product;

(8) to build a corporate company image; and

(9) to give information on price change, special offers, etc.

Meaning of Marketing

There can be no precise, all-purpose definition of marketing. This is owing to two reasons. One, at each stage of its evolution, hitherto unknown potentialities of the marketing function came to light. Secondly, marketing does not thus far have recognised theoretical base.

The following definition highlight different aspects of marketing:

(1) **Edward Cundiff and Richard Still:** "Marketing is the managerial process by which products are matched with markets and through which the consumer is enabled to use or enjoy the product."

(2) **E.F.L Brech:** "Marketing is the process of determing consumer demand for a product or service, motivating it sales, and distributing in into ultimate consumption at a profit."

(3) **Philip Kotler:** "Marketing is specifically concerned with how transactions are created, stimulated, facilitated and valued."

(4) **William Stanton:** "Marketing is a total system of interacting business activities designed to plan, price, promote and distribute want satisfying products and services to present and potential customer."

These definitions bring into focus the following features of marketing:

Marketing as Management Functions

Marketing as an operational management function is as important as production, personnel or finance functions. For this reason, it involves planning, organisation, direction, coordination and control of activities concerning marketing of goods and services produced by an enterprise.

- **Meaning of Marketing Management**
- **As Management Function**
- **Products being Subject-matter of Marketing**
- **Buying/Consumption an Essential Pre-requisite**
- **Motivations of Sales**
- **Instrument of Improved Standards of Living**

Marketing and production activities are highly interlocked. Only those goods and services can be marketed that can be produce, and only those goods and services should be produce which can be marketed. In this sense, marketing is a managerial function which is concerned with matching specific products with specific markets. In association with the production department, the marketing department is involved in decision-making concerning selection, manufacture and marketing of products that posses as many of the characteristics as are desired by the people who constitute the market while, at the sometime, seeking to achieve the profitability goals of the enterprise.

Products as Subject-matter of Marketing

Marketing is not concerned with tangible goods alone. It plays a similar role in respect of distribution of services. Thus, if a car manufacturer is interested in information as regards potential buyers, the types of care needed by them, as also the channels through which these could be made available to them, so is an insurance company which is in business of providing insurance coverage.

Buying/Consumption is Pre-requisite to Marketing

All marketing activity is directed at the existing and potential users and consumers of goods and services marketed by the producer. Movement of goods from the producer is in anticipation of the goods being bought by the users. Distribution of services is in anticipation of the services being consumed by the users. In other words, marketing will be a useless exercise if goods are not purchased by the users, or services are not consumed by the users.

Movement of goods from the producer to the final user results in transfer of ownership. In case the goods move through various channels of distribution, there is transfer of ownership every time the goods change hands. As regards services, the consumers obtain the right to consume or enjoy the services. But whether it is acquisition of ownership by the buyer, or right of consumption by the user, it is always in consideration of payment of the price demanded by the producer/supplier.

Motivation of Sales

Having been instrumental in ensuring production of desired products, marketing management is next concerned with decision-making as regards pricing, selling, advertising, other promotional activities, transport, etc., to motivate and facilitate sales.

Instrument of Improved Standards of Living

Through creation of time, place and possession utilities, marketing process makes it possible for consumers to use and enjoy the products of their choice at the time and place of their liking. By marketing available useful and quality goods at reasonable prices, marketing helps in improving living standards of people.

When the term "Marketing or distribution is used in the physical distribution it conveys the meaning of 'transporting' the goods to ultimate consumers through different channels of distribution of direct from the producer." Marketing, thus, assumes the role of customer satisfying process, which is quite distinct from that of goods-producing process. The marketing management has, therefore, to strike a balance between the production and distribution in such a manner which helps both the producer to get his produce moving and the consumer to get his satisfaction with fair amount of consumers surplus.

Marketing as a Business Function

In traditional sense, says F.E. Clark, "marketing consists of those efforts which affect transfers in ownership goods and care for their physical distribution." When viewed in economic terms marketing is "creation of time, place and ownership utilities."

Marketing as a business function is "the movement of goods and services from the producer to the user." To produce is not sufficient. Neither it is the acid test of business success unless it is sold at a reasonable profit to those who are prepared to buy at a reasonable price which for them is satisfying and worth parting with. Marketing as a philosophy is "a customers'-satisfying process."

Definition of Marketing

(1) "Marketing is the delivery of a standard of living to society." **—Paul Mazur**

(2) "Marketing is the creation and delivery of a standard of living to society." **—Professor McNair**

(3) "Marketing is the performance of business activities that direct the flow of goods and services from producer to consumer or user." **—American Marketing Association**

(4) "Marketing involves the design of products acceptable to the consumers and the transfer of ownership between seller and buyer." **—Herry Hansen**

(5) "Marketing is a total system of interacting business activities designed to plan, price, promote, and distribute want-satisfying products and services to present and potential customers." **—William Stanton**

From the above definitions, it is clear that different thinkers have defined the terms in different contexts. But all agree that marketing is s business activity which directs the flow of goods and services from producer to the user. Marketing as a function has been viewed from different angles by different thinkers. Different views as expressed above in the five definitions may be summarised in the following few words:

(1) From Society's Points of View: Marketing is a creation and distribution of standard of living to the society. Marketing is instrumental in spreading the civilisation throughout the world.

(2) As a Factual, Descriptive and Operative Thinking: Marketing is nothing but transfer of goods and services to those, who are prepared to pay for the same.

(3) From Legal Point of View: Marketing is considered to be the transfer of ownership from producer to user against payment.

(4) As a Combination of Traditional and Modern Concepts: Marketing is an activity of satisfying the consumer by selling the goods and services to him.

(5) From Management's Point of View: Marketing is planning, promoting and distributing the goods and services in a manner in which it satisfies ultimate consumer. "Marketing is not any activity," opines *M.C. Shukla*, "nor is it exactly the sum of several, rather, it is the result of the interaction of many activities. "For him marketing is a *Managerial function which starts with the product and ends with the complete satisfaction of the consumer's want.*

Modern Concept of Marketing

Above discussions make it abundantly clear that traditionally marketing a business function which is engaged in bringing together both the seller and the buyer at a place where they can meet and transact business to the mutual satisfaction of both. But marketing has now crossed the traditional barrier. It is something more than what the traditionalists have thought of. The modern concept views marketing as the entire business process and not as an isolated and separate functional process.

The total or modern concept is 'marketing-minded' and it considers the consumer as the sole factor around whom the whole business activity clusters. Nothing in the modern concept is considered in isolation. Every action is consumer-oriented. What he wants, at what price he wants, what satisfies him and to what extent competitors are trying to allure him are some of the questions which every marketing management is to answer. Today marketing is not considered to be a meeting ground to both buyers and sellers but it is now considered in its totality taking the consumer as a moving factor. Modern concept of marketing is consumer-oriented. It is a *state of mind* of both owners and managers to plan and to execute the production and distribution plans making the consumer a *constant focal point* of all their business activities.

Functions of Marketing

The total or modern concept of marketing envisages the adjustment of production of goods and services to the needs of consumers.

Consumption is the sole aim of any production. Adam Smith, the noted economist, has said long ago that "consumption is the sole end and purpose of all production." Marketing management considers the journey through which the goods and services produced passed before reaching to the hands of the ultimate consumer. It is the entire journey of goods and services which forms the marketing functions.

Firstly, marketing function can broadly be divided into the following two processes.

(1) **The Process of Concentration:** Which consists of collection of goods and services at a place where the sellers and buyers are expected to meet for transacting the business.

(2) **The Process of Dispersion:** Which comprises the distribution activity. The process delivers the goods and services to the ultimate consumer after the deal is struck between the seller and the purchaser.

The above two processes involve many auxiliary functions which facilitate the marketing of goods and services. The whole of marketing functions may be depicted with the help of the following chart.

Functions of Marketing
(Two Processes)

↓

Process of Concentration — Process of Dispersion

↓ ↓

→ **Auxiliary Functions** ←

Merchandising Functions	General Functions	Distribution Functions of Sales Functions or Actual Selling
(1) Buying: Determining Needs	(1) Financing	(1) Creation of Demand
-Source of Supply	(2) Record Keeping	(2) Source of Demand
-Negotiating Terms	(3) Future Trading	(3) Educating the Buyer
-Transfer of Title	(4) Insuring against Risks Involved	(4) Setting the Terms
-Payment or Arrangement for credit		(5) Transfer of Title, i.e., the Delivery
(2) Assembling		(6) Receipt of Payment, i.e., Collection or Extension of Credit and/or Maturity Arranging for Receipt of Payment
(3) Standardising		
(4) Grading and branding		
(5) Storing		
(6) Transporting		
(7) Packing, Packaging and Processing		

Importance of Marketing

The process of marketing is concerned with relating the needs and desires of people with the goods and services offered by the producer. While there can be no marketing without production, similarly there can be no production without effective and efficient marketing.

The importance of marketing is brought out by the following:

(1) Increase in National Income: Efficient marketing of goods and services results in substantial reduction in the cost of distribution, thus leading to lower prices for the consumers. In turn, this results in an increase in national income.

(2) Production of Socially Useful Products: Marketing involves a regular interactio with the present and potential users and consumers of goods and services with a view to ascertaining their needs and desires. This facilitates production of socially useful goods and services.

(3) Improvement in Living Standards: The marketing process aims at making available to the consumers goods and services which have been perfected after years of intensive research and experimentation. This has the effect of raising living standards and improving quality of life in general.

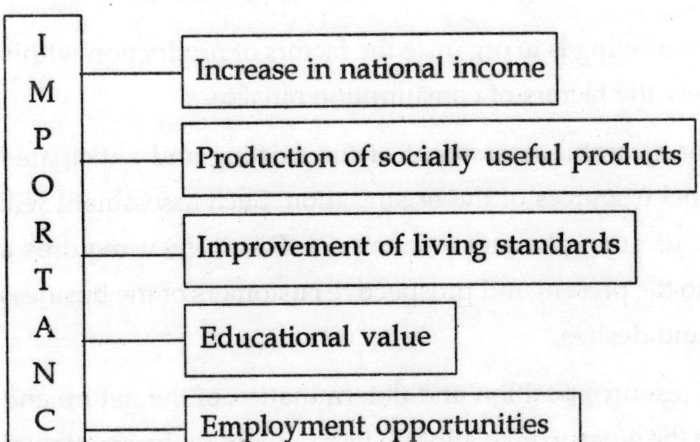

(4) Educational Value: Through competent advertising and salesmanship, marketing serves to educate the people about the availability of goods and services which would best fulfil their needs and desires. It is only due to marketing that goods and services which were till recently considered as a luxury, have become necessaries today.

(5) **Employment Opportunities:** Marketing has created substantial employment opportunities. In India, around 40 million people are engaged in wholesale and retail business alone. Add to it those engaged in transportation of goods, warehousing, advertising and salesmanship, and one can have an idea about the huge employment potential that marketing has.

In the USA, about one-third of people employed are engaged in the field of marketing.

Objectives of Marketing

The main objectives of marketing may be stated as follows:

(1) To secure consumer satisfaction.

(2) To achieve organisational integration.

(3) To attain profitability of operations.

(4) To serve the society.

Consumer Satisfaction

An important objective of marketing is to organise the factors of production within the organisation keeping in view the factors of consumption outside.

To begin with, this calls for a careful assessment of the existing and anticipated physical, financial and personnel resources of the organisation. Such assessment will enable the enterprise to know its strengths and weaknesses. Secondly, it requires a thorough understanding of who the present and prospective customers of the business are, and what are their wants and desires.

Assessment of the internal resource position and determination of the nature and strength of demand will enable the enterprise to allocate its resources to the creation of supplies of the required goods and services. The next step is to adopt suitable pricing, distribution and promotion policies to ensure that the goods and services do, in fact, reach the consumers for who they are intended.

Consumers are the targets of the marketing function. All marketing activities begin and end with the consumer. In the present-day world, it is not possible to sell whatever one produces. It is not the products but the satisfactions are sold. It would be suicidal for an enterprise to view marketing in terms of its product offering. It should rather see it in a larger perspective of the fundamental needs and desires of customers which its products are going to satisfy.

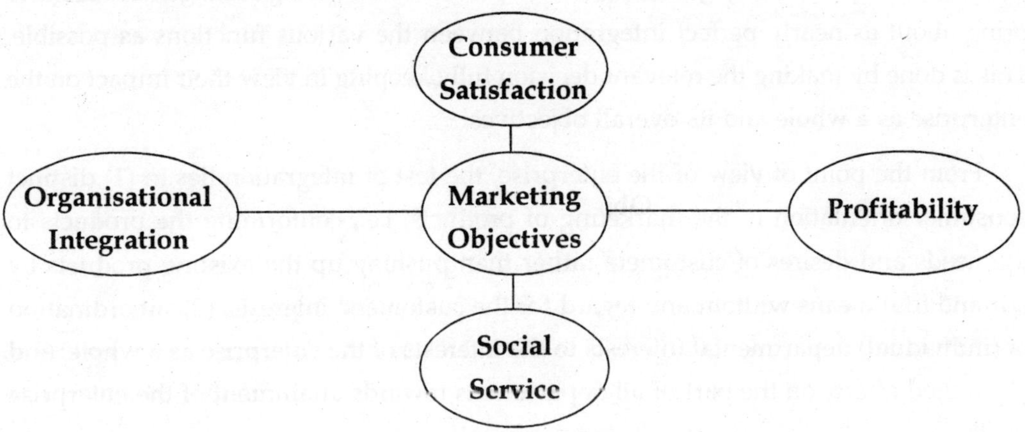

Organisational Integration

As an enterprise grows, function such as production, finance, and marketing get more complex and are, therefore, split in to smaller parts.

While the object of such sub-division is to benefit from specialisation, and unintended consequence is decreasing communication between functional department, and between sub-departments within the same functional department. This often leads to conflict as regards departmental goals.

Thus, while the production department is excessively interested in reduction of costs, the sales department seeks single-mindedly to increase sales. The production department's emphasis is on reduction in the number of products, standardisation of the product variety, longer time-interval between the model changes, and all such measures as would minimise costs of production. The sales department seeks to pursue wholly opposite goals, such as, increasing the number of products, wider variety, frequent model changes, lower pricing, and so on. The finance department may come forth with its own priorities which may be contrary to the goals of both production and sales department. It may, for example, oppose expenditure on research and development or innovation which, though beneficial in the long-run, may cost a large sum in the initial years. On top of it, it may prefer to go in for short-term small gains to keep the shareholders satisfied even if this is at the expense of customer's interests.

To be able to accomplish its objective of assuring consumer satisfaction within the framework of profitability goals of the enterprise, the marketing management seeks to bring about as nearly perfect integration between the various functions as possible. This is done by making the relevant decision fully keeping in view their impact on the enterprise as a whole and its overall objectives.

From the point of view of the enterprise, the test of integration lies in (1) distinct consumer orientation in the marketing of products, i.e., conforming the products to the needs and desires of customers rather than pushing up the existing products by fair and foul means without any regard for the customers' interests; (2) subordination of (individual) departmental interests to the interests of the enterprise as a whole; and (3) unified efforts on the part of all departments towards attainment of the enterprise goals.

Profitability

A business enterprise is an economic institution. It is required to generate profits from sale of the goods and services produced by it. Moreover, it has to earn profits on a sufficiently regular basis so as to be able to pay a return on the capital invested by the owners (shareholders), as also to set apart funds for future growth and to meet unforeseen business situations.

The profit goal of an enterprise is of vital interest to its marketing department. This is because profits materialise from sale of goods and services and it is the responsibility of the marketing department to affect the sales. However, sales will be possible only when customers are created and retained, and customers can be created and retained only if the goods and services produced by the enterprise satisfy them in terms of meeting their needs and desires. Thus, profitability of an enterprise is intimately linked with ability to provide customer satisfaction.

Profitability to an enterprise can be increased by either increasing the sales volume or by cutting down the costs production and distribution. Increase in sales will result in increase in profits, irrespective of smallness of the profit margin in the price. Increased efficiency in production and distribution methods will result in increase in profits even if the sales volume remains unchanged. It should be the objective of the marketing function to adopt both the strategies simultaneously to increase profitability of the enterprise.

Increase in sales volume can be brought about by (1) *market development,* i.e., selling of existing products in new markets; (2) *product development,* i.e., developing new products for sale in existing markets; (3) *market penetration,* i.e., increasing the sales of existing production in the existing markets; and (4) *diversification,* i.e., developing new products for sale in new markets. However, in each case, careful cost benefit analysis will have to be made for the strategy to be adopted to push up profitability. In other worlds, not only the financial costs of the proposed strategy but also the social, legal and ethical implications will have to be taken into account.

The question of pricing the products also has an important bearing on profitability. Pricing of the goods may be cost-based, demand-based or competition based. Cost-based pricing takes into account the production and distribution costs of the goods and services, with an appropriate profit margin added to these while determining the price. Demand-based pricing means adjustment of the price to the market conditions such that a higher price may be charged for goods and services with greater demand without consideration to the costs incurred. Under competition-based pricing, goods and services may be priced at a level which may be higher, lower or equal to that charged by competitors. However, while marketing a decision on pricing, it is useful to remember that marketing involves an exchange— and an exchange beneficial to both, the enterprise and customer.

To sum up, it should be an important objective of the enterprise to ensure that the profits made by it from the marketing of goods and service should be judged by customers, government, and the public at large as a fair return achieved by fair means.

Social Service

There are two distinctly opposite views as regards the social aspect of marketing. According to the first, marketing is a tool to be used to justify as well as to stimulate, unbounded consumption and self-indulgence. According to the second, marketing must develop social consciousness, in other words, it must become involved in vital issues and provide important public services.

It is clear that in the present-day world, promotion of limitless consumption and self-indulgence cannot be justified as an objective of marketing. In any case, existence of several laws and effective consumer protection groups will make it difficult for any enterprise to indulge in manipulation and exploitation of consumers as well as the public at large.

The social objectives of marketing may be listed as follows:

(1) It should set and maintain highest standards of quality of goods and services.

(2) It should only provide goods which are socially useful and not hoodwink people into buying goods which are frivolous and of no benefit to the buyers or the public at large.

(3) It should aim at minimising the costs of distribution, thus, lowering its effect on the price of goods and service.

(4) It should not resort to unfair trade practices, like profiteering, deliberate low pricing to edge out competitors, etc.

(5) It should not make false claims while advertising its products.

(6) It should not add to environmental pollution through development and promotion of disposable products like paper napkins, or by switching to disposable or throw packages.

(7) It should be ever attentive to consumer grievances as regards over-pricing, substandard quality, or faulty packaging of goods.

(8) It should abide by the laws of the land as regards regulation of patents, trade marks, packaging, labelling, weights and measurements.

(9) It should maintain reasonably high ethical standards in dealings with consumers and the public at large.

Distinction between Selling and Marketing

When used in the ordinary sense, marketing refers to the functions and activities involved in the production and distribution of such goods and services as are needed by the consumers. Assessment of the consumer needs is a necessary first step towards production of goods and services that would satisfy those needs. Thus, changes in the product-line, quality shape, size, design, price, channels of distribution, etc., are made only after information has been gathered from the market in a regular and systematic manner.

Selling, on the other hand, refers, to the functions and activities which are undertaken to affect the sale or distribution of the goods and services produced by an enterprise. In other words, selling is only concerned with the sale or distribution of goods and services; it has no hand whatever in attuning the production activity in accordance with consumer needs and desires.

The basic difference between marketing and selling lies in the orientation or approach of each. Marketing is basically consumer-oriented. Selling on the other hand is product-oriented. Marketing is involved in both—production of goods and services as per the customer's needs and then selling and distribution of whatever has already been produced.

Marketing	Selling
(1) It is oriented to satisfying *customers' needs* and *desires.*	(1) It is oriented to satisfying the *seller's needs.*
(2) The *customer* occupied the pride of place in any marketing Scheme.	(2) The product occupies the pride of place in any selling scheme.
(3) It is concerned with planning and development of products to match the market requirements.	(3) It is only concerned with selling whatever has already been produced.
(4) It represents an *integrated approach* to achieve long-term goals.	(4) It represents a piecemeal approach to achieve short-term goals.
(5) It is concerned with converting customers' needs into *products.*	(5) It is concerned with converting products into cash.
(6) Profit are sought by ensuring *customer satisfactions.*	(6) Profit by ensuring higher *sales volume.*

Organisation of Marketing Function

In a small concern, executives may have to attend to all types of problems whether relating to production, finance, personnel, or marketing. However, in a large enterprise, division of work based on specialisation is not only desirable but also in a way essential for the proper execution of diverse functions.

In the marketing department of a large enterprise, there may be several executives with specialised knowledge and training in various fields, such as marketing research, physical distribution, advertising, and so on. The division of work among these executives based on their skills and aptitude is the responsibility of the chief marketing executive, who may be variously designated as Vice President, General Manager, Director, etc.

The marketing manager in this case will mainly be discharging staff functions being an expert in the fields of activities assigned to him. The sales manager will be the principal line executive managing the sales force, though he will also be discharging certain staff functions such as looking after training. The products manager will coordinate and control all marketing activities concerning the product. The subject has been discussed at length in chapter 2.

Marketing Management

Today, producers and consumers both are undertaking one or the other kind of marketing activities to facilitate convenient transfer of goods. Marketing management has become very important for promotion of sales as well as consumers' satisfaction. Marketing Management involves planning, organising, directing and controlling of all marketing activities. It is an important operative function of management. It performs all managerial functions in the field of marketing. It is concerned with the direction of purposeful activities towards the achievement of marketing goals. It has to look after the production and sales of those goods and services which provide maximum satisfaction to the consumer. It increases the efficiency and effectiveness of the marketing activities of the organisation. It implies coordination of several factors for mutual gain.

(1) "Marketing management is concerned with the direction of purposeful activities towards the attainment of marketing goals." — **E.W. Cundiff and R.R. Still.**

(2) "Marketing management is the analysis, planning, implementation and control of programmes designed to bring about desired exchanges with target audiences for the purpose of mutual or personal gain. It relies heavily on the

adaptation and coordination of product, price, promotion and place of achieving effective response." **—Philip Kotler.**

(3) "Marketing management is a process of planning, organising, implementing and controlling marketing activities in order to effectively and efficiently facilitate and expedite exchanges." **—Pride and Farell.**

Marketing management includes all activities which are necessary to determine the needs of customers and supply goods and services to satisfy their needs in order to achieve the objectives of the business. The basic goal of all marketing management is the satisfaction of needs of the customers and generation of revenue for the business. Marketing management is the marketing concept in action.

Objectives of Marketing Management

The term 'Marketing' means different things to different people. For a housewife, it means buying family requirements at the market place. For a salesman, it means persuading customers to buying goods and services. A sales manger may interpret it in terms of selling. An advertising executive may equate it with advertising. A lawyer may perceive it as comprising all those efforts which have the effect of transfer of ownership in goods and their physical distribution. An economists may describe it as a function which creates time, place and possession utilities, and so on. The fact that marketing means all these activities and function and a lot more.

The concept of marketing has evolved over a long period and has undergone several changes. That explains why there is no single definition of the term. Among the several stages of evolution of marketing, the barter system prevailing in the early phases of civilisation may be said to be the first, since it necessitated the coming together of producers and consumers at a central place at a mutually convenient time. The invention of money as a common medium of exchange solved the problems of the barter systems, but it further added to the important of the marketing function.

The second stage in the evolution of marketing came with the onset of the Industrial Revolution. The various technological developments had made it possible to produce goods on a mass scale. But marketing was basically production-oriented, the assumption being that if a product possessed the qualities of being good and reasonable priced, it was bound to have a ready demand and that whatever could produced, could also effortlessly be sold.

The third stage in the evolution process was market by sales or market-oriented approach. This was largely the result of various socio-economic changes that had taken place in society, such as, production in anticipation of demand, keen competition among producers to reach out to consumers, improvement in the means of transport and communication, etc. But while the importance of the consumer had come to be recognised there was not much effort to tailor production to the satisfaction of individual consumer needs, the emphasis being only on increasing the sales rather than consumer satisfaction.

The fourth stage witnessed a major change in the outlook of producers toward marketing. With production being far exceeding the demand, and consumers rapidly shifting from one product to another due to increased awareness, the producers were quick to realise that in order to survive in the market they had to adopt consumer-oriented approach to marketing. For this purpose, assessment of consumer needs and behaviour was not enough. It was necessary to aim at consumer satisfaction by means of production of the right kind of goods as also a whole cluster of things associated with creating, delivering and finally consuming the goods.

The present management-oriented approach to marketing can be said to be natural consequence of increasing attention to consumer satisfaction. Today, the marketing factor has become crucial to all business planning and decision-making. Thus, in the present highly competitive and changing world, marketing function has come to be associated with first determining the type and quantity of goods which could be sold, and then finding the best way to make the consumer to buy those goods.

The basic objectives of marketing is to achieve the goals of business, i.e., earning reasonable profits by satisfying the needs of the customers. The main objective of marketing management are as follows:

(1) **Creation of Demand:** Marketing tries to creat demand through to various methods. It creates new customers for the business. It attracts customers to buy the products and services of the firm. The usefulness of the products and services are made known to the customers in advance. If facilitate increased sales by creating demand for the product in the market. Steady demand enables regular production.

(2) **Larger Market Share:** The primary objective of every business is to increase its

sales and to capture biggest share in the market for its products. In order to establish supremacy in the market, the entrepreneur may have to face severe competition and may have to adopt various strategies to make his goods most popular among the consumers. He may have to resort to aggressive sales techniques to secure larger market share for his products. He may have to make necessary changes in the quality, price, packaging, etc., of his products or even in his publicity policy.

(3) **Establishing Goodwill:** Goodwill is the most valuable assets that every business-house would like to earn for itself and its products. Businessmen earn goodwill by providing maximum satisfaction to their customers, by selling quality goods to them at reasonable price, by adopting fair trade practices and by courteous and honest dealings with their clientele. Marketing management must add to the image of the enterprise.

(4) **Increasing Profits:** Marketing management aims at securing stability, profitability, growth and expansion to business by customer's satisfaction. Business produces goods and services on the demand of the consumers and earn profit by supplying them to the consumers to satisfy their needs. Marketing management begins with the customers and ends with the customer.

Functions of Marketing Management

Marketing management is primarily concerned with the stimulation of sales and promotion of consumer satisfaction. It includes, analysis of markets, determination of marketing goals, sales forecasting and formulation of marketing plans, policies and procedures. An important function of marketing management is to evolve an appropriate marketing mix, i.e., planning and development of a satisfactory product for a particular market demand and fixation of its prices. It includes all efforts directed towards sales promotion.

To improve the efficiency and effectiveness of its marketing management, an enterprise has to determine the objective of its activities in term of sales and profits and lay down the manner in which the goals are to be achieved. This may involve sales forecasting, selection of channels of distribution, methods of sales promotion, marketing research, customers services, etc. Marketing management may also undertake collection of feedback and evaluation of performance against the established performance standards. However, all through the costs of marketing management must be kept within reasonable limits.

Organisation of Marketing Management

Organisation of marketing research has to take care of sales as well as the satisfaction of the consumers. Sales manager looks after the sales of the product. He looks after product designing, sales promotion, transportation, credit control, etc. He is assisted in his task by production managers, advertising managers, etc. Study of consumer needs, forecasting of demand, securing maximum satisfaction, building up goodwill for the products, etc., are the function of marketing manager. Both the sales manager and marketing manager work under the control and guidance of the chief executive of the organisation.

Marketing Mix

Marketing mix is a technique of marketing management wherein production of goods promotion activities distributing actual or maximum consumer satisfaction can be secured by business only with the help of an appropriate marketing mix. Marketing mix is the cornerstone of modern marketing. It is a dynamic concept as it keeps on changing with changes in the market conditions and the environment achieving the directed objectives.

(1) "Marketing mix is the set of marketing tools that the firm uses to pursue its marketing objectives in the target market." —**Kotler.**

(2) "The sum of elements of business activity that can be used by a firm to fulfil its marketing strategy is called the marketing mix." —**Greyson and Olson.**

(3) "Marketing mix is the term used to describe the combination of the four inputs which constitute the core of a company's marketing systems: the product, the price structure, the promotional activities and the distribution systems." —**William J. Stanton.**

Marketing mix refers to the combination of four basic elements, viz., Product, Price, Promotion and Physical Distribution, known as four Ps of marketing. These four Ps form the core of the marketing system. They help in optimising the level of productivity and satisfaction.

Elements of Marketing Mix

Product

Product element of marketing mix refers to the activities relating to the product and after sales service which satisfy customers' needs. Product includes not only the physical objects but also services capable of satisfying consumer's wants. *It involves decision with regard to quality, features, packaging, size, services, branding and warranties, etc. It must match with the customers' needs and expectations. Product must have good number of varieties to cater to the needs of all shades of customers.* It must cater to rich and poor, conservative and progressive consumers, all alike. Minor variation may be introduced to make the product acceptable by different classes of people.

Elements of Marketing Mix

Product	Price	Physical Distribution	Promotion
Quality	Special Discount	Channels	Advertising
Style	Allowances	Coverage	Personal Selling
Brand Name	Terms of Credit	Locations	Sales Promotion
Sales Services		Inventory	Public Relations
Warranties		Transport	
Packaging			

Good Quality of products must be available to the consumers at reasonable prices whenever and wherever they need them. Products must easily be identifiable. It may be given simple and easy brand name to gain popularity. It may be registered with a trade mark to avoid duplicity and deception of any kind. It must be presented in a useful and attractive packaging. Good packaging must provide for the protection and easy handling of the product. It must be economical. Real pre and post sales services facilitate marketing. It increases customers' satisfaction and sales and goodwill for the business.

Pricing

Price element of marketing mix covers pricing objectives and pricing policies. Price is the monetary value of a product. It also includes discounts, allowances and terms of credit or period of payment. Price is an effective means of competition. Hence, cost, demand, competition, government control should be considered before taking any significant decision on price. Price can also act as device for sales promotion.

Price must cover the cost of production and selling of the products. It must provide for liberal trade discounts, credit terms, etc., to attract more customers. It must favourably compare with the price charged by the competitors. To keep the price low, efforts should be made to reduce the number of middlemen. Pricing policy, which may be adopted by the enterprise, may be cost-based, demand-based or competition-based.

Promotion

Promotion mix refers to the activities relating to promotion of the sale of the products. It covers all means of marketing communications. Its purpose is to inform and persuade the customers about the product of the business concern. The various elements of promotional mix include personal selling, advertising, sales promotion, publicity and public relations.

(1) **Personal Selling:** Personal selling is face-to-face two-way oral communication with the potential customers to persuade them to buy goods. It may be adopted for introducing and creating demand for the new product or by ensuring satisfaction to the customers, to obtain repeat orders from them.

(2) **Advertising:** Advertising refers to those non-personal activities, visual or oral which are aimed at informing the prospective customers regarding a product, service or idea. It is conducted through media of press (newspapers and magazines), radio, television, films and so on and is paid for by the seller. Besides increasing demand for the product by resorted to şupport and facilitate salesmanship. It creates demand for the products by attracting attention and suggesting action.

(3) **Sales Promotion:** Sales promotion is the method of increasing the sales

through displays, show, exhibitions, demonstrations and various non-recurring selling efforts like contests, special discounts, coupons, etc. It consists for those activities that stimulate consumer purchasing and dealer's effectiveness.

(4) Publicity: Publicity refers to a non-personal stimulation of demand for a product, service of an idea by placing significant news about it in trade journals, newspapers, radio, etc., that is not paid for by the sponsor. It is also called 'free advertising.'

Physical Distribution

This element of marketing mix is concerned with linking the seller and buyer. It covers channels of distribution involving in getting the possession and the title to products to consumers and physical distribution, concerning with transporting, warehousing, storing and handling of the products. It also includes inventory control. The choice of the channels of distributions is determined by the need to provide to the customers; goods at the right time and at the right place.

The channels of distribution are those routes through which goods move from the producer to the consumer. The marketing manager has to decide the system of handling and transporting the products through these channels.

Delivering goods to and distribution of products amongst the prospective consumer is usually done by the various channels of distribution. They may be (1) direct, such as multiple, shop, mail order selling or home delivery service, etc., or (2) indirect, such as wholesalers, retailers and middlemen, etc. Selection of the channel of distribution is an important element of any marketing mix. It is guided by the nature of the product and its market, custom of trade, availability of middlemen and tendency of the producers.

Cheaper and standardised products are usually sold through longer and diversified channels of distribution. Perishable, bulky or technical goods are generally distributed through short channels. Manufactures generally prefer to sell new products directly to the consumers since they are required to educate the customer about utility.

Longer channels are preferable for handling small quantities or attending to large number of customers. Credit facilities usually need intermediaries as compared to cash sales. Consumer habits also affect the selection of channels of distribution.

Selection of the channels of distribution also depends upon the availability of middlemen, comparative costs, government regulation and the custom of trade. It is also affected by the policy and the competence of the management, financial positions of the manufacturers, quantity of production and the distribution policy of the producer of the goods.

Process of Marketing Mix

The purpose of determing the marketing mix is to satisfy the needs, values, habits, feelings and hopes of the customers. As the needs and habits of the customers and the environmental factors change, the marketing mix also changes. It cannot remain static. The following steps are involved in the process of determining the marketing mix:

(1) **Identification:** The marketing department of the firm must identify the present and potential customer to whom the product is to sold, i.e., the target market.

(2) **Analysis:** Once the present and potential customers are identified the next step is to find out the needs and wants of the customers as the market concept changes the orientation from "take what we produce and sell it" to "find out what they want and make it." All roads lead to consumer satisfaction. Marketing research is used to locate customers and potential areas, territories, relative profitability, data on competitors and general economic and market conditions, etc.

(3) **Designing:** On the basis of identification, an analysis of relevant information, an appropriate mix of product, price promotion and place is designed.

(4) **Testing:** After designing the marketing mix, the firm conceives the idea of a product, develops the product on a limited scale and tests its profitability before finally deciding to introduce it in the market. The reaction of customers will indicate the adjustment of required marketing mix and improving the entire development process.

(5) **Adoptor:** After the necessary improvement in development process, the marketing mix is adopted and put into use. The adopted mix should be

evaluated from time to time to find out the changes in the marketing environment.

The element of 'Marketing Mix' as described by Neil H. Borden involve two different kinds of factors:

(1) Elements of the marketing mix for a manufacturer of products.

(2) Forces that affect the marketing operations of a firm.

Element of marketing mix for manufacturer may be summarised as follows:

(1) **Product Planning Mix:**

(a) Product line to be followed in relation to qualities, design, etc.

(b) Markets-whom, where, when and in what quantity.

(c) Research and development programme relating to any product.

(2) **Pricing Mix:**

(a) Level of price to be adopted.

(b) Any specific price to be adopted.

(c) Price policy discrimination or one lot pricing to be followed.

(d) Margins to be allowed:

(3) **Branding:**

(a) Selection of trade marks.

(b) Individualised or family brands to be chosen.

(c) Sale of unbranded product or product under private labels.

(4) **Distribution Channels:**

(a) Determination of channels to be used between the producer/marketeer and consumer.

(b) Selection of wholesalers and retailers.

(5) **Packing:** Policy formulation regarding package and lable.

(6) **Servicing:** Policy and procedures to be formulated for providing service after sales, if required.

(7) **Handling of Goods:** Policies and procedures to be laid down for warehousing, transportation and inventory controls.

(8) **Advertising and Sales Promotion:**

(a) Formulation of policies relating to personal selling and selection of media to establish product image as well corporate image.

(b) Formulation of policies regarding special selling plans, etc.

(c) Amount to be spent and objective to be achieved—consumer promotion or trade promotion.

The following are the market forces determining the marketing mix:

(1) Consumers' Buying behaviour as determined by their

(a) buying habits,

(b) motivation in purchasing,

(c) buying capacity,

(d) attitude towards products.

(2) Traders' behaviour, i.e., wholesalers and retailers behaviour as influenced by their

(a) structure, practices and attitudes,

(b) motivations.

(3) Competitor's behaviour as influenced by

(a) size and strength of competitors,

(b) number of competitors,

(c) competition from other product—product choices offered such as competitor's in relation of quality, price, service, etc.,

(d) competitor's demand position of the product,

(e) supply and demand position of the product.

(4) Government behaviour as reflected by regulations over

(a) production.

(b) pricing.

(c) competitive practices.

(d) advertising and promotion.

It may be noted that if one is to consider all the above forces and weigh them in the correct perspective, it would not easy to devise a judicious combination of all the forces mentioned above. However, the important forces which bear on producers or marketeers are all arising from the behaviour of individuals or groups and as such their behavioural pattern needs a close study and analysis. It should always be remembered that any firm is only a small part of the total market complex with very many forces determining their role and evidently, therefore, marketing mix is pivotal in establishing and furthering the march of any establishment.

Marketing behaviour is very much affected by the behaviour of consumers, traders, competitors and government. Changes may take place in the buying and living habits of the consumers, their purchasing power, motivation and attitudes of the traders, intensity of competition, regulation of business by government, etc. All these changes will change the marketing mix. A good marketing mix should be able to adjust itself quickly with the changing internal and external environment.

The Marketing Mix of Manufacturers

(Mixing of marketing functions from the point of view of manufacturers)

Marketing is not a science. It is still an art wherein the management tries to marshall all its resourses to enhance the goodwill of the business enterprise and further its interest so that its competitors may not forge ahead. It is because of this reason the management is required to develop a 'concept of marketing mix' by mixing all the marketing functions, with a view to build a marketing structure for the entire enterprise. Prof. Neil H. Borden has suggested the following mix of manufactures. (As quoted by M.C. Shukla, *Business Organisation and Management)*.

(1) Product Planning: Policies and procedures relating to:

(a) Products line to be offered—qualities, designs, etc.

(b) Markets to sell—whom, where, when and in what quantity.

(c) New product Policy—research and development programme.

(2) Pricing: Policies and procedures relating to:

(a) Price level to adopt.

(b) Specific prices to adopt.

(c) Price policy, e.g., one price varying price maintenance, etc.

(d) Margins to adopt—for the company; for the trade.

(3) Branding: Policies and procedures relating to:

(a) Selections of trade mark.

(b) Brand Policy—individualised or family brand.

(c) Sale under private label of unbounded.

(4) Channels of Distribution: Policies and procedures relating to:

(a) Channels to use between plant and consumer.

(b) Degree of selectivity among wholesalers and retailers.

(c) Efforts to gain cooperation of the trade.

(5) Personal Selling: Policies and procedures relating to:

(a) Burden to be placed on personal selling and methods to be employed in:

(i) Manufacturer's organisation.

(ii) Wholesale segment of the trade.

(iii) Retail segment of the trade.

(6) Advertising: Policies and procedures relating to:

(a) Amount to be spent, i.e., the burden to be placed on advertising.

(b) Copy platform to adopt:

(i) Product image desired.

(ii) Corporate image desired.

(c) Mix of advertising to the trade; through the trade; to the consumer.

(7) Promotion: Policies and procedures relating to:

(a) Burden to place on special selling plans or devices directed at or through the trade.

(b) Form of these devices for consumer promotions, for trade promotions.

(8) Packing: Policies and procedures relating to:

(a) Formulation of packing and label.

(9) Display: Policies and procedures relating to:

(a) Burden to be put on display to help affect the sale.

(b) Methods to adopt to secure display.

(10) Servicing: Policies and procedures relating to:

(a) Providing service needed.

(11) Physical Handling: Policies and procedures relating to:

(a) Warehousing.

(b) Transporting.

(c) Investors.

(12) Fact Finding and Analysis: Policies and procedures relating to: securing, analysis, and use of facts in marketing operations.

Marketing Research

Collection of accurate, reliable and useful information about the market for planning and growth of business enterprise is termed as marketing research. Marketing research serves the purpose of an intelligence wing of the marketing management which form the essential part of the marketing management. It provides a scope for scientific study of all problems relating to purchase, sale and distribution of goods and minimise the marketing rise. "Marketing research," in the words of Vaile and Slagsnold "is an organised attempt to reduce the market risks—principal task of market research is to widen the basis of facts upon which business plans are laid."

Nature and Scope of Marketing Research

Goods and services cannot sale themselves. They are to be sold for which efforts are to be made. The first effort is to elicit information about the market. Such eliciting of information forms the subject matter of marketing research. The present and potential customers, the ultimate consumer, its products and determination of products to be produced, the ways and means of offering the product to the consumer are some of the problems which a marketing division of an organisation faces in its day-to-day affairs. Marketing research wing offers solution to all these problems on systematic manner. A systematic and impartial marketing research helps the marketing division to evaluate the results without bias which certainly provides the very basis of marketing process.

What, when, where and how to sell the end product and the service are four questions to which marketing research wing provides answer and the efforts for providing answer to these questions are the nature and scope of the marketing research. It is in the nature of marketing research to collect market information systematically and impartially so as to evaluate the results without prejudice and use the collected information for the benefits of the organisation.

Objectives of Marketing Research

From the above discussion on marketing research we may come to the following objectives of marketing research:

(1) To discover the need of the people—the present and potential customers and also ultimate consumers.

(2) To determine the goods to be produced in the light of the need of the people.

(3) To examine the reaction of the people when the product is already in the market.

(4) To suggest corrective measures in accordance with the scrutiny and analysis of the reaction of the people.

(5) To ascertain the future need and suggest to the organisation suitable product if the product in the market is not being accepted by the people whole-heartedly.

(6) To ascertain the reasons for non-acceptance of goods offered to people.

(7) To try to capture the foreign market.

Functions of Marketing Research

The main functions of marketing research may broadly be divide into following five parts:

(1) Describing.

(2) Evaluating.

(3) Explaining.

(4) Predicting.

(5) Assisting

The above five functions abbreviated as DEEPA actually forms the basis of any marketing research. *Describing* conveys the meaning of description of an event which has either taken place or expected to take place. Indeed description is the beginning of marketing research. The events described will afterwards be evaluated which gives rise to the function of *evaluation.* The goods produced, the acceptance given the product already in the market, customers' reaction, competitors' product and its performance in the market, etc., are first described and then evaluated which after a careful study 'explained' giving rise to the function of *explaining.* Explaining leads the organisation to some of the point where it comes to know as to why a particular event has taken place? Where the organisation has gone wrong? What has taken always the customers from the products? Which sales territory is doing better and the performance of which one is not upto the expectations and why? After explaining the market research wing comes to its most important function of marketing predictions. *Predicting,* in fact, is the focal point around which other functions of this wing cluster. Prediction, indeed, is the aim of description, evaluation and explanation. The market research wing predicts regarding what the sales volume might, will or should be in a future date (or period), what might, will or should be the future product needs, what distribution procedure should be adopted in future and what competition our product is going to face and what should be done to face the competitor's challenge, etc., are to be predicted by this wing. Once predication is made the whole organisation believes in it and acts in accordance with such predictions. But it is expected that the marketing research will come to the help of the organisation is acting according to the prediction. Such an assistance is, if forthcoming, helps the organisation in taking proper decision at a time when it is needed most. *Assisting* the decision-making helps the marketing research wing grow in strature. Here the marketing research wing functions as an advisor to the marketing management.

Marketing Research Methodology

It is natural that marketing research wing is interested in getting its recommendations accepted and acted upon. For acceptance and action on the recommendations the marketing research wing has to work scientifically so that it may come to an impartial conclusion. This it can do if it adopts certain methodology for its research activities. Though the methodology may differ from one research organisation to another but it is essential that a marketing research division of a marketing management department should adopt a flexible methodology. The following methodology may be suggested:

(1) Understanding the problem.
(2) Setting out specific objectives.
(3) Preparing a research framework.
(4) Defining the research goals.
(5) Developing the research plan including questionnaire, if any.
(6) Choosing the sample after careful analysis.
(7) Determing the statistical needs.
(8) Determing the information required and purpose which they would serve.
(9) Analysing the collected information after proper tabulation, etc.
(10) Drawing conclusions.
(11) Preparing recommendations.
(12) Preparing reports and then submission to the management.

Areas of Activity of Marketing Research

Solving and foretelling the marketing problem are two important proposes of a marketing research. To attain the purpose, areas of activity of marketing research are clearly demarcated into the following activities as has been enumerated by M.C. Shukla:

(1) Product or services.
(2) Market.
(3) Distribution.
(4) Pricing.
(5) Sales Organisation.
(6) Service.
(7) Advertising and sales promotion.
(8) Packaging.
(9) Brand names.
(10) Acquisitions.

Benefits and Uses of Marketing Research

Benefits

The following are the major benefits of a marketing research:

(1) Production as per requirement. Whatever the consumer wants, i.e., the market accepts is produced. This ensures better understanding between the producer and the consumer on the one hand and good investment climate and encouraging capital market on the other.

(2) Sales promotion is accelerate. It becomes the order. Marketing research helps in producing what is accepted by the market. This certainly stops unwanted production. Sales naturally is accelerated.

(3) Reduction in market expenses due to non-rejection and larger turnover.

(4) Policies, programmes and procedure are coordinated and interrelated which facilitate the appraisal of production plans and its schedules.

(5) Creation of new opportunity, better understanding and a field for coordinated production efforts.

Uses of Marketing Research

R.D. Crips has described the following uses of a marketing research:

(1) Position of the Enterprise: Marketing research enables the company to know its position as to where it stands in the industry.

(2) Trends of the Market: Marketing research reveals the prevailing trends of the market and, thus, the management comes to know as to what the trend is and what trends they are likely to adopt in future.

(3) Introduction of New Production: Marketing research comes to an aid to the management in taking a decision in connection with present product and introduction of the new products.

(4) Market Condition: Marketing research tells the management regarding market condition, finds out new uses of the product, ascertains unsatisfied needs of the customers, measures the extent of market, checks the efficiency of distributors, wholesalers and retailers and above all, plans the sales organisation for better results.

(5) **Improves the Sales Management:** Marketing research helps in improving the effectiveness of the sales management.

Marketing and Distribution Decisions

The marketing manager must constantly analyse and evaluate alternative situations and choose among them. To do so requires the implication of marketing reality and the resolution of conflicts. Given conflicting marketing situations, choice is after difficult and involves balancing risks and payoffs the knowledge, attitudes, opinions, feelings, judgements and facts, and current situations and future opportunities. The decision-making process includes more than the decision—the actual choice or cut-off point. The decision-making process shapes an organisation's destiny, since decisions are a prelude to tomorrow's marketing situations.

In recent years, more effective decision-making in marketing has been advanced through the application of the behavioural sciences, computers and quantitative techniques. Many aspects of marketing are emerging from a 'hit-or-miss' stage and are becoming quantifiable, measurable and more scientific. Linear programming, dynamic programming, marketing processes and expected value theory are used to increase the effectiveness of the problem-solving and decision-making process.

The marketing manager tries to reach decision that minimise the inputs required to achieve specified output or to minimise output from specified inputs. As a decision-maker, marketing manager is concerned with marketing decisions that alter the scope and direction of the whole organisation as well as those that pertain directly to marketing. Marketing decision have been classified in many ways. A common classification distinguishes between decision related to objectives and those that pertain to more specific goals. The latter can he judged on the basis of efficiency, the former depend on normative values. Strategic decisions regarding major directions of a business are contrasted with tactical decisions that carry out the strategies. Reciprocal decisions, in which one individual interacts with another and causes a reaction, are distinguished from controlling decisions, in which one person's actions control the actions of another without interaction. Sequential decision involving multiple actions and reaction, like those in the marketplace, are differentiated from single decisions.

Marketing decision form a spectrum from the programmed or highly rigid, routine, repetitions, specific type at one extreme to the non-programmed, less definite, unknown, uncertain, loosely constructed type at the other. The former can be handled by habit, clerical routines, standard operating producers, and mathematical calculations, whereas the latter require creativity, intuition, judgement and persuasive problem-solving techniques. While there may not be perfect solutions to complex marketing problems, there may be optional solution to a number of sub-problems or at least acceptable solution to the total problem.

Marketing decisions may also be classified according to management's degree of certainty information about choices. Where complete information is assumed. The decision is made under conditions of certainty. Here the outcomes of each management action can be announced explicitly and the particular state that will exist in the future can be completely identified. Wrong decisions can be eliminated. At the other extreme, decisions may be made under conditions of complete uncertainty, the decision-maker brings nothing to the actual choice by way of experience or other marketing information that helps in selecting among choices. This situation is unrealistic one and is closely approximated in marketing by an absolutely new product with no marketing-research information available. Choices here might be made on a random basis.

Some of these decisions call for estimates of the costs associated with individual segments of company's revenues. For example, the company's management may wish to have information on the profitability of individual sales territories or of small orders of sale made through its own retail stores. Other marketing problems call for estimates of the costs and revenues associated with new ways of doing business. For example, a company which now sells through wholesale is thinking of setting up its own wholesale operation to deal directly with retailers and needs estimates of the effect of this action on its total costs and total revenues.

Nature of Distribution Function

The marketing and distribution may be defined broadly as the task of getting the manufactured product to the firm's customer in return for the agreed monetary remuneration. It includes both marketing and transportation. For cost measurement and control purposes, the total distribution function may be divided into the functions of:

(1) demand creation and demand sustaining (advertising and sales promotion);

(2) storage and warehousing; and

(3) customer financing and collection.

Costs in function 1 often are called 'order-getting costs' and those in 2, 3 and 4 are known, 'order filling costs.' Within the firm, this decision frequently is the basis for organisation and assignment of responsibility.

Need for Proper Analysis and Accounting of Selling and Distribution Costs

The necessity for proper accounting of selling and distribution costs arises from the following:

(1) Determination of the cost of sales of jobs and production and the extent of the profitability of each. Costs are not completed and profits cannot be worked out correctly, unless selling and distribution costs are included.

(2) Control of selling and distribution costs.

(3) Price fixation and formulation of sales price policy.

(4) Fixation of optimum sales level.

The purposes of distribution cost analysis is to enable the management of the firm of determine the answers to some or all of such questions as these: "Which products are most profitable to sell?" In which territories are the most profitable sales made? What customer's accounts are profitable? What are the most profitable methods of distribution or what salesmen are making the most profitable sales records? In order to give answers to these questions, the following classification of distribution costs may be resorted to:

(1) The cost of distribution of each product.

(2) The cost of distribution within each territory.

(3) The cost of distribution for classes of customers, which may be further sub-divided as follows:

(a) According to size of sale.

(b) According to territorial classification—urban or rural.

(c) According to type of customer organisation – chain stores, mail order house, etc.

(d) According to type of store.

(4) The cost of distribution for each method of sale, through branch offices, salesman, cash sale, credit sale, etc.

Thus, we will discuss selected distribution decisions in the following pages.

Product Line Evaluation

In evaluating a product or product line, many factors must be considered including growth trend, competition and capital employed, besides profitability. Product profitability statements are a major source of information. They indicate products which should be pushed or eliminated and suggest areas of cost reduction. It is this analysis, which will illustrate product profitability and the fact that volume of sales is not the some thing as profit. Indeed, if a product upon which a loss is being made is sold, in greater and greater quantity, it is bringing the day of bankruptcy nearer. It may be that a product or group of products is unprofitable. The use of differential costing techniques will spot-light this, but it must be remembered that although generally, if a product is not recovering all its variable costs, including those of selling and distribution, it should be discontinued. If management is convinced that the product which is failing to recover its variable costs, is a means of inducing customers to buy other profitable products of the company to an extent which more than offsets the loss, than it may pay to continue producing the unprofitable product.

Apart from drawing attention to those products making a definite loss, products are revealed which make only a small contribution towards fixed costs and profits. It may be that the sources devoted to the product which only just covers its variable cost can be devoted to another more profitable product. This is management decision. But, it must be borne in mind that the contribution the product did make, however small is an opportunity cost which must be taken into account in estimating the new contribution form the product it is proposed to substitute for it.

This type of analysis throws considerable light upon the problems of pricing. While the cost of production is kept in mind when fixing prices, the price generally is more affected by the state of market. Analysis by products, showing relative profitability, puts production cost in their true prospective being merely one element out of several. Pricing must be carried out so as to yield the maximum profit in the long run and to ensure that the prices of all the firms products fit into a logical price structure which will be subject to the least amount of alternation.

Example 1

This will illustrate the analysis of income by products.

Products

	A	B	C	D	Total
	Rs.	Rs.	Rs.	Rs.	Rs.
Sales	68,000	2,92,000	80,000	60,000	5,00,000
Less variable cost of Sales	40,000	57,000	55,000	58,000	2,10,000
Gross Contribution	28,000	2,35,000	25,000	2,000	2,90,000
Less Variable selling distribution costs:					
Salesman	5,000	7,000	7,000	2,000	21,000
Warehouse	4,000	7,000	6,000	1,000	18,000
Packing	3,000	2,000	5,000	200	10,200
Delivery	3,000	3,000	4,000	800	10,800
	15,000	19,000	22,000	4,000	60,000
Contribution	13,000	2,16,000	3,000	(-2,000)	2,30,000
Less fixed selling and Distribution cost					1,10,000
					1,20,000
Less Fixed Admn. Costs					1,13,000
Net Profit					7,000

The analysis reveals that Product D has failed to meet its variable costs and so should be discontinued unless there are exceptional circumstances to justify its continued production. Product C shows a good gross contribution, but the variable selling and distribution costs reduce the net contribution to Rs. 3,000 only and it may be worth considering whether or not it is possible and profitable to divert the productive resources and selling and distribution organisation to the marketing of something else.

Example 2

There are three lines of production and their production cost per unit and selling price per unit are given.

	Products		
	X	Y	Z
	Rs.	Rs.	Rs.
Materials	18	26	30
Wages	7	9	10
Variable overheads	2	3	3
Fixed overheads	5	8	9
	32	46	52
Selling Price	40	60	61
Add Profit	8	14	9
Production in Units	4,000	2,000	5,000

The production manager wants to discontinue one line and guarantee the production in two other lines shall rise by 50 per cent. He wants to discontinue X as it appears to be least profitable.

(a) Do you agree to the scheme in principle?

(b) If so, do you think that X should be discontinued?

Solution

As all the products are being manufactured in the same factory, the total fixed expenses will be as follows:

Product X: 4,000 × 5	Rs. 20,000
Product Y: 2,000 × 8	Rs. 16,000
Product Z: 5,000 × 9	Rs, 45,000
Total Fixed Overheads	Rs. 81,000

It has been assumed that the fixed overheads will not decrease on the discontinuance of the one production and the facilities available can be utilised in the development of other products.

Calculation of contribution on each product

	Products X	Y	Z
	Rs.	Rs.	Rs.
Material	18	26	30
Wages	7	9	10
Variable	2	3	3
Marginal Cost	27	38	43
Selling Price	40	60	61
Contribution	13	22	18
Contribution Ratio (in %)	35.5	36.7	29.5

Now we will consider the alternative arrangements:

(1) If all products continued:

Product	Sales	Marginal Cost	Contribution
	Rs.	Rs.	Rs.
X	1,60,000	1,08,000	52,000
Y	1,20,000	76,000	44,000
Z	3,05,000	2,15,000	90,000
	5,85,000	3,99,000	1,86,000
Less Fixed Overhead			81,000
Net Profit			1,05,000

(2) If X is discontinued (50% increase in Y & Z)

Product	Sales	Marginal Cost	Contribution
	Rs.	Rs.	Rs.
Y 3,000 Units	1,80,000	1,14,000	66,000
Z 7,500 Units	4,57, 000	3,22, 500	1,35,000
	6,37,000	4,36,500	2,01,000
Less Fixed overheads			81,000
Net Profit			1,20,000

(3) If Y is discontinued (50% increase in X & Y)

Product	Sales	Marginal cost	Contribution
	Rs.	Rs.	Rs.
X 6,000 Units	2,40,000	1,62,000	78,000
Y 7,500 Units	4,57,000	3,22,500	1,35,000
	6,97,500	4,84,500	2,13,000
Less Fixed overheads			81,000
Net Profit			1,32,000

(4) If Z discontinued (50% increase in X & Y)

Product	Sales	Marginal Cost	Contribution
	Rs.	Rs.	Rs.
X 6,000 Units	2,40,000	1,62,000	78,000
Y 3,000 Units	1,80,000	1,14,000	66,000
	4,20,000	2,76,000	1,44,000
Less Fixed overhead			81,000
Net Profit			63,000

(a) It is not true that discontinuance of one product will improve the situation. If Z is discontinued, the profit will go down to Rs. 63,000 only and it will be very serious.

(b) If X is discontinued, the situation can improve as the profit will increase to Rs. 1,20,000 from Rs. 1,05,000. But if Y is discontinued, it will increase the profits to its maximum, i.e., to Rs. 1,32,000. This is the best alternative to be launched upon.

Order-size Profitability

Small orders are less profitable than large orders because, costs do not rise proportionately to increase in the size of order. Certain costs remain completely unchanged regardless of the size of the order, for example, accounting costs involved in maintaining ledger accounts, sending involves and statements and also the expenses and time of salesmen who solicit the orders. Other costs per unit may actually decrease with bigger orders, for example, transportation costs is generally lower per unit when large quantities are despatched at the same time.

It follows, therefore, that some order may be unprofitable and a customer who always orders in small quantities may be an unprofitable customer even though his annual turnover may be adequate. Take an example of a bookseller who is asked to supply a book, retailing at Rs. 30 The gross profit of the book-seller on the volume may be about Rs. 5 and for this order forms must be made, postage cost incurred. There remain clearly a negligible profit but the bookseller will wish to supply to provide a service and goodwill for the future may justify his actions.

Bearing in mind this question of goodwill and the fact that small unprofitable orders now may lead to something better in future, it will be seen that small orders create their own problems. Some manufacturers stipulate minimum orders size by value or quantity, others charge a price which varies with the size of the order and thus, while discouraging small orders, they ensure that costs are covered when small orders are received.

(1) **Trial Orders:** Small orders placed by customers to test the demand for the products. This may well result in profitable future business.

(2) **The Emergency Order by:** A customer who is faced with an unexpected and critical need.

(3) **Oversight Orders:** Small items committed by oversight from a previous order.

(4) **Full-in-orders:** Orders required to fill in and balance customers stock.

(5) **Hand-to-mouth Buying Orders:** Arising from lack of inventory control or poor buying habits of customers.

(6) **The Small Account:** Small accounts will have a tendency to submit proportionately smaller orders.

In attempting to measure profitability, it is first necessary to establish the order size classification. This will vary in different companies, since a large order for one company may be a small one for another. Perhaps the most logical methods for establishing the order-size categories is to make a statistical sampling of invoices. Quantity or value may be the criterion, whichever may suit the convenience of the individual company. Grouping may be, for example, below Rs. 5, Rs. 5 and under Rs. 10 and under Rs. 10 and under Rs. 100, Rs. 100< and over. It is then necessary to determine the total sales in each order size. Now after total sale have been determined, it is necessary to associate relevant costs with the order size. In the analysis of selling and distribution costs between order size, some departure from differential methods will be advisable, because some fixed costs should be analysed along with variable, for example, salesmen's salaries, depreciation of delivery vans. Only those costs which are affected by the size of order need be analysed, and costs unaffected can be ignored. For example, the rent of the Accounts Department need not be analysed, because it is unaffected by the size of the order. Similarly, if by eliminating the small orders, it is possible to reduce the number of delivery trucks used, the cost of these trucks become a relevant cost and must be analysed.

Example 3

Analysis by size of order

	Basis of Apportionment	Under Rs. 5	Rs. 5 but less than Rs. 20	Rs. 20 but less than Rs. 40	Rs. 40 and over	Total
Sales		1,00,000	3,00,000	6,00,000	4,00,000	14,00,000
Less: Cost of sales		59,000	1,77,000	3,54,000	2,36,000	8,26,000
Gross profit		41,000	1,23,000	2,46,000	1,64,000	5,74,000
Selling and Distribution Costs:						
Salaries of Salesman Commission	No. of Customers	35,000	16,000	11,250	4,000	66,250
Sales office Exp.	Direct	10,000	2,500	1,000	500	14,000
	No. of Customers	16,000	17,750	31,100	20,550	85,400
Warehouse etc.	No. of units despatched	3,525	10,575	21,150	14,100	49,350
Accounts	No. of orders	16,800	11,200	11,300	2,700	4,200
		81,325	58,025	75,800	41,850	2,57,000
Contribution		(-40,325)	64,975	1,70,200	1,22,150	3,17,000
Less Fixed cost						2,65,000
Net profit						52,000

The above analysis suggests that Rs. 5 is the minimum value of orders which should be accepted. The following possibilities may be explored to increase profits:

(1) Refuse to accept orders of a value of below a sum of Rs. 5.

(2) Encourage customers to order more at one time by introducing price differentials. This could be done by quoting different prices based upon quantities ordered. Alternatively a quantity discount may be offered which will be easy and favourable.

(3) Reduce the cost of handling a small customer's order by requiring cash to be paid with the order or upon delivery.

All other possibilities if any may also be explored to maximise profits.

Analysis by Areas of Salesman

Generally, a manufacturer will divide geographically into areas the territory in which he is selling his products. Depending upon the size of the firm and the nature of product each area may coincide with a specific salesman, one salesman for one area. Alternatively, an area sales manager may be appointed for each area, each controlling a number of salesmen.

It is essential to know the profitability of each area and of each salesman. Some areas will more profitable than others because of such factors as larger or smaller populations the comparative disposable incomes of the population of the different area, the incidence of competition. Sales promotion programmes may take different forms in different areas. Having regard to all these factors, profit can be forecasted by areas and actual results measured against forecasts.

Analysis of costs so as to show the profitability of each area and individual salesman is not difficult. Most costs such as salesmen's salaries, commissions and travelling expenses, delivery charges, area sales offices, etc., can be directly analysed. Charges of a more general nature such as head office, sales and distribution expenses, general sales management, advertising on a national basis must be apportioned upon an equitable basis.

Delivery Route Decisions

In many industries, it is customary of delivery product to customers in company owned trucks. Where this occurs, delivery costs often represent a sizeable portion of total cost of products sold and should be controlled carefully. Proper cost control requires the segregation of all costs directly related to delivery routes certain of those costs such as trucks depreciation, insurance, and garage space are fixed. Other costs such as gas and oil, repairs, maintenance and drivers commission are variable.

Route Profit and Loss statements are useful. They suggest cost reduction or other possibilities for profit improvement. These statements should disclose the revenue earned on each route less variable factory costs. Itemwise route costs should then be deducted to yield the direct route profits.

Selecting among Alternative Channels of Distribution

A manufacturing company may market its products in several different ways. It may employ its own salesman. It may utilise the services of middlemen such as wholesalers of commission agents. It may establish its own retail outlets. It may even sell directly to the ultimate consumer by combining its factory and sales efforts at a single location as in the case of small factory. Frequently a company employs two or more different marketing methods simultaneously. The selection of appropriate channels of distribution constitutes an important marketing decision since the final choice generally will have a significant impact on profits and growths.

The following factors may affect the selection of suitable channels of sales outlet.

(1) Financial status of the firm.

(2) Product characteristics.

(3) Nature of market.

(4) Industry Pattern.

(5) Profitability.

The relative profitability of alternative marketing channels is a basic consideration. The profit for each should show the volume, costs and profits for the alternative channels. Only those costs which vary with the alternative channels are relevant. The technique of marginal cost is used to estimate the profitability.

Example 4

A company is supplying its products to consumers through wholesalers. The managing director of the company thinks that if the company starts selling through retailers or to consumer direct, it can increase its sales, charge higher prices and make more profit.

On the basis of information given below, you are required to advise the Managing Director whether the company should change its channel of distribution and if so what mode it should follow:

	Wholesaler	Retailer	Consumer
	Rs.	Rs.	Rs.
Sales price per unit	4.00	4.50	5.00
Estimated sales per year (Unit)	8,00,000	8,60,000	9,20,000
Selling and distributions cost per unit	0.70	1.05	1.75

Cost of production – variable cost Rs. 2 per unit and fixed cost Rs. 8,00,000.

Statement of Profitability of various Channels

	Wholesaler	Retailer	Consumer
No. of units sold	8,00,000	8,60,000	9,20,000
Sales in Rupees	3,20,000	38,70,000	46,00,000
Variable costs Rs. 2 per unit	16,00,000	17,20,000	18,40,000
Selling and distribution costs	5,60,000	9,03,000	16,10,000
Marginal costs	21,60,000	26,23,000	34,50,000
Contribution	10,40,000	12,47,000	11,50,000
Less fixed costs	8,00,000	8,00,000	8,00,000
Profit	2,40,000	4,47,000	3,50,000

It is apparent from the above analysis that if goods are sold through retailers the company can earn maximum of profits.

❑❑❑

2

Marketing Management Organisation

Introduction

Like organisation in the private sector, public service organisations are facing a more dynamic and more turbulent environment. Writing from a generic perspective, the American management theorist Rosabeth Moss Kanter (1990) has argued that:

"If the new game of business is indeed like Alice-in-Wonderland croquet, then winning it requires faster action, more creative manoeuvering, more flexibility, and closer partnerships with employees and customers than was typical in the traditional corporate bureaucracy. It requires more agile, limber management that pursues opportunity without being bogged down by cumbersome structures or weighty procedures that impede action. Corporate giants, in short, must learn now to dance."

Similar sentiments have been expressed in a public service context by Osborne and Gaebler (1992) in their work on American Public Services. In their call to 'reinvent government' they argue that the adoption of ten principles can transform a bureaucratic government into an innovative one:

(1) Government should seek to act as a catalyst to allow other organisations to provide services. It should seek to steer rather than to row.

(2) Citizens should be empowered by transferring control from bureaucracies to the community.

(3) Government should promote competition between service providers.

(4) Government should be driven by its mission – what it is there to do – rather than by rules and regulations.

(5) The performance of government should be judged by the outcomes - what it achieves - rather than by inputs - what it swallows up.

(6) By focusing on the customer, government will ensure that the needs of the customer and not the bureaucracy are being met.

(7) Government should become an enterprise, earning rather than spending money.

(8) Government should be proactive rather than reactive, looking to prevent problems rather than to cure them.

(9) Government should be decentralised and participatory management should be encouraged.

(10) Market mechanisms should be preferred to bureaucratic mechanisms.

In this environment, marketing managers are enjoined to be more responsive, more flexible, more entrepreneurial and innovative. At the same time, it is argued, structures must support these new roles and organisations will require flatter, more flexible and customer-responsive organisations, where decentralisation will have a key role to play.

There are a number of assumptions evident in such arguments:

(1) Public service organisations should be responsive, flexible and innovative and, as public service organisations are bureaucratic they are unsuitable vehicles for delivering public services.

(2) Bureaucracy is essentially seen as, in some sense, a bad thing.

(3) The key value of public service organisations should be responsive to customers though the marketplace and traditional values of accountability, probity and procedural justice enshrined in a hierarchical structure are of diminishing importance.

The merits of bureaucratic structure have been questioned because of their costs, their lack of responsiveness and their 'deadening' effect on staff motivation and morale. Flatter organisations will allow, so it is argued, a quicker and more flexible response to the outside environment. We shall examine the status of arguments, and the assumptions upon which they are based.

Bureaucracy and the Public Services

However, before we move on, we need to examine briefly the status of bureaucracy. Discussions of bureaucracy start with Max Weber. Beetham (1987) summarises the basic features of a bureaucratic system as propounded by Weber:

(1) Hierarchy: Each official has a clearly defined competence within a hierarchical division of labour, and is answerable for its performance to a superior.

(2) Continuity: The office constitutes a full-time salaried occupation, with a career structure which offers the prospects of regular advancement.

(3) Impersonality: The work is conducted according to prescribed rules, without arbitrariness or favouritism, and a written record is kept of each transaction.

(4) Expertise: Officials are selected according to merit, are trained for their function, and control access to the knowledge stored in the files.

According to Weber, bureaucracy has the potential to be more efficient than any other form of organisational structure. Bureaucracies ensure control, uniform treatment, consistency and clarity in applying rules and reduce arbitrary decision- making. However, in the period since the Second World War a substantial body of literature emerged showing that as well as producing intended consequences, bureaucracies also produced unintended consequences. These are also known as the dysfunctions of bureaucracy. These include:

(1) Rules can become ends in themselves; managers may hide behind them and use them as an excuse for not exercising judgement. "I was only following the rules" does not remove the need to individual judgement (Merton, 1940).

(2) Rules can increase the power of public officials, who may use the knowledge of the rules to circumscribe the desires of politicians. In this sense it is argued that bureaucracy undermines the democratic process. Bureaucracy is not a neutral machine for the transmission of politicians' wishes into public policies (Thompson, 1983).

(3) Rules can lead to rigidity and to lack of motivation among staff, particularly where, for example, promotion is based on seniority and position in the hierarchy rather than ability (Gouldner, 1954 and Crozier, 1964).

(4) Informal rules may be more efficient for achieving organisational goals; sometimes rules can be too rigid and not allow the discretion necessary for officials to make decision. 'Red tape' sometimes has to be by-passed (Blau, 1963).

What is clear, however, is that discussions of structure turn on an assumption that it is closely linked with strategy. We will discuss strategy in detail later. For the moment, we need to be supported by its structures and that as goals change then it is likely that there will be pressure for structural change.

Strategy and Structure

Public service organisations define themselves in different ways. For example, local authorities can play the role of direct service provider, they can adopt a commercial approach or a neighbourhood approach or define themselves in terms of community government. Each role may require a different organisational structure as the following analysis indicates:

(1) Direct service provider may be based on traditional departments carrying out a particular function such as education or social services. Control may be located in the hands of professionals at the top of a hierarchical structure (Leach *et al.,* 1994).

(2) The commercial-style organisation may deliver services through a range of other bodies all kept at arm's length on a contractual basis. A strong central core will be concerned with contract specifications, tendering and monitoring functions (Leach *et al.,* 1994).

(3) A neighbourhood approach may require power to be developed to neighbourhood offices at the local level, with a small central core (Leach *et al.,* 1994).

(4) A community approach may require that the organisation be structured on matrix lines where programme teams rather than departments deliver services which cut across traditional departmental or geographical boundaries.

The key issue is what the organisation does and how its structures can best support it. Strategy is concerned with where an organisation is going and structures are concerned with how to get the organisation there. Strategy is not given and strategic processes are iterative in nature.

Let us return to the example of bureaucracy and compare it with an alternative structure, with what Kanter (1990) calls 'post-entrepreneurialism' (*see* Table 1).

Table – 1

Bureaucracy and Kanter's 'Post-entrepreneurialism'

	Bureaucracy	**Corporate ideal**
Authority system	Position-centred, status or rank critical	Person-centred, authority derives from expertise and/or relationships
Task focus	Repetition-oriented	Creation-oriented, seeks innovation and efficiency
Orientation	Rules-oriented	Results-oriented
Reward system	Payment for status	Payment for contribution and value added
Information flows	Formal structures, restricting information	Communication and coalitions
Style	Creates mandates and teritories	Opportunities developed by network relations
Direction	Seeks ownership and control	Seeks leverage and experimentation

One conclusion that we can draw from the analysis presented in Table 1 is that bureaucracy as an organisational form may be suited to a particular context. Thus, it may be appropriate where, for example, large amounts of information need to be stored for long period of time, where organisational tasks are repetitive and the external context of the organisation is stable and likely to remain so.

Structures do not stand alone but involve people, processes, outcomes and tasks. Kanter's post-entrepreneurial model implies that organisations need to move from:

(1) an emphasis on hierarchical decision-making to an approach stressing delegation and personal responsibility;

(2) a focus on quantity to a focus on quality;

(3) being a service provider to having a user orientation;

(4) an emphasis on internal procedures to an emphasis on outcomes;

(5) an emphasis on professional judgement to an emphasis on management of contracts and trading relationships within an internal market; and

(6) stability and conformity to innovation and diversity.

Internal Strategies and Structures

The classical management theorists were concerned with the enduring principles of organisation structure. From Taylor onwards, through Fayol to Burns and Stalker (Lawton and Rose, 1994), structures have reflected a concern with:

(1) rules, processes and work tasks;

(2) division and specialisation of labour;

(3) allocation of duties and responsibilities;

(4) relationships between the centre and departments and/or field offices in terms of control;

(5) communication;

(6) configuration in terms of size, functions, clients, place, knowledge and skills;

(7) vertical and horizontal integration; and

(8) coordination.

One of the key internal roles of structure is to ensure coordination between the different parts of the organisation. Traditional approaches to public services assume that an organisation structured in hierarchical terms, such as a bureaucracy, is best placed to achieve this. According to Mitchell (1993):

> "Hierarchy is a structural mechanism for bringing about coordination, of running a large and complex organisation, of making a large number of individuals act together for a collective purpose of producing desired end results, in short, it is a way of 'getting things done'."

Whether coordination is best carried out by hierarchy is, however, open to question and later we examine the role of markets in coordination. However, many organisations have tinkered with their structure and then found a rationale for so doing; strategy has followed structure. Under the guise of speedier decision-making, or encouraging and empowering frontline staff, organisations have sought to cut costs by 'de-layering.' Tiers of middle management have disappeared. Advocates argue that de-layering gets rid of unnecessary tiers of management and empowers staff to take on more responsibility and become more involved in organisation decisions. Others argue that de-layering expands responsibilities but often not resources, reduces career opportunities and leads to bigger workloads and increased stress. Whatever the arguments, it is clear that the workplace is changing.

The Local Government Management Board (1996) argued for:

(1) smaller corporate management teams;

(2) the appointment of specialist policy advisers to support decision-making;

(3) decentralisation and a move towards multifunctional directorates;

(4) the establishment of contracting units staffed by councillors with a remit to seek value for money and service quality;

(5) increased use of joint officer/member working groups;

(6) partnerships and alliances with a variety of organisations

Equally obvious are the costs involved in changing one from of structure to another. Kanter argues that there are many by-products of significant organisational restructuring, including discontinuity, disorder and distraction.

> If mismanaged, restructuring can all too easily make people feel helpless, anxious startled, embarrassed, dumb, overworked, cynical, hostile or hurt. Restructuring thus produces a window of vulnerability at a time when exposure to disease is increased at precisely the same time as the corporate body is temporarily weakened. This threatens not only current productivity, but also the foundation of the future, the organisation's credibility, culminating in *a crisis of commitment and a need for people to reaffirm their membership.* Every time the basis of the relationship of employee and company changes, a recommitment is necessary. It is especially ironic that more commitment is needed at the very time when the basis for commitment itself is temporarily weakened (Kanter, 1990, emphasis in original).

New Decentralised Organisations

Organisations are not value neutral; that is, a belief in efficiency, responsiveness, control or whatever is not just about improving organisational effectiveness but is also a concern with a preferred way of conducting business. As we saw above, advocates of de-layering argue that it is a good thing in so far as it empowers frontline workers. Values are an enduring feature of public services organisations and one expression of these is in terms of the balance between political ideals (in Western countries, the ideals of democracy and organisational effectiveness). Those who support decentralisation argue that not only does it encourage the organisation to be more flexible and responsive but it is also more democratic. For example, Burns *et al.* (1994) argue that "Decentralisation offers glimpses of a new vision for local government which is rather different from the current obsession with markets and quasi-markets."

Decentralisation is seen as strengthening 'voice' in local government by:

(1) improving representative democracy through voter registration drives, open government, giving citizens rights at meetings and providing better support for councillors;

(2) extending representative democracy in area committees of councillors based onwards or groups, and strengthening parish councils;

(3) fusing representative with participatory democracy by co-option on to committees, neighbourhood committees and user groups; and

(4) extending participatory democracy through the funding of non-statutory groups, community development and user groups and valuing grass-roots participation (Burns *et al.*, 1994).

Jeffrey (1997) argues that the traditional local authority committee is an inappropriate vehicle for participation. She says that local authorities which have widened the scope of participatory democracy through the encouragement of community involvement in decision-making have become dominated by a community elite. Jeffrey argues that structures tend to limit committee membership, that discussion has often taken place elsewhere, that papers are only circulated to key members and that the local authority committee cycle means that time is a key constraint. She concludes (1997) that "The cumulative effect of the way the structures operate is to reinforce the creation of a community elite of 'gatekeepers' into the system. They become pseudo-councillors, but with none of the councillor's requirements of accountability and adherence to a party manifesto." This illustrates the way in which structures can be used to further individual ends. Structures, ideally, will support strategy. Organisations are not, however, rational bodies, but places where power is played out.

Decentralisation can be seen in terms of power transferred from a central body to subunits or operational agencies. The centre gives up some of its power and decisions are taken lower down the organisational hierarchy. In contrast, deconcentration is carried out for administrative reasons where it is considered that a service could be more effectively administered by local or regional bodies; power is still held at the centre. Local bodies become more effective in carrying out national policies rather than determining policies for themselves. Mintzberg (1993) identifies three different types of decentralisation:

(1) *Vertical decentralisation,* where power is located down the chain of command.

(2) *Horizontal decentralisation,* where decision-making powers are transferred to people outside the line structure.

(3) *Dispersal,* involving the physical relocations of services. This is often referred to as field administration.

However, even administrative relocation may not be 'power neutral,' as new regional offices of central government may conflict with local government or may impose greater central control over local government, for example, through Single Regeneration Budget allocations.

In two cases of decentralisation of fictional local authorities in a city a number of problems may be encountered. These include fears about deskilling and worries about redundancy, on the part of staff, and an unwillingness of areas to take on functions. Often there is a perception that insufficient resources are being devolved with the responsibility. Factors leading to success include devolving functions only when it is clearly cost effective to do so and the development of improved management information systems. Management of the area to which functions are devolved must accept the responsibility and their accountability for performance. Quality control should be provided, together with feedback. Customer care strategies also need to be developed.

So far we have concentrated on decentralisation in terms of area. It is also possible to reorganise on the basis of function, and it is this which underpins the creation of business or trading units. Consider the advantages and disadvantages of creating a direct service organisation (DSO) (*see* Exhibit 1.1)

Exhibit 1.1

Direct Service Organisation: Functional Decentralisation

Advantages:

- large enough to recruit competent managers;
- large enough to influence the rest of the authority in the pursuit of its interest;
- economies of scale;
- ability to use its staff flexibly;
- easier to identify and allocate the cost of DSO services;
- easier to allocate capital, buildings and land;
- easier to allocate central overheads.

Disadvantages:

- it may become too dominant in the affairs of the authority;
- possible duplication of functions and staff;
- establishing a radically different structure will involve considerable disruption to the authority;
- possible difficulty in recruiting managers to manage large DSOs;
- it will contain a very wide range of functions that may bear little relationship to each other.

Source: *Local Government Training Board,* 1988, p. 8.

Decentralisation has been experimented with throughout in liberal democracies. In Australia, for example, the public sector has undergone major reforms in recent years. One aspect of this reform has been the creation of devolved agencies at all levels of government. The Management Advisory Board conducted a comprehensive survey of decentralisation in central government. Its findings are set out in Exhibit 1.2.

Exhibit 1.2

Advantages and Disadvantages of Decentralisation

Benefits:

- Devolution is a powerful tool to promote and implement change.
- Managers are more in control of achieving outcomes.
- Managers become more familiar with corporate management issues.
- Managers have more scope in determining the level and type of service delivery and the method of delivery.
- Managers can be more responsive to stakeholders.
- Service providers are closer to their clients and have a better understanding of needs.
- There are opportunities of increased job satisfaction.
- Managers have the opportunity to acquire new and marketable skills.

Costs:

- Loss of quality and increased inconsistency in decision-making.
- Loss of purchasing power and other economies of scale.
- Duplication of tasks or functions.
- Reduction in number of people skilled in providing corporate services.
- Diminution of expertise, for example in personnel matters.
- Loss of corporate identity.

Findings:

1. Commitment from the Chief executive is crucial.
2. Communication, transparency and openness are needed.
3. Training for all staff is crucial.
4. Appropriate time must be allowed, plus monitoring and evaluation.
5. Line managers must be given real choices about how they will obtain or undertake corporate service functions.
6. Accountability must be taken into consideration.
7. There is no one best way; each agency needs to find its own way.
8. There is a need for good management information systems.
9. Trust line managers.

Source: *Management Advisory Board,* 1992.

The Core and the Periphery

In the rhetoric surrounding decentralisation it is easy to forget that there are certain advantages in centralisation. These include:

(1) easier implementation of a common policy for the organisation as a whole;

(2) prevention of subunits becoming too independent;

(3) easier coordination;

(4) improving economies of scale and a reduction in overhead costs;

(5) greater use of specialisation;

(6) improved decision-making, which might otherwise be slower and a result of compromise because of differentiated authority; and

(7) uniform and equitable treatment of clients.

Some local authorities are experimenting with the development of a stronger strategic core which is responsible for controlling the core values of the organisation and the strategies which it wishes to pursue. Service units are controlled through strict performance management systems. Thus there appear to be two trends: one with a strong corporate centre and another in which organisations are being encouraged to change their structures in favour of giving responsibility (though not always power) to those lower down the organisation. Winstanley *et al.* (1995) describe public services restructuring as involving change from:

(1) centralised management to local management of service provisions;

(2) direct hierarchical control to arm's length regulation;

(3) a smaller number of large hierarchies to more complex networks of organisations;

(4) being state owned and run to being characterised by a contracting out of services, CCT and the development of quasi-markets; and

(5) a unified service to a splitting of the purchaser and provider roles.

Such changes are deemed to be desirable. Consider the LGMB's view of good management in local government (1993): The well-managed authority is one which:

(1) undertakes structural change only when it has established a real need for it and avoids cosmetic changes;

(2) establishes a relatively small management team of officers (five to eight members) whose primary role is strategic and encourages a strong sense of corporate identity;

(3) relies on informal networks of staff throughout the organisation to deal with corporate problems and spread corporate messages;

(4) develops a clear view of the role of the centre of the organisation in the new local government context; and

(5) achieves a balance between central direction and devolution of managerial control.

Whether such authorities exist is a moot point. Research carried out by Rao and Young found that:

> There were also indications that regrouping the authority around a set of trading units exposed the lacunae in the overall strategic management of authorities. The externalisation of parts of technical services, or the loss of a competitive bid by an in-house team under CCT, could have an impact on the authorities' central departments as they reduce the customer base. In one authority it was recognised that while certain aspects of central service provision would be carried out externally, such as payroll, accountancy, legal and personnel advice, and personnel records, the authority should seen to retain a significant proportion of the central support services "to enable the client and regulators services to carry out its statutory, democratic and strategic functions." (1995)

Of course, such structural change are not 'people neutral' in their effects. Charles Handy (1990) uses the imagery of the shamrock to show how organisations may be composed of three different kinds of staff:

(1) The first leaf is the core professionals; it is shrinking.

(2) Non-essential work is contracted out so that much of the work of an organisation is carried out by people not in the organisation. The risks are thus outside the organisation.

(3) Flexible labour force, part-timers and temporary staff.

Each group of people will have a different kind of commitment to the organisation, a different contractual arrangement and a different set of expectations. A core group, whose contribution is deemed to be essential and which would be difficult to replace, will sit alongside others who are more peripheral, in the sense of being more easily replaceable or whose work adds little extra value to the organisation.

Much of what has been happening in public services organisations in recent years poses questions for the boundary of the organisation. These relate to the practice of outsourcing, where an organisation contracts to another supplier work that was previously done in house. Under competitive tendering, many authorities have outsourced activities such as payroll, catering, security, cleaning, IT services. One driving factor is legislation, but other reasons include political motivations, so as to give, for example, at least the illusion of reducing the size of the public sector; a belief in the private sector; or a requirement to cut costs. Invariably the contracting out of work provides an incentive for firms to win contracts through offering lower tender prices, often based on lower labour costs. It may also allow access to specialist services, or may eliminate peripheral activities which distract from the core business.

The issues for management in outsourcing include contract negotiation, confidentially and risk sharing. Outsourcing may result in the loss of expertise in certain areas which is difficult to recover. There is a danger of 'hollowing out' the organisation, the loss of come capabilities, leaving nothing in their place.

According to Bahrami (1992):

> "The emerging organisational systems of high-technology firms is more akin to a 'federation' or a 'constellation' of business units that are typically interdependent, relying on one another for critical expertise and know-how. Moreover they have a peer-to-peer relationship with the centre. The centre's role is to orchestrate the broad strategic vision, develop the shared organisational and administrative infrastructure, and create and cultural glue which can create synergies, and ensure unity of mission and purpose."

From Hierarchy to Markets

As indicated above, outsourcing or contracting out can be given an economic justification. Before we turn to consider that aspect, however, let us consider the role of hierarchies in organisations. It is assumed that hierarchy should give way to either markets on networks as a means of organising the delivery of public services. Jaques (1990) offers an alternative view: "managerial hierarchy is the most efficient, the hardiest and, in fact, the most natural structure ever devised for large organisations."

According to Jaques, a hierarchy meets four fundamental needs:

(1) To add value to work as it moves through the organisation.

(2) To identify and nail down accountability at each stage of the value-adding process.

(3) To place people with the necessary competence at each organisational layer.

(4) To build a general consensus and an acceptance of the managerial structure that achieves these ends.

He argues that the managerial role has three key features. First, every manager must be held accountable for the work of subordinates and for adding value to their work. Second, every manager must be held accountable for sustaining a team of subordinates capable of doing this work. Third, every manager must be held accountable for setting a direction and getting subordinates to follow willingly.

There are boundaries between successive managerial layers and these have a time-span element to them. The more distant the time-span, the heavier the weight of responsibility. Senior managers are looking at a direction for the next three years, the production supervision at a direction for the next three months. Jaques argues that managerial boundaries occur at a specific time-span increment. Similarly, the higher up the hierarchy, the more complex are the problems to be solved. Jaques (1990) argues that "What we need is not some new kind of organisation. What we need is managerial hierarchy that understands its own nature and purpose."

However, Leach *et al.* (1994) argue that the public services have moved from hierarchy to markets: "The relationship between the centre and direct service providers has moved from one of distribution on the basis of command, towards allocation on the basis of exchange, that is, from hierarchy towards market processes."

The centre no longer retains control through hierarchy but through a mixture of subcontracting, franchising and partnership arrangements. Williamson (1975) contrasts the co-ordinating role of the market, in contrast to hierarchy, and provides a theoretical underpinning for contracting out. Williamson argues that hierarchial coordination is more efficient under certain conditions:

(1) Where there is insufficient information to specify a market contract, that is, where *bounded rationality* exists, with the result that future contingencies cannot be specified or it is costly to do so.

(2) Where *opportunism* exists, so that parties to a contract will try and take advantage of any loopholes. By internalising the transaction the firm gains more information. Also, where there are a large number of competitors, opportunists would have more difficulty in renewing contracts than where there is no alternative.

(3) Where *asset specificity* (specialised equipment or skills) exists, that is, where resources are committed to a specific activity and have little value in any alternative use. A small number of suppliers and buyers increases asset specificity since there are few alternatives and price can be affected. A component supplier would charge a higher price to compensate for the risk of the investment.

Where these conditions are internal to an organisation risks are reduced and transaction costs are lowered. Williamson argues that a firm has a role to play in the economic system if transactions can be organised within the firm at less cost than if the same transactions were carried out through the market. The limit to the size of the firm is reached when the costs of organising additional transactions within the firm exceed the costs of carrying out the same transactions through the market. Transaction costs economics adopts a comparative contractual approach to the study of economic organisation in which the transaction is made the basic unit of analysis.

The approach employs two critical behavioural assumptions:

(1) Human agents are assumed to be independently rational but only in a limited way. Bounded rationality means that comprehensive contracting is not feasible.

(2) Human agents are given to opportunism. Therefore costs of safeguards may be high.

Bartlett (1991) examines contracting in the NHS using the transaction costs approach. He argues that the NHS reforms move away from vertical integration to more market-like considerations. It is, though, a quasi-market in which consumers' decisions are mediated through a variety of intervening agents, the District Health Authority or fundholding GPs.

Bartlett argues that many of the defects of market exchange associated with uncertainty, bonded rationality, opportunism and asset specificity apple to the NHS. He examines different types of contract — block, cost per case, cost and volume (a mixture of the other two):

(1) Complete contracts, which cater for every possible act of nature, are difficult and costly to write, implement and enforce. Therefore transaction costs will be relatively high.

(2) Incomplete block contracts (which the NHS prefers) are the answer, but they do allow opportunistic strategies and they shift the risk on to the provider unit.

However, as Stewart (1993) points out, contracting for the public services involves more than economic considerations. He considers the advantages claimed for the contract model:

(1) It separates the political process of determination of objectives from their delivery, removing the conflict of interest which occurs when those specifying a service are also its deliverers.

(2) It reduces the public phenomenon of lobbying for bureaucratic expansion by introducing built-in competitive pressures.

(3) It strengthens opportunities for quality control.

(4) It makes funding transparent.

(5) It regularises relationships between central government, local authorities and competing agencies.

(6) It establishes a set of guarantees with reciprocal responsibilities.

Could any of these be achieved without contracts or with existing relationships? Stewart accepts that, in the past, public services have been too much producer led. Yet is government by contract the only response?

It cannot be assumed that the introduction of contracts into public services is unproblematic or that contracts can play the same role in relation to public services as they do in the private sector. They have to be judged by criteria grounded in government. The local council, for example, is responsible for everything done in its name; the DSO or a business unit is not in the same legal position. Stewart (1993) argues that:

> "The process of government has its distinctive role as the arena of collective action in society on which the functioning of society depends. In the public domain the process of government enables values to be realised the purposes pursued that are beyond the capacity of private action. Insofar as contracts enable that process, they can promote governmental effectiveness as well as efficiency of service delivery, but there are limits. Government cannot be reduced to a series of contracts."

Public sector organisations, particularly in the NHS, tend to operate in quasi-markets where the boundary between public and private is blurred. The existence of hybrid organisations which both provide tax-supported services and rely on income from the commercial market leads, according to Paton (1993), to a dual logic. The logic of the quasi-market is different from that of the commercial market. Quasi-markets involve:

(1) a fixed pot of tax finance, now distributed more on the basis of competitive bidding;

(2) a mixed bag of competition and collaboration;

(3) fragmentation of the organisation and between units in terms of service-level agreements (internal contracts);

(4) continued existence as non-profit organisations.

Hybrid managers compete in two markets – quasi and the real thing. Paton identifies a number of key questions. First, how much of the resources of the organisation are to be devoted to the two sides? Second, where are funds reinvested? Third, what products are developed? Fourth, what pricing policy is appropriate? Fifth, what are the internal transfer prices?

Rather than a enhance responsiveness, it could be argued that the introduction of markets creates increased organisational formality. Services are more strictly specified. Payment systems are precisely defined - involving orders and invoices. Record systems are central to the management of contracts. There also needs to be a system of arbitration for the resolution of differences between the parties. All of this leads to increased costs.

Does transaction costs analysis cater for this? There are also the costs of disruption and the costs to morale that Kanter (1990) highlighted and which are described above.

Conclusions

Organisational structure is not a given and it is not just concerned with centralisation or decentralisation, hierarchies or markets. It is more problematic and involves people— power, culture, processes and so on. In the NHS management by hierarchy has been replaced by management by contract. This may shift the fundamental rationale of the organisation from being based upon a division of labour to being based on a division of knowledge and power - that is, who has the purchasing power. With any change we can ask who has lost and who won in terms of power, resources, or status.

In local government we have seen the division of role between client and contractor but also the need to develop a greater capacity for strategy and cohesion. How fragmentation has taken place and what has been its effect on strategy are key questions. Has the role of the core strategic management cadre been reinforced at the expense of service professionals? To what extent is the centre driven by a resource-led view rather than any consideration of public service? Is the relationship between members and officers now one of contract specification, penalty points and service monitoring?

In education there are some signs of a return to centralised provision, particularly in specialist education services, curriculum advice, the careers service, education psychology. This seems likely to have occurred as a result of pressures to streamline services.

However, in general, where central services have been retained their provision has been subject to service-level agreement with user departments.

A concern with structure cannot be separated from power; Winstanley *et al.* (1995) identify restructuring as resulting in a restriction of local political accountability, an attack on the monopoly power of the provider professions and an emphasis on consumer power. They define two aspects to power:

(1) *Criteria power* is concerned with the ability of stakeholders to define aims and purposes, design overall systems, set or influence performance criteria and evaluate performance on the basis of these.

(2) *Operational power* is concerned with the ability to provide the service and change the way the service is delivered, allocating limited resources and using knowledge and key skills.

They provide a power matrix and map various services on this matrix (*see* Fig. 1).

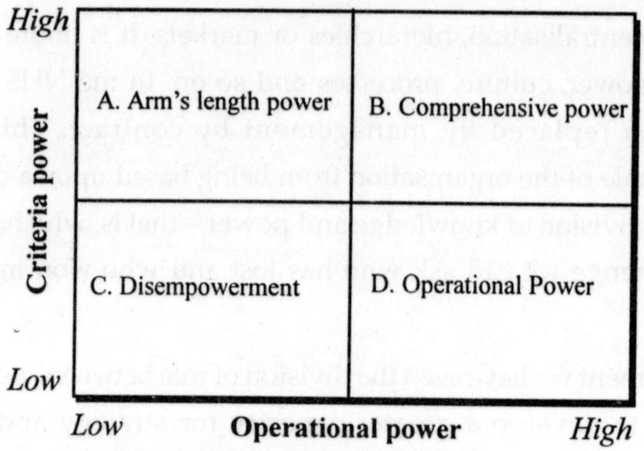

Fig. 1 Power Matrix

Thus, in the NHS restructuring, regional health authorities have reduced criteria power since they have become regional offices of the NHS. They have retained accountability for purchasers and monitor trusts. District health authorities have become commissioning agencies and have increased their power in setting local criteria for service delivery but have lost direct operational power.

In much the same way, other public services could be mapped, to show that local education authorities (LEAs) have moved from B to C. In other words what are the implications of structural change from a power/stakeholder perspective? Winstanley *et al.* (1995) consider that Generally, government will move from B to C and from A to D.

Of course, the devolution of power may be more evident in rhetoric than in reality. In the NHS, the creation of clinical directorates could be seen as an example of forcing the medical profession to make unpalatable decisions concerning rationing.

Paton (1993) contends that:

"Decentralisation and devolution may be strategies to pass responsibility for the management of limited resources to those providers responsible for using them. This has been an interpretation by some sceptical doctors of the policy to establish clinical directorates. It is in effect an attenuated example from the developed world of a phenomenon life in health care systems within the developing world – decentralisation to communities as a means of admitting that resources do not exist at the central level to allow a nationally planned system."

The discussion of power illustrates the tensions and paradoxes that exist within organisations. Structures are part of the tension. These tensions pull in different directions:

(1) central control and decentralisation;
(2) integration and differentiation, reflecting the problems of coordination mechanisms, strategy and operations when the roles of purchaser and provider are differentiated;
(3) management and democracy;
(4) continuity and flexibility, knowing what to discard and what to retain;
(5) uniformity and diversity; and
(6) specialisation and generalisation, and the relationship between professionals and managers.

Organisational balance is crucial. Some of these tensions are captured by the chief executive of an American corporation quoted by Bahrami (1992):

> We want an environment that enhances individual creativity, but we do not want chaos . . . we want people involved in decisions that affect their work and we want teamwork, yet we want our employees to have a bias towards action . . . we want small groups of dedicated workers (decentralisation) but such groups may feel aimless or may be charging in the wrong direction with hidden agendas . . . we want people to stretch to reach tough goals, so our real emphasis is on easily-measured short-terms growth and profits – but we should also have time to develop out employees for the longer haul, to promote from within, to monitor the atmosphere for creativity.

Contradictory demands are made upon employees. There are institutionalised inequalities of power and opportunity. We respect individuality but also expect conformity. Organisational structures will need to reflect these contradictions.

□□□

3

Personal-marketing

Introduction

Personal-marketing is a form of promotion, and it is marketing management's responsibility to determine the role of personal selling in the promotional mix. Fig. 1 shows how personal selling fit into the promotional programme. While an occasional marketer shifts the entire personal-selling activity to middlemen, most must concern themselves with setting personal-selling objectives, determining sales policies, formulating personal selling strategies, and determining sales budgets, as well as with managing their own sales forces. As Fig. 1 indicates, these interrelated tasks collectively make up the personal selling portion of the promotional programme.

There are both qualitative and quantitative personal-selling objectives. The qualitative objectives generally are long-term objectives and mainly concern the contributions management expects personal selling to make in achieving overall long-term company objectives. Such objectives change very little over time and essentially are carried over from one period's promotional programme to the next. Depending upon the overall long-term company objectives and the nature of the promotional mix, personal-selling may be assigned such qualitative objectives as:

(1) To do the entire job (as when there are no other elements in the promotional mix).

(2) To 'service' existing accounts (that is, to maintain contacts with present customers, take orders, etc.)

(3) To search out and obtain new customers.

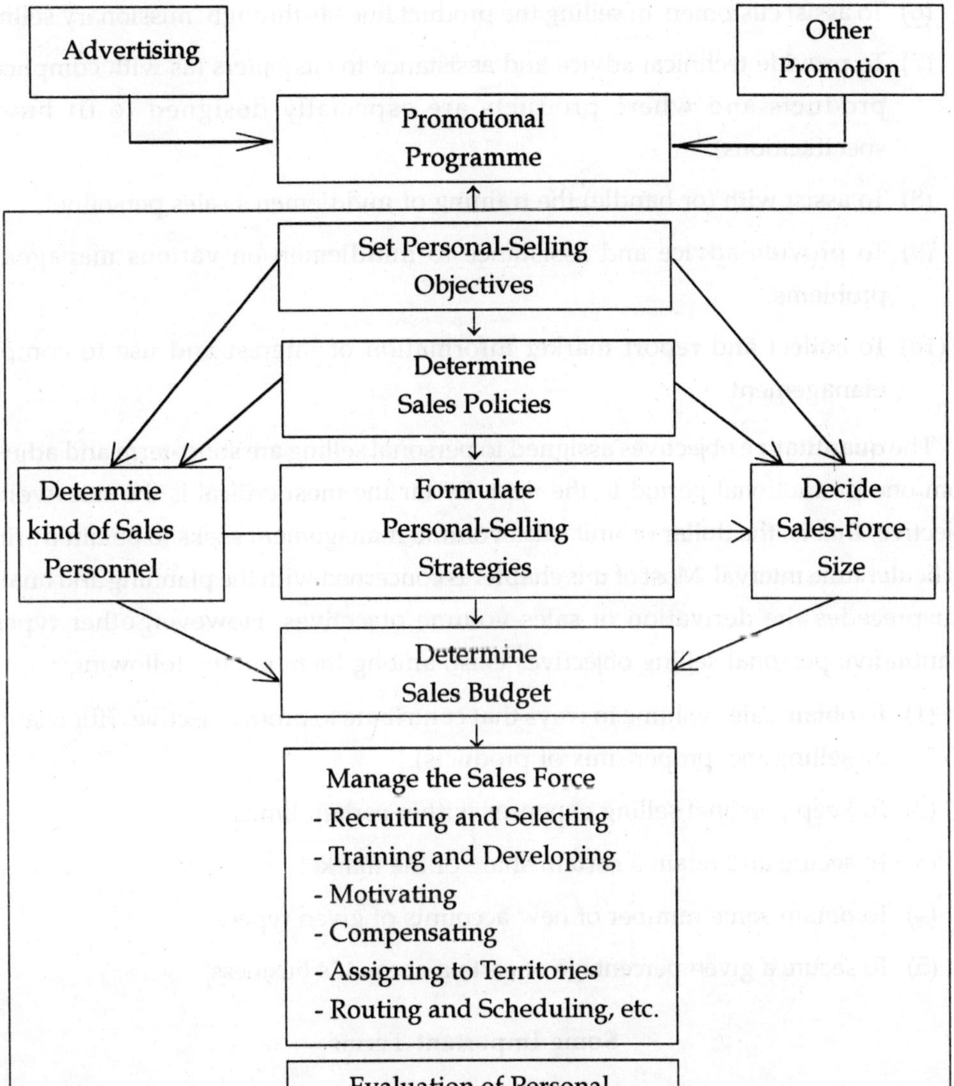

Fig. 1 Personal Selling as Part of the Promotion Programme

(4) To secure and maintain customers' cooperation in stocking and promoting the product line.

(5) To keep customers informed on changes in the product line and other aspects of marketing strategy.

(6) To assist customers in selling the product line (as through 'missionary selling').

(7) To provide technical advice and assistance to customers (as with complicated products and where products are especially designed to fit buyer's specifications).

(8) To assist with (or handle) the training of middlemen's sales personnel.

(9) To provide advice and assistance to middlemen on various management problems.

(10) To collect and report market information of interest and use to company management.

The quantitative objectives assigned to personal selling are short-term and adjusted from one promotional period to the next. By far the most critical is the sales-volume objective, that is, the dollar or unit sales volume management seeks to obtain during a particular time interval. Most of this chapter is concerned with the planning and analysis that precedes the derivation of sales-volume objectives. However, other types of quantitative personal-selling objectives exist, among them are the following:

(1) To obtain sales volume in ways that contribute to profit objectives (for example, by selling the 'proper' mix of products).

(2) To keep personal selling expenses within certain limits.

(3) To secure and retain a certain share of the market.

(4) To obtain some number of new accounts of given types.

(5) To secure a given percentage of certain account's business.

Some Important Terms

Before we examine the planning and analytical work that lies behind the setting of sales-volume objectives, it is necessary to define three important terms: market potential, sales potential, and sales forecast. Up until recently, it was common for executives to use these terms synonymously. However, as the following discussion indicates, there are good reasons to distinguish among them.

Market Potential

A market potential is a quantitative estimate of the maximum possible sales opportunities present in a particular market segment and open to all sellers of a good or service during a stated future period. Thus, an estimate of the maximum number of low-priced pocked cameras that might be sold in San Mateo Country, California, during the calendar year 2006 by all sellers competing for this market would represent the 2006 San Mateo County market potential for low-priced pocket cameras. A market potential indicates how much of a particular product can be sold to a particular market segment over some future period, assuming the application of appropriate marketing methods.

Sales Potential

A sales potential is a quantitative estimate of the maximum possible sales opportunities present in a particular market segment open to a specified company selling a good or service during a stated future period. To illustrate, an estimate of the number of low-priced pocket cameras that might be sold in San Mateo County, California, during the calendar year 2006 by the Eastman Kodak Company would be the 2006 San Mateo County sales potential for Eastman Kodak low-priced pocket cameras. Note carefully that a sales potential represents sale opportunities available to a particular manufacturer, such as to Eastman Kodak Company, while a market potential indicates sales opportunities available to an entire industry.

Sales Forecast

A sales forecast is a estimate of sales, in dollars or physical units, for a specified future period under a proposed marketing plan or programme and under an assumed set of economic and other forces outside the unit for which the forecast is made. A sales forecast may be, for a single product, or for the entire product line. Similarly, a sales forecast may be for a manufacturer's entire marketing area, or for any subdivision of it. More precisely, such forecasts are known as short-term, or operating, sales forecasts to distinguish them from long-range sale forecasts, which are used mainly for planning changes in production capacity and for assisting in long-run financial planning. Predictions of the probable sales experience of the firm in the comparatively distant future, although naturally of interest, are normally so tentative that sales planners given them only passing attention. It is the short-term, or operating, sales forecast with which the sales executive is mainly concerned. Keep in mind, then, that the basic purpose of an operating sales forecast is to predict how much of a company's particular product (or product line) can be sold during a specified future period in certain markets under a given marketing plan or programme and under an assumed set of economic and other outside forces.

Determining Market Potential

Market Identification

An essential step in determining a product's market potential is to identify its market. Market identification requires finding answers to one or more of these questions:

(1) Who buys the product?

(2) Who uses it?

(3) Who are the prospective buyers and/or users?

Occasionally these questions are at least partially answered through analysing internal company records; but in most companies, especially those that use long marketing channels, more complete answers are obtained only through field research. In consumer-goods marketing, buyers, users, and prospects are identified and classified according to such characteristics as age, sex, education, income, and social class. In industrial-goods marketing, buyers, and prospects are identified and classified by such characteristics as size of firm, geographical location, and type of industry.

Marketing identification studies reveal the characteristics that distinguish the various market segments making up the products' total market potential. Frequently they uncover unexploited market segments whose patronage might be obtained by, for example, redirecting personal-selling efforts or changing promotional strategy. Sometimes, market identification studies provide, as a side result, customer data on such factors as purchase frequency, searching time expended, unit of purchase, and seasonal buying habits. When these data are assembled and analysed, they are helpful in estimating market potential.

Market Motivation

A second important step in determining a product's market potential relates to the determination of buying reasons. Market motivation studies are aimed at answering twin questions: Why do people buy? Why don't people buy? Answers to these questions provide information that is helpful not only in estimating a product's market potential but is of immense value of the sales executive seeking to improve promotional programmes and to increase their effectiveness.

Motivation research techniques vary, but all derive from psychological theory. Probably the most widely used are the protective techniques, in which respondents project themselves, their feelings, and desires, into interpretations of special materials presented by the researcher. Motivation researchers use such information-gathering devices as sentence-completion tests, thematic-appreciation tests, and world-association tests. Most motivation research studies make no use, or minimal use, of formal questionnaires; and interviews are usually of the 'depth' type, the interviewer's main role being that of keeping the respondent talking, sometimes for several hours.

Later analysis of interview results by trained specialists seeks to lay bare what actually goes in buyers' minds, including, importantly, the real reasons for buying or not buying the product under study. Most motivation studies have been directed toward explaining the buying behaviour of ultimate consumers rather than that of industrial users. Information derived from motivation studies is helpful not only in estimating a product's market potential but assists in deciding:

(1) How to present the product in sales talk?

(2) The relative effectiveness of different selling appeals.

(3) The relative appropriateness of various promotional methods and advertising media.

Measuring Market Potential

Market identification and market motivation data provide important insights on a product, but they do not indicate the size of its potential market. Having identified the types of potential buyers and with information available about their buying behaviour, it is necessary next to measure the market potential. Generally, it is not possible to measure market potential directly, so the analyst approaches the measurement task by using market factors (a market factor is a feature of characteristic of a market that is related to the demand of the product). For instance, the number of males reaching shaving age each years is a market factor influencing the demand for men's electric shavers. However, not every male reaching shaving age is a given year is a prospective buyer of an electric shaver—some will be late in starting to shave, others will adopt other shaving methods, many will either not have the money to buy a shaver or will prefer to use the money for something else, and still others will borrowed shavers or, perhaps, simply not shave at all. This demonstrates, then, that using marketing factors for measuring a product's market potential is a two step process:

(1) Select the market factor (s) most closely associated with the product's demand.

(2) Eliminate those market segments that for one reason or another are not prospective buyers of the product.

Measurements of market potential usually are expressed in relative terms, such as in percentages or index form, rather than in absolute numbers of units or dollar value. One reason for this has already been implied-only rarely is it possible to find market factors directly related to a product's demand; most market factors relate indirectly to the demands of specific products. Another important reason for expressing market-potential measurements in relative terms is that estimates of absolute market size are obtained through sale forecasting (described later in this chapter).

Manufacturers of consumer products are fortunate in that several market-potential indexes are readily available. The most widely used index are population as a percentage of the Indian total, effective buying income as a percentage of the Indian total, and retail sales as a percentage of the Indian total. Many companies refine these index further by breaking them down into greater detail; for example, the population index may be divided into sub-indexes covering various are groups and the income index into sub indexes for different income groups.

The well-known *Sales Management Buying Power Index* combines effective buying income, retail sales, and population into a single index using weighting of factors of five for income, three for retail sales, and two for population. This particular combination and weighting of market factors serves as a satisfactory measure of market potential for many consumer-products manufacturers but many others construct their own index, including different or additional market factors and using different weighing systems. One manufacturer of lighting fixtures, for instance, includes data on new housing starts as a factor, and a maker of automobile seat covers includes motor vehicle registrations. Other market factors frequently used in constructing consumer-goods indexes of market potential are: registrations of new automobiles, home ownership, marriage licences issued, births, and deaths. Manufactures of industrial products construct their index of market potentials using such market factors as value added by manufacture, number of employees engaged in certain types of manufacturing, number of manufacturing establishments, man-hours worked, total value of shipments of various items, and capital expenditures for new plant and equipment.

Sales Potential and Sales Forecasting

Sales potentials, as defined earlier, are quantitative estimates of the maximum possible sales opportunities present in particular market segments open to a specified company selling a goods or service during a stated future period. They are generally derived from market potentials after analysis of historical market -share relationships and through the making of adjustments for recent or impending changes in company and competitors' selling strategies are not usually identical—in most instances, the sales potential will be greater than the sales forecast. There are several possible reasons for this. Some companies do not have sufficient production capacity to capitalise on the full sales potential; other firms have not yet developed their distributive networks to the point where they are capable of reaching every potential customers; others do not attempt to realise their total sales potentials because of limited financial resources; and other, being more profit-oriented than sales-oriented, seek to maximise profitable sales and not possible sales. The estimate for sales potential indicates how much a company could sell if it had all the necessary resources and desired to use them for this purpose. The sales forecast is a related but different estimate—it indicates how much a company with a give amount of resources can sell if it implements a particular marketing programme. Thus, the sales-potential estimate is a much more speculative figure than is the sales forecast.

Sales Forecasting Methods

There are two main classes of forecasting methods: unsophisticated and sophisticated. The unsophisticated methods rely primarily on judgement to produce sale forecasts; the basic reasoning underlying these methods is easily understood. The sophisticated methods, in contrast, involve applying statistical techniques or varying degrees of difficulty. In the following sections we consider six methods at some length:

the jury of executive opinion and the poll of sales force opinion (both unsophisticated methods); projection of past sales and survey of customers' buying plans (both of which may be either unsophisticated or sophisticated, depending upon how they are applied); and regression analysis and econometric model building and simulation (both sophisticated methods).

Jury of Executive Opinion

There are two steps in this forecasting method: (1) a small number of high-ranking executives register their individual opinions concerning the probable future level of sales, and (2) the forecast is derived from a rough averaging of these opinions. The executives whose opinions are solicited should be ones who are well informed about the industry outlook and the company's relative market position and capabilities. All participating executives should support their estimates with factual material to the maximum extent possible and be prepared to supply the rational behind their estimates.

Companies using the jury-of-executive opinion method generally do so for one or more of four reasons:

(1) This is a relatively easy way to turn out a forecast in a short time.

(2) This is a way to pool the experience and judgement of people who 'are in a position to know.'

(3) This may be the only feasible approach to forecasting if the company is so young that it has not yet accumulated the experience necessary to use other methods.

(4) This method may have to be used when adequate sales and market statistics are missing, or when these figure have not yet been put into the form required for more sophisticated forecasting methods.

The jury-of-executive-opinion approach to sales forecasting has some obvious weaknesses. As the name indicates, its findings are based primarily on opinion, and factual evidence to support the forecast is often sketchy. Using the approach adds to the workload of key executives, requiring them to spend time that they would otherwise devote to their areas of primary responsibility. And a forecast made by this method is difficult to break down into estimates of probable sales by products, by time intervals, by markets, by customers, and so on; if the sales forecast is to be of maximum value for operating purposes breakdown of this sort are needed.

Poll of Sales-force Opinion

Under the poll-of-sales-force-opinion method, often tagged 'the grass-roots approach,' individual sales personnel forecast sales for their respective territories; then these individual forecast are combined and modified, as management thinks necessary, to form the company sales forecast. The logic underlying this approach is that forecasting responsibility is assigned to those who must later produce the results. Furthermore, this method has the merit of utilising the specialised knowledge of those company personnel who are in the closest touch with market conditions. In addition, because the salespeople have helped to develop the forecast, it seems reasonable that they should have greater confidence in any quotas based upon it that are later assigned to them. Still another attractive feature is that forecasts developed by this method are easy to break down according to products, territories, customers, middlemen, and sales force.

But the poll-of-sales-force-opinion approach to sale forecasting has basic weaknesses. Not generally trained to do forecasting, and heavily influenced by current business conditions in their territories, salespersons tend to be overoptimistic or overpessimistic about their prospects for making future sales. They are entirely too near the trees to see the forest—they often are unaware of broad changes taking place in the economy and of trends in business conditions outside their own territories. Furthermore, if the 'forecasts' of the sales staff are used in setting quotas, some sales personnel deliberately underestimate so that they can reach their quotas more easily. To some extent these weaknesses can be overcome through training the sales force in forecasting techniques, by orienting them on factors influencing company sales, and by adjusting for consistent biases in individual salespersons' forecasts detected through analysis of their forecasting records. For most companies, however, implementing such corrective actions is an almost endless task, because turnover among sales personnel is constantly going on and new staff members (whose biases are unknown at the start) submit their forecasts along with the forecasts of long-experienced sales personnel with known forecasting biases. In short, this method is based to such a large extent on judgement that it is an unreliable approach for most companies to use as their only forecasting method. The poll sales-force opinion, where used, usually serves as a method of getting an alternative estimate of sales for use as a check of a sales forecast obtained through some other approach.

Projection of Past Sales

The projection-of-past-sales methods of sales forecasting takes a varity of forms. In its simplest form, the sales forecast for the coming year may be set at the same figure as the current year's actual sales. Alternatively, the forecast may be made merely by adding a set percentage to last year's sales or to a moving average of the sales figures for several past years. For instance, if it is assumed that there will be the same percentage sales increase next year as this year, the forecaster might utilise a naïve-model projection such as:

$$\text{next year's sales} = \text{this year's sales} \times \frac{\text{this year's sales}}{\text{last year's sales}}$$

This year's sales are inevitably related to last year's. Similarly, next year's sales are related to this year's and to those of all preceding years. Projecting present sales levels is a simple and inexpensive forecasting method and it may be appropriate for companies in more or less stable or 'mature' industries – it is rare in such industries for a company's sales to vary more than 15 per cent plus or minus from the preceding year's experience.

Time Series Analysis

Not greatly different in principle from the simple projection of past sales is time-series analysis, a statistical procedure for studying historical sales data. This procedure involves isolating and measuring four chief types of sales variations: long-term trends, cyclical changes, seasonal variations, and irregular fluctuations. Then a mathematical model describing the past behaviour of the series is selected, assumed values for each type of sales variation are inserted, and the sales forecast is 'cranked out'.

For companies in most industries, time-series analysis finds practical application mainly in the making of long-range forecasts. The results obtained may be reliable for a period of several years ahead; but the chances are great that predictions on a year-to-year basis, such as are necessary for an operating sales forecast, will not be reliable. Only where sale patterns are clearly defined and relatively stable from year to year is time-series analysis used successfully for making short-terms operating sales forecasts.

Another drawback of time-series analysis is that it is extremely difficult to 'call the turns'. Trend and cycle analysis often makes it possible to do a good job in explaining why a trend, once it is under way, continues in a certain direction; but it is predicting the turns that is important. On their correct prognostication depends to a large extent the maximisation of sales opportunities when the trend is favourable, and the minimisation of losses when the reverses itself.

Exponential Smoothing

A statistical technique for short-range sales for forecasting, which has received increasing acceptance in recent years, is called 'exponential smoothing.' Exponential smoothing is a type of moving average which represents a weighted sum of all past numbers in a time series, with the heaviest weight placed on the most recent data. To illustrate, consider this relatively simple but widely used form of exponential smoothing—a weighted average of this year's sales is combined with the forecast of this year's sales to arrive at the forecast for next year's sales. The forecasting equation, in other words, is:

$$\text{Next years sales} = a\ (\text{this year's sales}) + (1-a)\ (\text{this year's forecast})$$

The *a* in the equation is called the *smoothing constant* and is set at a value between 0.0 and 1.0. If, for example, actual sales for year came to 320 units of product, the sales forecast for this year was 350 units, and the smoothing constant was 0.3, the forecast for next year's sales is:

$$(0.3)\ (320) + (0.7)\ (350) = 341 \text{ units of product}$$

Determining the value of *a* is the main problem in using exponential smoothing. If the series of sales data changes slowly, *a* should be small to retain the effect of earlier observations. If the series changes rapidly, *a* should be large so that the forecasts respond to these change. In practice *a* is estimated by trying several values and making retrospective tests of the associated forecast error. The *a* value leading to the smallest forecast error is then chosen for future smoothing.

Evaluation of Past Sales Projection Methods

The main limitation of all forecasting method involving projections of past sales is that past sales history is assumed to be the only factor influencing future sales. No allowance is made for sharp and rapid upswings or downturns in business activity, nor is it usual to make corrections for poor sales performance extending over previous periods. Another difficulty encountered in using past-sales projection methods is that the accuracy of the forecast may depend largely upon how close the company is to the market saturation point. If the markets is entirely saturated, it sometimes is defensible to predict sales by applying, for instance, a certain percentage figure which is equivalent to the annual replacement demand. More often, however, the firm whose product has achieved full market saturation is likely to find, since most companies of this type market durables or semidurables, that its prospective customers can postpone or accelerate their purchases to a considerable degree. However, because numerous computer programmes are available for using such statistical techniques as time-series analysis and exponential smoothing, many companies rely, to some extent at least, on past-sales projections of making their sales forecasts.

Survey of Customer's Buying Plans

What could seem more like a sensible sales forecasting approach than that of asking customers about their future buying plans? Industrial marketers use this approach more than consumer-goods marketers, probably because it is best adapted for use in situations where the potential market consists of small numbers of customers and prospects, substantial sales are made to individual customers, the manufacture sells direct to users, and customers are concentrate in a few geographical areas. In such instances, it is relatively easy and inexpensive to survey a sample of customers and prospects to obtain their estimated requirements for the product during the next operating period, and to project the sample results in order to obtain a sales forecast. The results of such surveys, however, need to be tempered by management's specialised knowledge, and few companies are willing to base their forecasts exclusively on a survey of customer's buying plans.

The main reasons lies in the assumptions inherent in this forecasting method—that customers know what they are going to do and, in addition, the buyer's plans, once made, will not change. At least part of the time, either or both assumption are likely to be unwarranted.

Even though the survey of customers' buying plans is generally classified as an unsophisticated forecasting method, it can be rather sophisticated, that is, if it is a true survey (in the marketing research sense) and if the selection of respondents is made by probability sampling techniques. However, since it gathers opinions rather than measuring actions, substantial amounts of nonsampling error are likely to be present in the results. Respondents do not always have well-formulated buying plans and, even if they do, they are not always willing to relate them to an interviewer. In actual practice, most companies using this approach appear to pay little attention to the composition of the sample and devote minimum effort to measuring sampling and nonsampling errors.

Regression Analysis

Regression analysis is a statistical process and, as used in sales forecasting, determines and measures the association between company sales and other variables. Briefly stated, the method involves the fitting of an equation to explain the fluctuations in sales in terms of related and presumably causal variables, substituting for these variable values considered likely during the period to be forecasted, and solving for the value of sales. In other words, there are three major steps in forecasting sales by use of regression analysis:

(1) Identify variables causally related to company sales.

(2) Determine or estimate the values of these variables related to sales.

(3) Derive the sales forecast from these estimates.

Computers and improved computer programmes have made it relatively easy to use regression analysis for sales forecasting. One tire manufacturer, for instance, used simple regression analysis to determine the association between various economic variables and its own sales. This company quickly discovered that a positive correlation existed between gross national product and its own sales, but the correlation coefficient was too low to use in forecasting company sales. The same was found to be true of personal disposable income and retail sales; their correlation coefficients with company sales were too low to use in forecasting company sales. Fig. 2 is a scatter diagram illustrating the relation between total Indian retail sales and the tyre manufacturer's sales. The straight line is the result of the mathematical computation of the correlation between the two series of data. If the correlation has been perfect, all the dots would have fallen on the line. The tire manufacturer also measured the relationship between its own sales and the sales of new automobiles and found a much higher degree of correlation (see Fig. 3); notice that the dots on this scatter diagram cluster closely around the line.

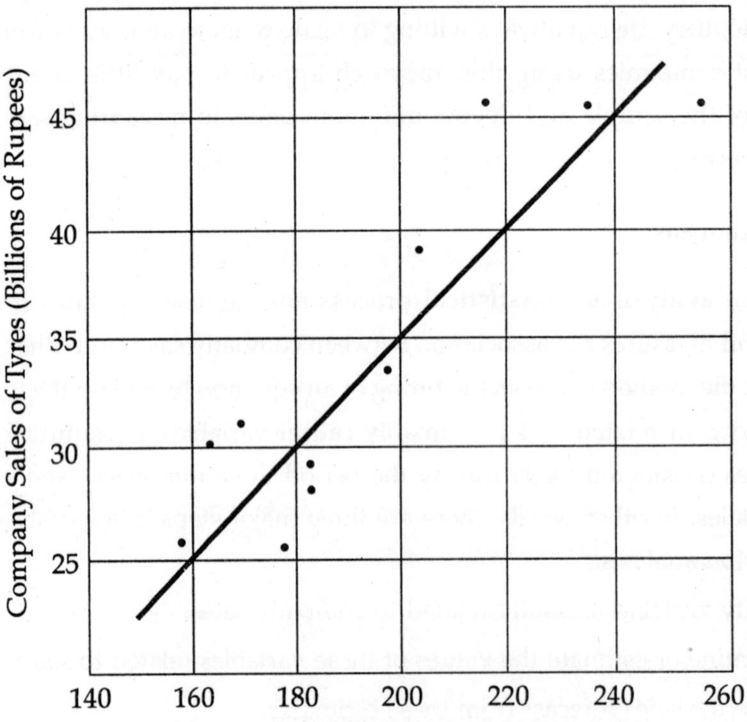

Fig. 2 Relation between Company Sales of Tyres and Indian Retail Sales

In forecasting situations where sales are influenced by two or more independent variables acting together, multiple-regression-analysis techniques are applied (generally through use of computer). To illustrate, consider the following situation. An appliance manufacturer was considering adding an automatic dishwasher to its line and, in the course of studying the feasibility of adding this product, decided to develop a forecasting equation for use in predicting industry sales of dishwashers. From published sources, such as the *Statistical Abstract of the India,* data collected of manufacture's sales of dishwashers for a period of 20 years (the dependent variable). Also collected from similar sources were data on four possible independent variables:

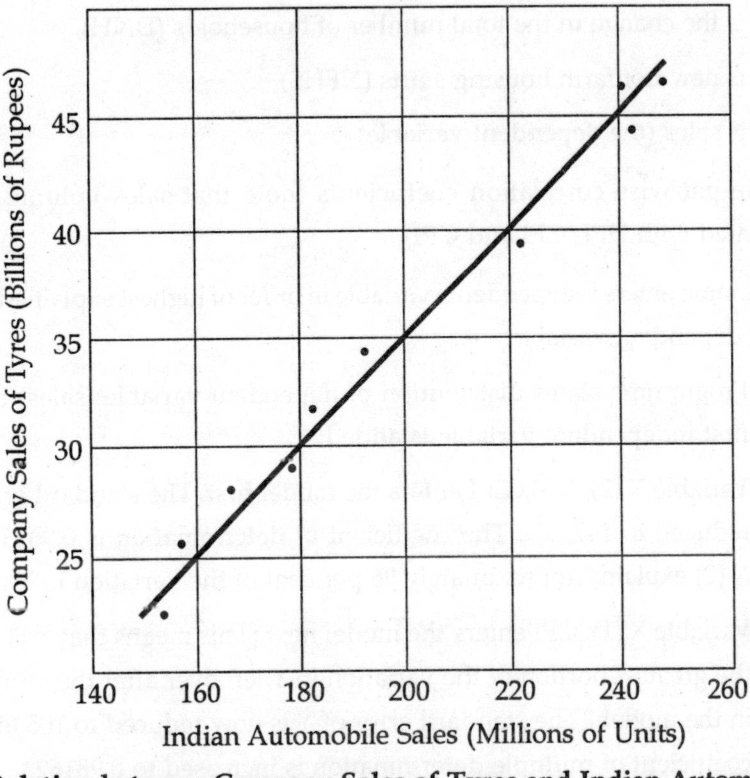

Fig. 3 Relation between Company Sales of Tyres and Indian Automobile Sales

(1) The Consumer Price Index for durables.

(2) Disposable personal income deflated by the Consumer Price Index in terms of 2000-01 rupees.

(3) The change in the total number of households.

(4) New nonfarm housing starts.

Then, the analysis decided to use a stepwise multiple-linear-regression technique to estimate the relationship among the variable. Fig. 4 shows the computer printout used in developing the forecasting equation. The following is a step-by-step explanation of the programme output.

(1) Means and standards deviations for all variables:

X (1) is Consumer price Index for durables (CPI)

X (2) is disposable personal income deflated by the Consumer Price Index (DPI/CPI)

X (3) is the change in the total number of households (DNH)

X (4) is new nonfarm housing starts (NFHS)

X (5) is sales (the dependent variable)

(2) Simple pairwise correlation coefficients (note that sales volume is highly correlated with DPI/CPI and CPI).

(3) Programme enters independents variable in order of highest explained variation of the dependent variable.

(3.1) Programme states distribution of dependent variable (sales) before the first independent variable is added.

(3.2) Variable X (2): DPI/CPI enters the model first. The standard error of Y is reduced to 147.209. The coefficient of determination is 0.96234; that is, X (2) explains approximately 96 per cent of the variation in Y.

(3.3) Variable X (1): CPI enters the model next [This means that X (1) explains the greatest portion of the variation in Y left over after the entry of X (2) in the model.] The standard error of Y is now reduced to 105.65553. The coefficient of multiple determination is increased to 0.98162.

(3.4) After the addition of variable X (2) and, X (1), less than 2 per cent of the variation in Y is left to be explained.

(3.5) The results of the additions of X (3) DNH and of X (4) NFHS indicate that these variables are not statistically significant; this is shown by the low F values as well as by the low *t* values

$$t = \frac{\text{coefficient}}{\text{standard error of coefficient}}$$

Therefore, the effect of adding these two variable to the model is not to reduce the standard error of Y, but, in fact, in this case, it is increased slightly.

These results indicated, then, that the forecasting equation was as follows:

$$\frac{\text{Manufacturers' sales of}}{\text{dishwashers (in thousands)}} = -4{,}404.97 + 28.85\ \text{CPI} + 6.36\ \text{DPI/CPI}$$

So if the manufacturer had estimates for the coming year the CPI would be 125 and DPI/CPI would be 550, its forecast of industry sales of dishwashers (in thousands) would be:

$$\begin{aligned}\text{Sales} &= -4{,}404.97 + (28.85)\,(125) + (6.36)\,(550)\\ &= 2{,}699.28 \text{ (or approximately 2,700,000 dishwashers)}\end{aligned}$$

Evaluation of Regression Analysis for Sales Forecasting

If high coefficients of correlation exist between company sales and certain independent variable, the forecasting problem may be simplified, especially if the related variable 'lead' company sales. The probable course of sales may then be charted on an apparently reliable basis, and the forecaster's attention can be concentrated on factors that might cause deviations from the indicated movement. But it is still necessary for the forecaster to examine other circumstances that might upset relationships upon which the correlations are based. A forecast made through regression analysis techniques is found on the assumption that relations which the variables have brone to each other in the past will also hold for the future. To have a 'lead-lag' association in which deviations regularly occur in the related independent variable(s) prior to a change in company sales is a near-ideal situation; unfortunately it rarely holds expect over short periods. Although lead-lag relationships are fairly common, associations between the lead variables and sales in which the intervening time intervals remain relatively stable are uncommon. These periods not only contract or expand without warning; they also exhibit great variations during different phases of the business cycle.

Multiple Regression Analysis: Grimes Project Title: Sales F(CPI, DPI/CPI, DNH, NFHS)

		Mean	Standard Deviation
Step 1	X	103.0000	6.5012
	X (2)	373.2286	89.4190
	X (3)	1.0299	0.3833
	X (4)	1428.8571	188.1014
	X (5)	939.9524	739.3600

Contd. . . .

Contd. . . .

Step 2 *Correlation Coefficients*

r(1,2)	0.836915
r(1,3)	0.415448
r(1,4)	0.486596
r(1,5)	0.897006
r(2,3)	0.443997
r(2,4)	0.229535
r(2,5)	0.980989
r(3,4)	0.240009
r(3,5)	0.469477
r(4,5)	0.316022

Step 3.1 *The Standard Error of Y will now be* 739.35996

	Coefficient	Standard Error of Coefficient
b(0)	938.95238	

Coefficient of Determination is 0.00000

Step 3.2 *The Variable* X(2) *now being entered into the model with an* F = 485.51400

The Standard Error of Y will now be 147.20898

	Coefficient	Standard Error of Coefficient
b(2)	8.11130	0.36812
b(0)	-2088.41491	

Coefficient of Determination is 0.96234

Step 3.3 *The Variable* X(1) *is now being entered into the model with an* F = 18.88398

The Standard Error of Y *will now be* 105.65553

	Coefficient	Standard Error of Coefficient
b(1)	28.85239	6.63949
b(2)	6.35570	0.48272
b(0)	-4404.97376	

Coefficient of Determination is 0.98162

Contd. . . .

Contd. . . .

Step 3.4 *The Variable* X(3) *is now being entered into the model with an* F = 0.62558

The Standard Error of Y *will now be* 106.77186

	Coefficient	Standard Error of Coefficient
b(1)	28.37586	6.73664
b(2)	6.27963	0.49721
b(3)	55.19663	69.78664
b(0)	-4384.34552	

Coefficient of Determination is 0.98227

Step 3.5 *The Variable* X(4) *is now being entered into the model with an* F = 0.25544

The Standard Error of Y *will now be* 109.18975

	Coefficient	Standard Error of Coefficient
b(1)	26.09639	8.23421
b(2)	6.38803	0.55185
b(3)	50.4226	71.98926
b(4)	0.08159	0.16143
b(0)	-4301.67933	

Coefficient of Determination is 0.98255

Fig. 4 Computer Printout Used in Developing an Equation for Forecasting Industry Sales of Automatic Dishwashers

If forecasters discover close associations between company sales and a reliable barometer, their estimates will be improved by the predictions of probable changes in the barometer made by expert analysis. However, one great danger in using regression analysis for forecasting is that forecasters may put too much faith in the statistical output; that is, they may be tempted to abandon independent appraisals of future events in favour of a forecast developed entirely by computer. It may be only natural to place blind faith in a method that seems infallible; but it is wise to check unaccountably good results with forecasts arrived at through other methods.

Econometric Model Building and Simulation

Econometric model building and simulation holds considerable promise as a sales forecasting method for companies marketing durable goods (consumer or industrial).

This approach uses a mathematical model in the form of an equation or system of equations to represent a set of relationship among different demand-determining independent variables and sales. Then, by 'plugging-in' values (or estimates) for each independent variable (that is, by 'simulating' the total situation), a sales forecast is produced. Forecasting equations derived through regression-analysis techniques resemble, but, strictly speaking, are not regarded as, econometric models. An econometric model (unlike regression model) is based upon an underlying theory about the relationship that exist among a set of variables and parameters are estimated by statistical analysis of past data. Thus, an econometric sales forecasting models is an abstraction of a real-world situation, expressed in equation form and used to predict sales. For example, the sales equation for a durable good can be written:

$$S = R + N$$

Where

S = total sales

R = replacement demand (i.e., purchase made to replace units of the good going out of use, as measured by the scrapple of old units).

N = new-owner demand (i.e., purchase made not to replace existing units of the product, but to add to the total stock of the product in users' possession).

Total sales of a durable good, in other words, consist of purchases made to replace units that have been scrapped and purchases by new owners. Thus, a family buys its first new automatic washing machine and becomes a part of the new-owner demand for that machine; another family, which has a five-year old machine, trades it to a dealer for a new machine and becomes part of the replacement demand (although only effectively so when the five-year-old machine, perhaps passing through several families hands in the process, finally comes to be owned by a family that goes ahead and consigns its even-older machine to the scrap heap).

Replacement demand, then, is normally measured by the scrappage of old units of products, that is, by the percentage of the total stock of the product in users' hands that is actually taken out of service either through consignment to the trash pile, by sale to a junk dealer, or merely by being stored away and never used again. So replacement demand in any one year does not necessarily include demand organising from the family that had a five-year old machine which it treaded to a dealer for a new machine, with the dealer reselling the old machine to another family who buys it second-hand. Only when the particular washing machine involved goes *completely out of service* is it considered as having been scrapped and, at that time (through a chain of purchased and trade-ins), some family becomes a part of the replacement demand. Econometricians estimate replacement demand by using life expectancy tables or survival tables, which are similar to the life (or mortality) tables used by life insurance actuaries. An example of such a survival table is shown in Figure-5.

Year	Survival Coefficient
1	1.0000
2	0.9995
3	0.9946
4	0.9656
5	0.8621
6	0.6406
7	0.3594
8	0.1379
9	0.0344
10	0.0054
11	0.0000

Fig. 5 Durable-Goods Survival Coefficients
(Maximum Service Life: 11 Years: Average Service Life: 6.5 Years)

If some durable good has a maximum service life of 11 years and 10,000 units of the good enter service in some year, the Fig. 5 indicated that five years later 8,621 will probably still be in service and ten years later, 54. For this batch of 10,000 product units, scrappage would amount to 1,035 in the fifth year (that is, 1,379-334, the difference between the accumulated total scrappage at the close of the fifth and fourth years, respectively). In the fifth year, then, 1,035 replacement sales would trace back to the batch of 10,000 products units that entered service five years before.

In this model, new-owner demand is defined as the net addition to users' stocks of the product which occurs during a given period. For instance, if 20,00,000 units of some appliance were in service at the start of a period and 25,00,000 at the end, new-owner demand would have been 5,00,000 during the period. Forecasting the number of sales to new owners is matter of treating the stock of durable good in the hands of users as a 'population' exhibiting 'birth' and 'death' characteristics, that is, thinking of this stock as behaving in ways analoguous to a human population.

Constructing an econometric model of the replacement demand + new-owner demand type involves going through a three-step procedure. First, the various independent variable affecting each demand category (replacement and new-owner) are studied and those that bear some logical relationship to sales (the dependent variable) are chosen for correlation analysis. Second, the forecaster detects (through correlation analysis) that combination of independent variable which correlates best with sales, some times including a time trend in this combination to represent other variables, which cannot measured directly. Third, a suitable mathematical expression is chosen to show the quantitative relationships among the various independent variable and sales, the dependent variable. This expression becomes, then, the econometric model that is used for sales forecasting.

The general procedure for building econometric models seems simple enough. But such models, when actually constructed, can take on rather formidable appearances. Consider, for example, the following econometric models for forecasting the sales of washing machines.

$$S_{tc} = Y_t - Y_t + Y_t \left\{ H_t \left[0.03 - 0.0157 \times \left(\frac{(I_t + 3C_t)1P_t}{10^{0.01818t-331143}} \right) \right] - 0.0000283 Y_t \right\}$$

Where

S_{tc} = calculated value for forecasted sales of washing machines during time period.

Y_t = level of consumers' stock of washing machines in any period (as of January 1).

Y_t = level of consumers' stock would occur in the following period (as of January 1) if no washing machines were sold and scrappage rates remained that same.

H_t = number of wired (i.e., electrified) dwelling units, in millions.

I_t = disposable personal income.

C_t = net credit extended (excluding credit extended for automobiles).

P_t = price index for house furnishings.

$10^{0.01818t-331143}$ = trend of real purchasing power over time

It + 3Ct/Pt real purchasing power.

Thus, new-owner demand in this models is represented by Y_t – Y_t both members of the expression being determined through application of appropriate survival coefficients to previous years sales of washing machines, and through estimation of consumers' total stock of washing machines in each year. Replacement demand is represented by other symbols in the remaining part of the expression, which takes into account the number of wired dwelling units (washing machines are not likely to be sold to people, who live in homes with no electricity), real purchasing power (disposable personal income plus credit availability divided by a price index), and real purchasing power adjusted for the historical trend of real purchasing power over time. Correlation-analysis techniques were used to derive the various numerical values in this model.

The econometric model-building approach seems a nearly ideal way to forecast sales. Not only does it take into account the interaction of independent variables that bear logical and measurable relationships to sale; it also uses correlation-analysis techniques to quantify these relationships. Such models, however, are used far more to forecast industry sales than they are to forecast the sales of individual company's sales are more numerous and more difficult to measure than those determine the sales of an entire industry. Many companies use an econometric model to forecast industry sales, and then apply an estimate of the company's share-of-the-market percentage to the industry forecast to arrive at the company's sales forecast.

Conversion of Industry Forecast into Company Sales Forecast

The sequence of forecasting procedure usually provides, first, for making an industry sales forecast and, second, for breaking down this forecast into a company sales forecast. Previous discussions reflects this usual sequence. We examined six main forecasting approaches, and only in two of them—the poll of sales force opinion (the most unsophisticated approach), and in some rather unsophisticated forms of past sales projections—is the industry sales forecast skipped and a company sales forecast arrived at directly. The other approaches—jury of executive opinion, survey of buying plans, regression analysis and econometric model building—usually result in industry forecasts.

Converting an industry sales forecasts into a company sales forecast requires that company strengths and weaknesses relative to those of competitors be appraised and a quantitative estimate of the company's share-of-the market by arrived at, which then can be used to derive a company sales forecast. The poll-of-sales-opinion approach leaves this appraisal largely up to the sales personnel-they focus on estimating how much the company can sell, not on how much the industry can sell. The unsophisticated form of the past-sales-projection approach carry the implicit assumption that no changes will occur in the company's strengths and weaknesses relative to those of its competitors. In the other four approaches, management makes this appraisal at the time it determines the company's probable share-of-the market percentage and, although some companies check such estimates with their sales personnel, the main appraisal of competitive position is made by executive who should be better informed on the overall sale outlook than any salesperson is likely to be.

Forecasting a company's market share varies greatly in complexity from one industry to another. In an industry such as steel, where the number of competitors is small and market share is fairly stable, determining a given company's market share is a relatively simple task—mostly a matter of projecting past trends and adjusting for anticipated changes in the company's relative strengths and weaknesses. But in an industry such as women's clothing, where the number of competitors is large and the market share fluctuates widely, determination of market share is difficult: The ability to evaluate a style's salability is a key element in forecasting, and this requires both through knowledge of market trends and keen judgement. Most, companies, however, operate in industries that lie somewhere between these two extremes, with market shares neither as stable as in steel nor as volatile as in women's apparel. Forecasters in most companies, therefore, need information on competitors' plans to launch new and improved products, advertising and selling plans, pricing strategies, and so on. When forecasters evaluate such information in relation to their own company's proposed marketing and selling plans, they are in a position to exercise, informed judgement in predicting the company's probable market share. If, for example, a forecaster known that a major competitor plans, a substantial price cut on a product than many buyers buy mainly on the basis of price, it will be necessary to lower the estimate of the company's market share accordingly unless management is willing to match the price cut. Forecasting a particular company's market share is a matter both of examining past trends and of appraising significant changes in competitive relationships which may alter these past trends.

Derivation of a Sales-volume Objective

A sales-volume objective for the coming operating periods is the hoped-for outcome of a company's short-range sales-forecasting procedure. In order to understand the relationship of the sales-volume objectives and the sales forecast, recall the two main parts of the definition of a sales forecast: (1) it contains as estimate of sales tied to a proposed marketing plan or programme, and (2) it assumes a particular set of economic and other forces outside the unit for which the forecast is made. Thus, the sales-forecast estimate does not necessarily and automatically become the company's sales-volume objective, but it does provide an orientation point for management's thinking. Further, adjustments in the sales-forecast estimate are usually necessary, perhaps because management decides to alter its marketing plan or programme or because changes appear to be occurring in competitor's marketing strategies.

The sales-volume objective finally established should be consistent with management's profit aspirations and the company's marketing capabilities. In other words, it must be attainable at costs low enough to permit the company to reach its net-profit objective, and for the company's marketing forces (that is, its sales force, the advertising programme, the dealer organisation, and so on) to be capable of reaching the objective set. All three of these items – the sales-volume objective, management's profit objectives, and the company's marketing capabilities – are interrelated. Using the sales estimate in the sales forecast as a point of departure, management juggles these three items until it satisfies it self that the relationship between them is the best that can be obtained. Only then does the sales forecast result in the setting of a sales-volume objective. And at that time, the chief sales executive (along with other marketing executives) accepts a major share of the responsibility for marketing the forecast 'come true.' Sales policies and selling strategies, formulated by the chief sales executive and subordinate sales executives, must be put into effect in the grand effort to reach the sales volume, profit, and other objectives derived from the sales forecast.

Evaluation of Forecasts

Before submitting forecasts to higher management, sales executives should evaluate them carefully, regardless of the extent of their personal involvement in the preparation. Since every forecast necessarily pertains to the future, all contain some element of uncertainty; consequently, all forecasts are based on assumptions. So a good first step in evaluating a sales forecast is to examine the assumptions (including any hidden ones) on which it is based. Sales executives should view each assumption critically and note particularly any that seem unwarranted, testing each by asking. If this assumption was removed, or changed, what would be the effect on the forecast? They should also evaluate the forecasting methods as objectively as possible, and then ask themselves such questions as: Are there any variations here from what past experience would seem to indicate? Has sufficient account been taken of trends in the competitive situation and of changes in competitors' marketing and selling strategies? Has account been taken of any new competitive products that might affect the industry's and company's sales? Have inventory movements at all distribution levels (including those at wholesale and retail levels) been considered? Sales executives should also continue evaluating the accuracy and economic value of the forecast as the forecast period advances. Forecasts should be checked against actual results, differences explained, and indicated adjustments made for the remainder of the period. When the period's sales results are all recorded, all variations should be explained and stored for possible future use in improving forecasting accuracy.

□□□

4

The Marketing Executive

Introduction

Basically, the marketing executive's job, like the jobs of other line executives, involves making decisions and then seeing to its that other carry out these decisions. What qualification must marketing executives have in order to make decision? They need a considerable base of experiential and other knowledge, much of which may not be very explicit; however, this knowledge base provides them with a 'feel' for problems and their possible solution. They need keen awareness of both company and marketing department goals – they must recognise the key features distinguishing the sort of company that top management is trying to build; and they must visualise the nature and type of contributions that the marketing department can and should make toward realising that future 'company image.' They need the ability to conceptualise problem situations clearly in area where they have the main decision-making responsibility, and in those where they help make decision that have implications in other marketing areas and/or in other parts of the business (such as in production or finance).

In other words, the decision that the marketing executive is involved in may affect only the marketing department, or they may have significant repercussion for executives elsewhere in the business. Therefore, in performance the job, marketing executives must know how to analyse information, how to combine its significance with their own experiential knowledge and judgement (and their willingness to accept a certain degree of risk), how to apply imagination in searching for alternative solutions to problems, how to predict the likely outcomes of different alternatives, and, finally how to choose that alternative with the best payoff in terms of company and departmental goals.

Nature of Marketing Management Positions

The requirement of the marketing executive's jobs vary from company to company and from position to position within companies. However, certain responsibilities are pretty typically assigned to the same types of executives in different companies. It is possible, therefore, to generalise to a considerable degree about the activities and responsibilities of marketing managers, district marketing managers, product managers, and other marketing or marketing executives. Some companies have formulated concise statements of the duties associated with various positions, known as position description or position guides. Typical position guides for the jobs of marketing manager and district marketing manager follows:

Marketing Manager

The marketing manager is responsible for securing maximum volume of rupee marketing through the effective development and execution of marketing programmes and marketing policies for all product marketed by his division. In addition to planning and administrative duties, the marketing manger is expected to develop working relations with other department heads and the marketing executives of other divisions of the company. The marketing manager reports to the senior marketing manager or vice-president for marketing.

In carrying out the job's responsibilities, this marketing executive is expected to be concerned with:

Marketing Programme

The marketing manager should take the initiative in the establishment of long range marketing objectives of the division, in collaboration with other department heads and the marketing manager, to assure achieving overall marketing objectives.

The marketing manager should arrange for the development of detailed marketing programmes designed to improve competitive positions, reduce distribution costs, and reach established marketing goals.

The marketing manager should review and approve marketing policies, marketing strategies, and pricing policies (to the extent of the job's responsibility) for all products to ensure that short-term operations are in accord with long-term profitability and do not jeopardise other phase of the company's operations.

Organisation

The executive managers should establish an effective plan of organisation, and methods of controlling the activities of members of the marketing organisation, that will provide sufficient time for carrying out the full line of departmental responsibilities.

The marketing manager should provides leadership to all levels of the marketing organisation in establishing a sound basis for each individual's self-development, and in making certain that compensation is in line with responsibilities and performance.

Management of Marketing Department Personnel

The marketing manager should identify permission sources for the recruitment of new marketing personnel and set standards for selection of the most promising new personnel from among recruits.

The marketing manager should provide for the training of new personnel so as to achieve high-level performance in the shortest possible time. At the same time the marketing manager should train marketing personnel, so as to have an adequate supply of marketing executive taken for replacement up through and including the marketing manager's own position. The development of human resources is the marketing manager's most important responsibility.

The marketing manager should ensure that marketing personnel are properly motivated, so as to achieve optimum marketing performance.

The marketing manager should establish a system of marketing supervision that will reduce waste and inefficiency and point marketing efforts into the most preferable channels.

Internal and External Relations

The marketing manager should develop effective working relations with other department heads and the marketing manager so that every significant marketing development can be translated into an appropriate course of action.

The marketing manager should develop relationship with key customers that will provide maximum long-term participation in their available business.

Communications

The marketing manager should keep the general manager and the marketing manager fully informed on marketing results and future plans of operation.

The marketing manager should also establish a system of communication with other marketing management and supervisory personnel that will keep them informed of overall divisional marketing objectives, results, and problems and keep him informed of their needs and problems.

Control

The marketing manager should consult with the production manager so that production rates and inventories can be geared as closely as possible to actual marketing needs.

The marketing manager should review and approve marketing and expense budgets and evaluate periodically the performance of all marketing activities in relation to budgets and marketing goals and take such correlative action as are required.

The marketing manager should delegate authority and develop control records and performance standards to permit a proper balance of his own time spent on various activities in the position guide.

District Marketing Manager

The district marketing manager is responsible for the effective deployment of selling efforts and the maintenance of good trade relations in the assigned district. The district marketing manager is expected to secure maximum rupee marketing of the division's products in accordance with established marketing policies and marketing programmes, within the, limits of the marketing budget. The district marketing manager is responsible to the marketing manager for the overall district performance.

In carrying out the job responsibilities, the district marketing manager is expected to be concerned with:

Supervision of Marketing Personnel

The district marketing manager should accurately evaluate the marketing opportunities in the district and assign territories that have equitable workloads and that permit minimum travel costs, so as to secure maximum rupee marketing at minimum cost.

The district marketing manager should direct, assist, and supervise the marketing personnel in maintaining and improving the division's competitive position and in handling special marketing or competitive problems.

The district marketing manager should rate marketing-people in the performance of all their duties, and at least annually discuss these ratings with them to direct their attention toward areas where improvement is needed.

The district marketing manager should advise the marketing manager in important personnel problems.

The district marketing manager should evaluate the marketing-people's strategies for key accounts, helping each to plan strategy for all accounts assigned to him and to develop new accounts.

Control

The district marketing manger should forecast short-term marketing of the district and work with marketing personnel in estimating future marketing in their territories so that accurate marketing budgets and marketing quotas can be developed.

The district marketing manager should also prepare a periodic progress report on industry conditions, forward plans, and the progress made toward marketing objectives.

The district marketing manager should report immediately on significant marketing or competitive developments that may affect the company's future.

Administration

The district marketing manager should assume responsibility for the efficient administration of the district office operations and warehouse and stock facilities in accord with established policies and procedures.

The district marketing manager should develop effective working relations with technical personnel, other district managers, and home office personnel, so as to take full advantages of their help to achieve marketing goals, reduce costs, and effectively vary out marketing programmes.

Communication

The district marketing manager should study and analyse the plans, programmes, and policies originating in the home office and interpret them to the marketing staff so that these plans, programmes, and policies can be effectively coordinated in the district's activities.

The district marketing manager should communicate to the marketing manager and top administration any information about customers and market or about personnel that should be of interest to them.

The district marketing manager should maintain membership in professional organisation whose activities are of interest and concern to the division so as to promote better customer relations and develop intelligence source.

Time Management by the Marketing Executive

To gain a realistic appreciation of the marketing executive's job, one should consider not only the kinds of activities performed but also the amount of time allocated to each activity. One of the most comprehensive analysis of time apportionment among marketing executive was conducted by the Metropolitan Life Insurance Company. Although this study is now somewhat old, many of its finding are still valid. Table-1 shows how 60 chief marketing executives divided their time among eight major marketing functions. The table emphasised the composite average amount of time devoted to each function; it shows, however, average time allocations for marketing managers (1) of different types of product, (2) in companies of various sizes, (3) by types of supervisory organisations, that is, with direct or indirect supervision of the field force by the chief marketing executive. As might have been expected, most

Table-1

How Sixty Chief Marketing Executive Apportion their Time among Eight Major Marketing Activities

Company Classification		Operating Functions (%)					Planning Functions (%)					
	Number of Companies	Directing Markeing Organisation	Marketing Calls with Field Personnel	Trade Relations	Selling Personal Account	Marketing Plan Total Operating	Advertising and Research	Marketing Promotion	Product Merchandising	Marketing Training	Total Planning	Other (%)
All companies	60	28	14	8	4	54	13	10	9	8	40	6
By type of Product:												
Consumer goods	27	26	13	10	4	53	15	13	9	7	44	3
Industrial goods	28	31	16	7	6	60	9	7	7	8	31	9
Commercial goods*	5	26	3	6	1	36	23	15	16	7	61	3
By size of Company:												
Large (100 to 10,000 Marketing people)	18	28	13	7	4	52	15	11	10	7	43	5
Medium (26 to 86 Marketing people)	22	29	14	8	5	56	13	12	9	7	41	3
Small (4 to 25 Marketing people)	20	27	15	10	5	57	11	8	7	8	34	9
By type of Organisation:												
Direct supervision of the field force	24	36	13	9	4	62	10	9	6	5	30	8
Supervision through subordinates	24	21	13	9	4	47	17	11	11	10	49	4
Number of executives reporting each function	60	60	58	43	32	-	55	56	53	51	-	-

* Includes products materialed principally to offices and stores.

Source: *Function of the Marketing Executive,* Metropolitan Life Insurance Company, New York, p. 26, Reprinted by permission.

marketing managers developed more time to marketing direction than to any other activity, the average being 28 per cent.

This study also revealed that the significance attached to the different duties varied with the class of product marketed. Consumer goods marketing managers tended to spend more time than industrial marketing managers on marketing planning and research, advertising and marketing promotion, product merchandising, and trade relations. In contrast, industrial marketing managers placed relatively heavier emphasis on directing the marketing force, marketing calls with marketing people, and selling personal accounts. Consumer-goods marketing managers, in general, spent more time on planning and less on operating than did their counterparts in the industrial field. Commercial goods marketing managers spent far more time on planning and less on operating than did marketing managers in either of the their fields.

The amount of executive time devoted to each activity was greatly influenced by the size of the organisation. Marketing executives in small companies spent relatively less time on planning and more on miscellaneous, unclassified, activities. As the size of the company increased, more time was devoted to such planning functions as advertising and marketing planning, and research.

The type of supervisory organisation, the number and calibre of subordinate executives, and the manner of delegating authority also had important influences on the way chief marketing executives distributed their time and effort. When marketing executives supervised the field force directly, the additional time required for marketing direction resulted in their spending 62 per cent of their total time on operating functions. But when supervision of the field force was exercised through subordinate, the planning functions were more important, and marketing executives were less involved with actual operations.

Compensation Patterns for Marketing Executives

Because marketing is normally more important to the success of the enterprise than either production or finance, marketing and marketing executives often command substantially higher compensation payments. Chief marketing executives in large companies are likely to earn, on the average in lakhs or more rupees annually. Chief marketing executives average 70 per cent as much as the top marketing man. Top marketing, and marketing executives usually rank among the highest paid mean in the company. The main reason for this is that as much as one-third of their compensation is made up of bonuses for reaching predetermined marketing goals. Financial rewards in smaller companies are less spectacular, but even here the top marketing executive, along with the chief marketing executive, generally ranks among the highest-paid four or five men in the company.

Naturally, marketing executives at lower levels in the organisational hierarchy are paid less than their chiefs. Higher-ranking subordinates, such as regional and district marketing managers, have median earnings approximating 90 to 95 per cent of those of the chief marketing executive. Field marketing managers, those on the first step of the ladder in the marketing-force executive hierarchy, receive median earnings roughly two-thirds of those of the top marketing executive, while marketing people earn about half as much as the top marketing executive.

Most marketing executives receive a portion of their pay in the form of bonuses, commissions, or other 'incentive' payments. These incentive payments generally are based upon relative profit performance at higher levels in the marketing organisational hierchy and upon marketing volumes achieved (relative to marketing potential) at lower marketing executive levels. The prevalence of incentive payments in the compensation packages of marketing executives causes their earnings to fluctuate considerably from year to year.

Table-2 shows how top marketing executives in 15 large companies were compensated in a recent year. Notice that 11 of these 15 top marketing executives had stock options (which generally gives them the right to purchase company stock on advantageous terms) and ten received some of their compensation in form other than salaries-incentive bonuses, profit-sharing plans, stock-purchase plans, and deferred-compensation plans. These and other fringe benefits (such as retirement funds, company-paid insurance policies, and annuities) tend to be effective in reducing executive turnover. Most executives are reluctant to leave companies where they have accumulated sizeable fringe benefits.

Table-2

Compensation of Top Marketing Executives in Selected Large Companies in 2001

Company	Product Field(s)	2001 Marketing Vol. (in 000s)	Top Marketing Executive's Compensation		
			Total	Stock Options?	Other Non-salary Compensation from:
Simplicity Pattern Co., Inc.	Apparel patterns	$90,447	$64,583	Yes	
Jos. Schilitz Brewing Co.	Beer	522,094	133,100	Yes	
Abbott Laboratories	Pharmaceutical and drugs	124,117	73,859	Yes	Incentive bonus
Chicago Bridge & Iron Co.	Fabricated metals	394,000	76,520	Yes	Profit sharing
Snap-On Tools Corp.	Industrial equipment	88,399	110,389	Yes	
Chicago Pneumatic Tool Co.	Machinery	394,000	57,000	No	Deferred Compensation
Cowles Communications, Inc.	Publishing	171,000	39,154	No	Profit sharing
Inland Street Co.	Steel and Iron	1,253,610	119,836	Yes	Incentive bonus
Graniteville Co.	Textiles	135,204	95,975	Yes	
American Brands, Inc.	Tobacco and diversified	2,827,771	87,414	Yes	Profit sharing
Briggs & Stratton Corp.	Industrial parts	1,86,225	126,166	No	
Beeline Fashions, Inc.	Aparel	51,506	59,300	Yes	Profit sharing
Reichhold Chemical, Inc.	Chemicals	194,228	37,500	No	Profit sharing, Stock purchase
Stokely-Van Camp, Inc.	Food	280,836	60,000	Yes	Profit sharing
Clorox Co.	Household product	145,000	52,050	Yes	Profit sharing

Source: Extracted from "What Top Sales and Marketing Executives Earn," *Sales Management*, pp. 26-30.

Qualities of Good Sales Executives

What qualities should top-flight marketing executives possess that will enable them to perform effectively, both as managers and as important members of the marketing executive team? In a complex and variable field such as marketing management, it is difficult to list 'success' qualification applicable in all situations and all companies. Marketing executives' jobs cover a wide gamut of products, markets, and marketing channels, and there would seem to be few, if any, qualifications in common. Nevertheless, several qualities (or abilities) common to most successful marketing executives, whatever their fields, can be identified.

(1) **Ability to Define Clearly the Position's Exact Functions and Duties in Relation to the Goals the Company should Expect to Attain:** Too often, marketing executives neglect to calculate what is entailed in their responsibilities. Whether or not the company provides them with a position descriptions, marketing executives should draw up their own descriptions consistent with responsibilities assigned higher management. Revisions are necessary whenever changes occur in the assigned responsibility or in company goals.

(2) **Ability to Select and Train Capable Subordinates, and Willingness to Delegate Sufficient Authority to Enable them to Carry Out Assigned Tasks with Minimum Supervision:** Inability to delegate authority is a common weakness. Sometimes inexperienced executives select high-calibre subordinates but fail to provide them with authority to make decisions on any except the most routine matters. Such practice destroys the morale of subordinates, and it results in an unnecessarily heavy work load for the superior. Within existing policy limits, decisions should be made by subordinates; when an exception falling outside these limits occurs, the superior should decide. The more capable the subordinates, the wider policy limits can be and the more the superior's time is freed for planning.

(3) **Ability to Utilise Time Efficiently:** The time of marketing executives is valuable, and they should budget it and use it as carefully as they would money. They should allocate their working time to tasks yielding the greatest return to the company. They must, for instance, arrive at an optimum division between

office work and field supervision. To the marketing executive, even the use off-duty hours is important. Excessive work time and too little leisure reduces executive efficiency. Successful marketing executives consider the likely values both to themselves and to the company, then balances such leisure-time activities as community service and professional meetings against personal social activities, recreation, and self-improvement.

(4) **Ability to Allocate Sufficient Time for Thinking and Planning:** Able administrators make their major contributions through thinking and planning. They have know-how and are willing to think. They recognise that reviewing past performances is a prerequisite to planning. They strive continuously to gain new insight that will help brings problems into better focus. Too often, marketing executives are so involved in daily administrative tasks that little time remains for thinking and planning. Furthermore, it is easier to procrastinate than to think. Effective marketing executives find ways to shield themselves from routine task and interruption. Failing this, they retreat to Shangri-Las where surroundings are more conducive to thinking and planning.

(5) **Ability to Exercise Skilled Leadership:** Competent marketing executives develop and improve their skills in dealing with people. Although they necessarily rely to certain extent on an intuitive grasp of leadership skills, they depend far more on careful study of motivational factors, and shrewd analysis of the ever-changing patterns of unsatisfied needs among those with whom they work. They recognise that skilled leadership is important in dealing with subordinates and with everyone else with whom they come into contact.

Relations with Top Management

The most effective and successful executives are well above average in initiative and personal drive, and marketing executives should not be exceptions. Realising their potentials, however, depends largely upon their relations with top management. Marketing executives should want to get ahead, for personal goals are as vital to them as the objectives they set for the marketing department, but if they are to achieve these goals, not only must they know where they are going, but top management must be kept abreast of their progress.

Marketing executives must plan and implement their own self-development programmes, and setting definite career goals in an essential part of such programmes. Marketing executives must, however, strive to harmonise their own goals with those of the organisations, this being important condition for maximum progress of individuals and company alike. Whenever the marketing executive and the company cease to move toward mutually compatible goals, the resulting friction causes both to fall short of expected achievement levels. When this happens, either the two sets of goals must be reconciled, or the executive should leave the firm. Sometimes, marketing executive unilaterally reconcile such goals conflicts (usually by adjusting their personal goals to fit those of the organisation). More often, they reconcile them through interaction with company top management.

In their relations with management, marketing executives should readily accept responsibility for all activities related to their positions, but they should avoid becoming indispensable. Indispensability is undesirable for both the executive and the company. For the marketing executive, it means the blocking of opportunities for promotion; for the company, it means that too much is being staked on one individual, probably the best way for marketing executives to avoid becoming indispensable is to practice and advocate delegation of authority; and they should, concurrently, place high priority on training their own replacement.

At the same time, junior marketing executives climbing the management ladder are well advised to learn and master the duties and responsibilities of the positions immediately above theirs. Promotions come most readily to those prepared for them, and preparation largely consists of setting definite goals and adhering to a programme of continuing self-development.

Top management expects marketing executives as important members of managements, to be highly qualified as problem solvers and decision makers. Consequently, marketing executives should guard against taking too many of their problems to top management. Asking for help in deciding problems on which they clearly possess decision-making authority is tantamount to asking for closer supervision (and less authority). Competent marketing executives do not require a close watch over their activities, and those who have the confidence of top management enjoy considerable freedom in deciding things by themselves.

Nevertheless, chief marketing executives should keep top management informed on important decisions made and on the department's plans and accomplishments. They should transmit all required ordinary reports promptly, and special reports when appropriate. They should exercise some restraint in reporting their own activities, but they should see to it that their superiors have all the information needed to evaluate their personal effectiveness. Their reports should ensure that top management knows in broad outline the problems encountered in selling the company's products, the ways they are handled, and the results accomplished.

Chief marketing executives should pay careful attention to the manner in which they communicate with top management. They should not hesitate to give their superiors the benefits of their thinking, but, unless matters of high principle are involved, they should generally be willing to modify preconceived ideas. However, as the outstandingly successful executive *David Ogilvy* has written.

> "In the modern world of business, it is useless to be a creative original thinker unless you can also sell what you create. Management cannot always recognise a great idea unless it is presented to them by a good marketingman."

When the marketing executive has a great idea, is absolutely sure of it, and top management is unconvinced, the marketing executive must play the role of a super marketing person and 'sell' to those with the authority to decide. When the facts do not speak for themselves – when those in authority fail to grasp their full significance – the marketing executive, like any competent executive, should bring to bear his or her full powers of persuasion.

In all their dealings with top management, chief marketing executive should make a special effort to listen and learn. They should keep a dated record of important conversations. They should refrain voluntarily discussing the personal competence of fellow executives unless they can do so in a manner favourable to the executive involved. They should avoid relaying rumours. And they should exercise close control over their executive contacts, never missing scheduled engagements without justifiable reason. Marketing executives following such commonsense rules of conduct experience little difficulty in winning top management's confidence and respect.

Relations with Managers of Other Marketing Activities

Although chief marketing executives spend the greatest portion of their time on activities relating directly to management of the personal selling function, they also are concerned with other marketing activities. The degree of responsibility over these activities, and the amount of time allocated to them, vary with the particular job; but marketing executives are almost always concerned to some extent with product, promotion, pricing, and distribution management. They may also have an important role in aching control over these activities and coordination among them.

Relations with Product Management

Executives responsible for product planning and the formulation of product policies make numerous decisions. Periodically, each product in the line needs appraising in terms of its profitability and its ability to fulfil buyers' wants. When products come up for review, decision have to be made on whether each should be retained, changed or improved, or dropped from the line. Other decisions have to be made on adding new products and on changes in product design and other product features. Still other product decision concern product quality, services rendered in connection with product marketing and packaging.

Product decisions are often a shared responsibility of marketing, production, research and development, and financial executive, operating as a product committee. Chief marketing executives provide important inputs for such decisions. Their continuos contact with the market through subordinate and marketing personnel provide them with feedback about product performance and acceptance generally not available from other sources.

Relation with Promotional Management

While chief marketing executive are primarily responsible for setting promotional policies, chief marketing executives participate importantly in their formulations. Their knowledge of the market and their direct control over personal-selling activity make chief marketing executives a key source of information, and they occupy a highly strategic position in implementing promotional plans. Marketing personnel, for instance, are responsible not only for transmitting marketing messages directly to prospects but for securing the proper use of point-of-purchase displays and for coordinating dealer efforts with advertising programmes. Clearly, then, chief marketing executive, because of the key roles they play in making and implementing promotional policies, must coordinate very closely with other executives participating in the formulation and implementation of the promotional programme.

Almost every product marketing relies on personal selling as a necessary promotional method at one or more points in the marketing channel. Personal selling's effectiveness traces to the use of personal contacts in conveying the marketing message to prospective buyers. But, personal selling also is the most expensive promotional method in terms of cost per marketing message transmitted. For this reason, the proportion of personal selling in the promotional mix generally must be limited, and it is the marketing executive's responsibility to keep selling costs at a level regarded as reasonable by top management.

The chief marketing executive is responsible for marketing certain that marketing-people are kept abreast of important aspects of current advertising campaigns. Marketing personnel need briefing, for example, on the specific advertising appeals being used, enabling them, perhaps, to adapt their own selling approaches in way that enhance the total promotional impact. The marketing force should also known which media are scheduled to carry advertisements for which products, and the timing of each appearance. In addition, advertising personnel need ready access to the top marketing executive, since this executive is such an important source of information about customers, their needs, behaviour, and motives.

Relations with Pricing Management

When major decision on pricing policy are required, both the top marketing executive and the chief marketing executive occupy especially influential positions in top management councils. Relative to other high executives, they should have much clearer ideas of the prices final buyers are willing to pay, the marketing executive because of close and continuing contacts with the market, and the marketing executive because of knowledge of pricing information gathered and interpreted by the marketing research staff.

In spite of the fact that these two executives are particularly well qualified to speak with authority on pricing matters, price policies should be formulated and prices should be set by a group of executives. Each department affected should have some representation on this group, for policymaking in the pricing area is, by nature, an interdepartmental activity. Included in the policymaking group should be representatives not only of the marketing department but of such departments as production, cost accounting, credit, advertising, legal, and public relation. The pricing policies finally drafted should result from the comparative action of the group rather than form compromises among its individual member.

Once princing policy is established, its implementation is ordinarily the responsibility of the chief marketing executive for example, the pricing committe might decide to adopt a policy of resale price maintenance, but the chief marketing executive is responsible for informing distributors and dealers, obtaining their conformance, and initiating action against the nonconformers. Responsibility for administering prices should be assigned to a single line executive. Usually the chief marketing executive receives this assignment, becuase the marketing department has the closest relationship with the market.

Relation with Distribution Management

The distribution policies chosen by a firm are major determinations of the breadth and complexity of the marketing department's organisation and its functions. Selection of a marketing channel, or channels, sets the pattern for marketing force operations, but geographically and with respect to the classes of customers from whom marketing personnel are to solicit orders. But this is not the only aspect of distribution policymaking. It is also necessary to determine the number of outlets that are to handle the product at each distribution level, and this also affects the size and nature of the manufacturer's marketing organisation and the scope of its activities. Furthermore, marketing management determines policies in regard to the amount and extent of cooperation it desires to maintain with members of the distributive network—also influencing importantly, for example, the size of the marketing force, the nature of the marketing-person's job, the need for marketing supervision, and the like. Because of the significant impact, then, that distribution policy decisions have upon the marketing organisation and its activities, chief marketing executives must play a key role in providing information needed for their formulation, since they also bear major responsibility for the success of the implementation of distribution policy.

□□□

5

Theories and Techniques of Marketing

Introduction

The fully qualified marketing executive has a thorough understanding of the various activities that make up the marketing-person's job, is aware of the many problems that marketing-people are likely to encounter, and is prepared to make practical suggestions for their solution. The marketing executives must have a keen grasp of the theoretical aspects of marketing techniques; and should have learned, preferably through field experience, how the theories relate it and work out in practice. Although many marketing executives, some of them outstanding, have had little or no experience as marketing-persons, the normal progression to marketing management is through marketing. There are cases, however, of usually good marketing-people being utter failures as executives. The characteristics that make a person good at marketing do not necessarily make him or her a good executive. Nevertheless, all other things being equal, usually the person who has some marketing experience is likely to prove successful as a marketing executive.

Marketing executives must be in close and enough touch with actual marketing situations to have a sympathetic understanding of the problems faced daily by the marketing force. They realise that marketing-persons experience many frustrations. They know that marketing-people must cope with obstacles to marketing that often arise unexpectedly and require great ingenuity to surmount. Equipped with this understanding, marketing executives have the background needed to train marketing-personnel for maximum productivity; they should also be able to direct the marketing forces to make efforts efficiently, and to evaluate individual's achievements realistically.

Although the terms 'personal marketing' and 'personal selling' are often used interchangeably, there is an important difference. Personal marketing is the broader concept. Personal marketing may or may not be an important part of personal marketing; it is never all of it. Along with other key marketing elements such as pricing, advertising, product development and research, marketing channels, and physical distribution, personal marketing is a means through which marketing programmes are implemented. Combined and integrated into a marketing programme, these marketing elements become the strategy with which a firm seeks to active its marketing objectives. Whereas the broad purpose of marketing is to bring a firm's products into contact with markets and to affect profitable exchanges of products for money, the purpose of personal marketing is to bring the *right products*, into contact with the right customers, and to make certain that *ownership transfers* take place. Marketingmanship is one of the skills used in personal marketing; as defined by T.F. Stroh, it is a *direct, face-to-face, marketing-to-buyer influence which can communicate the facts necessary for making a buying decision; or it can utilise the psychology of persuasion to encourage the formation of a buying decision.* Salesmanship, then, is marketing-initiated effort that provides prospective buyers with information, and motivates or persuades them to make favourable buying decisions concerning the marketing's product or service. The marketing-person of today has to react and interact in many different ways to many different people. In addition to knowing the product thoroughly-regardless of how technical it may be, the marketing-person has to be a psychologist with one prospects, a human computer with another, an adviser with another, and at the same time a friend with some buyers. Marketing-persons must adjust their personalities on every call, making sure that what they say and do is compatible with the personality of each prospect.

Marketingmanship may be implemented not only through personal marketing but through advertising. In fact, advertising has been described as 'Marketingmanship in print.' The American Marketing Association defines advertising as any paid form of nonpersonal presentation and promotion of ideas, goods, or services by an identified sponsor. Modern advertising is planned with motivation and/or persuasion as the objective.

Personal marketing and advertising are simply two means that marketers use to inform and to motivate or persuade prospective buyers to buy; both means make use of marketingmanship techniques. Marketingmanship in advertising utilises nonpersonal presentations. Nonpersonal advertising type presentations are necessarily less flexible than those made by marketing-personnel. An advantage unique to personal marketing is that the marketing-person can usually identify differences among buyers and pattern his or her presentation according to individual peculiarities.

Buyer-Marketing-Dyads

Fundamental to an understanding of marketingmanship is recognition that it involves buyer-marketing interactions. Sociologists use the term 'dyad' to describe a situation in which two people interact with one another. The marketing-person and the prospect, personally interacting with each other, constitute on example of what we will call a 'buyer-marketing dyad.' Another example is provided by the interaction of a marketing using advertising with a particular prospect in the reading, listening, or viewing audience. In both the advertising and personal-marketing situations, the marketing, generally speaking, is trying to motivate or persuade the prospective buyer to behave favourably toward to marketing. Whether or not the buyer reacts as the marketing desires depends upon the nature of the interaction. The opportunity for interaction is obviously less in the advertising case then in the personal-marketing case, pointing up another advantage unique to personal marketing. You should recognise, however, that in many situations, advertising and personal marketingmanship supplement, or support each other, and the buyer's reaction results from the combined impact of both.

In one interesting piece of research, Franklin Evans studied buyer-marketing dyads in the life insurance business. This research revealed that prospects who bought insurance positively toward them, than prospects who did not buy. Furthermore, the more alike marketing-persons and their prospects were, the greater was the likelihood that a marketing would result. This was true for physical characteristics (age, height), other objective factors (income, religion, education), and variables that could be related to personality factors (politics, smoking). These findings have considerable significance for marketing management. Wherever possible, marketing personnel should be assigned to prospects whose characteristics are similar to their own, thus improving the change that successful dyadic relationships will result. However, pairing of marketing-persons with customers of similar backgrounds is more easily accomplished in industrial marketing, where there are fewer prospects about whom information is needed, than in consumer-goods marketing, where the number of prospects and customers per marketing-person is generally much larger.

In another interesting research project, Henry Tosi studied dyads made up of wholemarketing drug marketing-people and retail pharmacists, who made buying decisions. One apparent finding was that, when the buyer perceived the marketing-person's performance to be similar to his or her concept of 'ideal' performance, the number of sources from which purchases were made was low. Although this did not necessarily results in a larger percentage of purchases from the marketing-person, customer satisfaction with the marketing-person's behaviour did at least allow the marketing-person to get into the store. Tosi's suggested conclusion was that, in addition to the physical characteristics and objective factors cited by Evans, the customer's perception of how well the marketing-person's behaviour fits into the customer's conception of what the behaviour should be is a necessary condition for the continuation of dyadic interaction.

Another factor to be considered in these interactions among buyers and marketings is the buyer's initial conditioning with respect to marketing. Marketing-people have been maligned, and the butt of the nasty stories for generations. People are taught from childhood to beware of the tricky marketing-person.

There are also definite indications that marketing-people, not as stereotyped, but as they actually carry out their jobs, leave much to desired in the impact they make on customers. Studies of the attitudes of buyers and purchasing agents reveal that they are heavily critical of the marketing-person's lack of product knowledge, failure to follow up, general unreliability, slavish adherence to 'canned' presentations, blatant use of flattery, bad manners, commercial dishonesty, and so forth.

Degree of Difficulty in Marketing

The relative degree of difficulty encountered in making marketing varies considerable from one situation to another. In analysing this problem, it is helpful to distinguish between two kinds of marketing—service and developmental. In service marketing, the objective is to obtain marketing from people who are already customers and whose habits and patterns of thought are already conducive to such marketing.

The objective in developmental marketing is not so much the creation of marketing as the creation of customers out of people who do not at the moment view the markting-peron's company favourably, and who are undoubtedly resistant to change. McMurry points out that individual marketing positions require different amounts of service and developmental marketing, and he classified marketing positions according to their location on the spectrum involving degrees of developmental skill, from the very simple to the highly complex. McMurry identified seven main types of marketing positions:

(1) Positions where the marketing-person's predominantly to deliver the product, for example, milk, bread, fuel oil.

(2) Positions where the marketing-person is predominantely an inside order taker, for example, the marketing clerk behind the counter in dry-goods store.

(3) Positions where the marketing-person is also predominantly an order taker but works in the field, as the packing house, soap, or spice marketing-person does.

(4) Positions where the marketing-person is not expected or permitted to take an order but is called on only to build goodwill or to educate the actual or potential user, e.g., the distiller's 'missionary man,' or the 'detail man' representing an ethical pharmaceutical house.

(5) Positions where the major emphasis is placed on technical knowledge, for example the engineering marketing-person, who is primarily a consultant to the 'client' companies.

(6) Positions that demand the creative marketing of tangible products, such as vacuum cleaners, refrigerators, siding, and encyclopaedias.

(7) Positions requiring the creative marketing of intangible, such as insurance, advertising services, or education.

The more developmental marketing required in a particular marketing position, the more difficult it is to make marketing. The amount of developmental marketing required, in turn, depends upon the natures of the prospect (or customer) and the product. The easiest marketing are self-service marketing, which McMurry omits from his spectrum and rightly so; here the customers are aware of their needs, they know which products are capable of satisfying these needs, and they sell themselves. The most difficult marketings are those that involve intangibles—the customers usually are not fully aware of their needs; someone must explain the existence of these needs and how the intangible can satisfy them. Such marketing required effective explanations of the benefits to be derived from the intangible and the consequences of not buying it. The level of difficulty of the majority of marketing falls between these two extremes. The prospects has some awareness of the need; but, before the purchase is made, the marketing-person must further define the nature of the need and explain the product and its benefits.

Theoretical Aspects of Marketing

There is considerable disagreement as to the extent to which marketing can be described as a science with basic concepts that can be easily taught, or as an art that can be learned only through experience. In a survey of 173 marketing executives, 46 per cent perceived marketing as an art, only 8 per cent perceived it as a science, and 46 per cent perceived it as an art that is evolving into a science. The fact that some consider marketing an art and others consider it a science has product two theoretical approaches to explaining how marketing are made.

The first source involves the distillation of marketing theories from the experiences of successful marketing-people and, to a lesser extent, advertising professionals. Many such persons, of course, have succeeded because of their grasp of practical, or learned through experience psychology and their almost intuitive ability to apply it in actual marketing situations. Thus, it is not too surprising that such marketing theories emphasise the 'what to do' and 'how to do' rather than explaining 'why.' It is important to recognise that these theories based on an experiential kind of knowledge that is accumulated from years of "living in the market" rather than on a systematic, fundamental body of knowledge, are subject to Howard's dictum, "Experiential knowledge can be unreliable."

The second source, which has been tapes only comparatively recently, includes the behavioural sciences, whose research findings a growing number of marketing scholars have been attempting to apply to the problems of buying and marketing. The late E.K. Strong, Jr. Professor of Psychology at the Stanford Graduate School of Business, was one of the pioneers in this effort, and his 'buying formula' theory of marketing is resented later in the section. John A. Howard of the Columbia Graduate School of Business has been in the forefront of the group of marketing scholars concerned with borrowing and adapting the findings of research in behavioural science to the analysis of buying behaviour; his 'behavioural equation' represents an attempt to develop a unified theory of buying and marketing. This behavioural equation is also discussed later in this section.

The purpose of this section, then, is to acquaint the reader with four attempts to identify and explain the nature of the process of influencing others to buy. The first two, the 'AIDAS' theory and the 'right set of circumstances' theory, are marketing-person or marketing oriented. The third, the 'buying-formula' theory of marketing, is buyer oriented. And the fourth, the behavioural equation, emphasises the buyer's decision process but takes the marketing-person's influence process into account. Our intention is not to provide the reader with a secret formula for successful marketing; indeed, we are unaware of the existence of such a formula. Our belief is that readers will understand the marketing process better if they understand these four 'theories.'

AIDAS Theory of Marketing

The first theory—popularly known as the AIDAS theory, after the initials of the five words used to express it—forms the basis for many marketing and advertising texts and is the skeleton around which many training programmes in marketing are organised. Although some support for this theory is found in the psychological writings of William James, there is little doubt that the construct is based mainly upon experiential knowledge and, in fact, was in existence as early as 1898. During the successful marketing interview, according to this theory, the prospect's mind passes through five successive mental states; attention, interest, desire action, and satisfaction. Implicit in this theory is the notion that the prospect who buys goes through these five stages consciously; thus, the marketing-person's presentation must lead the prospect through them in the right sequence if a marketing is to result.

Securing Attention

In this phase the marketing-person's goal is to put the prospect into a receptive state of mined so that the main body of the presentation may be stated. The first few minutes of the interview are often crucial. The marketing-person has to have a reasons, or at least an excuse, for conducting the interview. If the marketing-person has made a previous appointment with the prospect, this phase should present no great problem; but experienced marketing-personnel say that even with such an appointment a marketing-person must possess considerable mental alertness, and be a skilled conversationalist, to survive the beginning of the interview. The prospect's guard is naturally up, since he or she realises that the caller is bent on marketing him or her something. So the marketing-person must establish good rapport at once. The marketing-person needs as ample supply of 'conversation openers,' and must strive to make a favourable first impression. Favourable first impressions are assured by, among other things, proper attire, neatness, friendliness, and a genuine smile. Skilled marketing-personnel often decide upon conversation openers just before the interview so that the gambits chosen will be as timely as possible. Generally it is considered advantageous if the opening remarks are about the prospect (people like to talk and hear about themselves), or if they are favourable comments about aspects of the prospect's business. A good conversation opener causes the prospect to relax his or her feeling of caution and sets the stage for succeeding phase of the marketing-person's presentation. Conversation openers that cannot be readily tied in with the remainder of the presentation should be avoided, for once the conversation starts to wander, great skill is required to return to the main thrust of the presentation.

Gaining Interest

The marketing-person's second goal is to intensify the prospect's attention so that it evolves into a state of strong interest. Many techniques are used for gainning interest. Some marketing-people develop a contagious enthusiasm for their product, becoming so inspired that the prospect's interest is built up almost automatically. Another technique is to let the prospect handle the product or as sample. When the product is bulky or technical, marketing portfolios, flipcharts, or other visual aids serve the same purpose.

Through the interest phase, one of the marketing-person's main purposes is to search out the marketing appeal that is most likely to be effective. If the marketing-person is fortunate, the prospect drops hints, which the marketing-person then uses in selecting the best approach. To encourage the prospect along this line, some marketing-people devise stratagems to elicit revealing question. Other draw out the prospect by asking questions designed to clarify attitudes feeling toward the product.

The more experienced the marketing-person the more he or she can rely for possible clues on what has been learned from other interviews with similar prospects. But even experienced marketing-personnel often must resort to considerable probing, usually of the question and answer variety, before identifying in the strongest appeal. It should be mentioned, too, that prospects' interest is also affected by such factors as their basic motivations, the closeness of the interview subject to their current problems, the timeliness of the subject, and their mood—receptive, skeptical, or hostile—and the marketing-person must take all these into account in selecting the marketing appeal that he or she will emphasise.

Kindling Desire

The marketing-person's third goals to kindle the prospect's desire to the ready-to-buy point. The marketing-person must remain in control of the situation and must keep the conversation running along the main line toward the marketing. The development of marketing obstacles, the prospect's objections, external interruptions, and digressive remarks are some of the factors tending to sidetrack the presentation during this phase. Obstacles have to be faced and ways found to get around them. Objections need answering to the prospect's satisfaction. Time frequently is saved, and the chance of making a marketing improves, if objections are anticipated and answered before the prospect has a chance to raise them. External interruptions cause breaks in the presentation; and when conversation resumes, bood marketing-people normally summarise what has been said earlier before continuing. Digressive remakes should generally be disposed of tactfully, with finesse, but something distracting digression is best handled bluntly: for example, "Well that's all very interesting, but to get back to the subject. . . ."

Inducing Action

If the presentation has been perfect, the prospect is ready to order. However, this action is not usually automatic and, as rule, must be induced. Experienced marketing-personnel rarely try for a close unit they are positive that the prospect is fully convinces of the merits of the proposition. Thus, it is necessary for the marketing-person to sense when the time is right to induce the prospect's buying action. Such devices as the trial close, the close on a minor point, and the trick close are used to test the prospect's reactions to the proposition. Some marketing-personnel never ask for a definite 'yes' or 'no' for fear of getting a 'no,' from which they think there is no retreat. But it is usually better to ask for the order straightforwardly. Most prospects find it easier to slide away from hints than from frank requests for an order.

Building Satisfaction

After the customer has given the order, the marketing-person should reassure the customer that the decision was correct one. The customer should be left with the impression that the marketing-person merely helped in making the decision. Building satisfaction means thanking the customer for the order, which should always be done, and attending to such matters as making certain that the order is correct as written, and following up on any promises made. Because the order is the climax of the marketing situation, the possibility of an anticlimax should be avoided—customers sometimes unsell themselves, and the marketing-person should not linger too long.

'Right Set of Circumstances' Theory of Marketing

Often a marketing-person comments, "Everything was right for the marketing to take place" and this sums up the popular version of the second theory. This theory, sometimes expressed by the term 'situation-response,' had its psychological origin in experiments with animals, and holds that the particular circumstances prevailing in a given marketing situation cause the prospect to respond in predictable way. More specifically stated—If the marketing-person succeeds in securing the attention and gaining the interest of the prospect, and if the marketing-person presents the proper stimuli or appeals, the desired response (that is, the marketing) will result. Furthermore, according to the theory, the more highly skilled the marketing-person is in handling the total set of circumstances, the more predictable will be the response.

The relevant set of circumstances, which the theory suggests that the marketing-person should try to control, includes factors external and internal to the prospect. To use a simplified example, suppose that the marketing-person says to the prospect, "Let's go out for a cup of coffee." The marketing-person and the remark represent external factors. But at least four internal factors related to the prospect affect the response. These are the presence or absence of desires: (1) to have a cup of coffee. (2) to have a cup of coffee now, (3) to go out for a cup of coffee, and (4) to go out with the marketing-person for a cup of coffee.

Proponents of this theory have been inclined to overstress the external factors and to neglect the importance of the internal factors. They have devoted their major efforts to seeking out marketing appeals that generally can be depended upon to evoke desired responses. Marketing-personnel who try to apply the theory commonly experience difficulties traceable to prospects' ingrained habits and instinctive behaviour. Although it is relatively easy to control the external factors in many marketing situations, the internal factors do not readily lend themselves to manipulation by marketing-people. Thus, this is a marketing-oriented theory, and from that emphasis derives its chief drawbacks: it stress the importance of the marketing-persons controlling the situation, does not adequately handle the problem of influencing factors internal to the prospect, and fails to assign appropriate weight to the significance of the response side of the situation-response interaction.

'Buying-Formula' Theory of Marketing

In market contrast to the two theories just discussed, the third places emphasis on the buyer's side of the buyer-marketing dyad. The buyer's needs or problems receive major attention, and the marketing-person's role is conceived as being one of helping the buyer find solution. This theory purports to answer the question: What thinking process goes on in the prospect's mind that causes the decision to buy or not buy? The buying formula itself is a schematic representation of a group of responses, arranged formula in feasible psychological sequence. The buying-formula theory, in other words, emphasises the prospect's responses (which, of course, are strongly influenced by internal factors) and de-emphasises the external factors, on the assumption that the marketing-person, being naturally conscious of the external factors, will not overlook them. Since the marketing-person's normal inclination is to neglect the internal factors, the formula is a convenient way to help the marketing-persons remember. The origin of this theory is somewhat obscure, but recognisable versions appear in a number of early books on advertising and marketing by authors who evidently had experiential knowledge of marketingmanship. Several psychologists also advanced explanation substantially similar to that contained in the buying formula. The name 'buying formula' was given to this theory by the late E.K. Strong Jr., and the following step-by-step explanation is adapted from his teaching and writings.

Reduced to their simplest elements, the mental process involved in a purchase are:

need (or problem) – solution – purchase

Because the outcome of a purchase affects the chance that a continuing relationship will develop between the buyers and the marketing, and because nearly all marketing organisations are interested in such continuing relationship, it is necessary to add a fourth element to our analysis of a purchase. The four elements, then, are:

need (or problems) – solution – purchase – satisfaction

Whenever a need is felt, or a problem recognised, it means that the individual is confronted with a difficulty or is conscious of a deficiency of satisfaction. In the world of marketing and buying, the solution to such a difficulty will always be a product or service. And the product or service will belong to a potential marketing.

In purchasing, then, the element 'solution' involves two parts: (1) product (or service), and (2) trade name (name of manufacturer, company, or marketing-person).

In buying, anything, the purchase proceeds mentally from need or problem to product or service, to trade name, to purchase; and, upon using the product or service, he or she experiences satisfaction or dissatisfaction. Thus, when a definite buying habit has been established, the buying formula covering the elements involved in buying can be diagrammed as follows:

<table>
<tr><td>need or
problem</td><td>–</td><td>product
or service</td><td>– trade name – purchase –</td><td>satisfaction
dissatisfaction</td></tr>
</table>

To ensure purchase, the product or service and the trade name (that is, the source of supply) must be considered adequate, and the buyer must experience a (pleasant) feeling of anticipated satisfaction when thinking of the product or service and the trade name. In a great many cases, a commodity viewed as adequate is also liked, and *vice versa,* but this is not always the case. Some products and services that have been found quite adequate are not liked, and some things are liked and bought that are admittedly not as good as competing items. Similar reasoning applies in the cases of trade names—some sources of supply are considered both adequate and liked; other are adequate but not liked; still others are liked but patronised in spite of the fact that they are inadequate compared to competing sources.

When adequacy and pleasant feeling are included in the buying formula, the following diagram results:

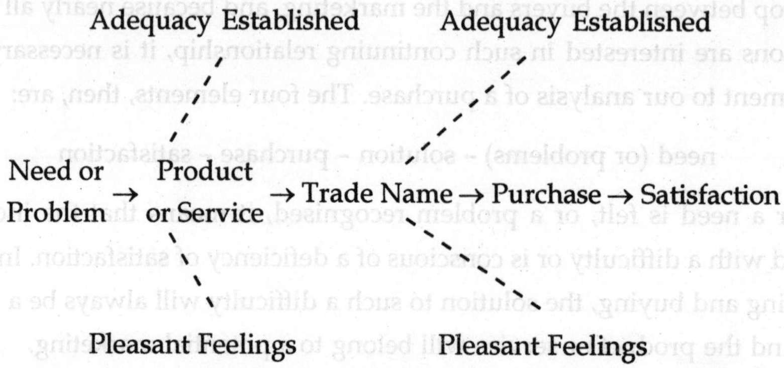

When a buying habit is being established, the buyer must be aware of the reason why the product or service is an adequate solution to the want or problem, and why the particular trade name is the best one to buy from. It is also necessary that the buyer have a pleasant feeling toward the product or service and the trade name.

Then, whenever the buyer's buying habit is challenged by a friend's remark, a marketing-person's presentation of a competing article, or a statement in an advertisement, it is essential that the buyer have reasons with which to defend the action, and that, in addition, he or she have a pleasant feeling toward both the product or service and the trade name. All this is represented by the dashed lines in the formula.

The primary elements in a well-established buying habit are those connected by solid lines, on the central line of the formula. Probably the majority of purchases are made with scarcely a thought as to why, and with a minimum of feeling. And it should be the constant aim of the marketing-person and advertiser to form such direct associations. Reasons, and pleasant feelings, are related to element on the central line by dashed lines to indicate that they constitute the elements of defence in the buying habit. As long as they are present, buying will continue as in the past.

The solution to each marketing problem is implied in the buying formula, and the differences among these various solutions are merely differences in the emphasis that is put upon the elements in the formula.

Where the emphasis should be placed depends upon a variety of circumstances. Without going into detail, it may be said that:

(1) If the prospect does not feel a need or recognise a problem that can be satisfied by the product or service, the need or problem must be emphasised.

(2) If the prospect does not think of the product or service when he or she feels the need or recognises the problems, the association between need or problem and product or service must be emphasised.

(3) If the prospect does not think of the trade name when he or she thinks of the product or service, the association between product or service and trade name must be emphasised.

(4) If need or problem, product or service, and trade name are well associates, emphasis must be put upon facilitating purchase and use.

(5) If competition is felt, emphasis must be put upon establishing in the prospects minds the adequacy of the trade named product or service, and pleasant feeling toward it.

(6) If marketing involving new prospects are desired, every element in the formula must be presented.

(7) If more marketing to old customers are desired, the latter must be reminded. (Developing new uses is comparable to selling to new customers.)

'Behavioural-Equation' Theory

Using a stimulus-response model (which is a much refined and highly sophisticated version of the 'right set of circumstances' theory discussed earlier), and incorporating numerous findings from behavioural science research. J.A. Howard explains buying behaviour in terms of the purchasing decision process, viewed as phases of the learning process.

Four essential elements of the learning process included in the stimulus-response model are drive, cue, response, and reinforcement. These elements are described as follows:

after analysing a number of findings from behavioural science research, says that there are at least two ways: (1) by repeating and re-emphasising the advantages of the product purchased, and stressing the relative disadvantages of the foregone alternatives; and (2) in cases of dissonance traceable to buyer's feelings that they have purchased items not sanctioned by the relevant reference groups, the marketing-person can try to show the many characteristics of the items are similar to products the buyers have forgone, but which are approved by their particular reference groups. In other words, the buyer experiencing cognitive dissonance should be reassured that the decision is or was a wise one; the marketing-person can exert influence by providing information that will permit the buyer to rationalise the decision.

Prospecting

Efficient organisation of their time and thorough planning of their work are earmarks of above average marketing person; only a small portion of their total time is devoted to actual marketing but they are ever alter for ways to 'stretch' this productive marketing time. Above-average marketing-persons do many things to stretch out the time available for marketing. They arrange their travel and call schedules to economise on time spent on route and distance travelled. They make advance appointments, to avoid prolonged waiting period and unnecessary callbacks. Most important, they make certain that they do not waste time trying to sell to people who cannot but or are not likely to do so. This planning work, which is essential in eliminating calls on nonbuyers from the itinerary, is called *prospecting*.

Improvement in prospecting is one of the most promising approaches toward more productive use of marketing time. Unfortunately, many marketing-personnel devote too little time to prospecting and, as a consequence, too much to calling on nonprospects. Even though prospecting is one of the surest methods for marketing-persons to increase their own incomes and their worth to the company, many marketing-people tend to neglect their prospecting duties. Marketing-persons who are proficient in prospecting are able to apply their marketing efforts more productivity; they waste less time in making calls on nonprospects, and devote more attention to those that are most likely to buy.

Some companies use specialised personnel for prospecting work, but most regard it as one of the marketing-person's normal responsibilities. Regardless of who performs the task, the steps involves are similar. Even though marketing-persons may not personally do prospecting, they should understand the process. They are the ones in closest touch with the customers, and they often have access to sources of information on likely prospects not available to central office personnel.

Steps in Prospecting

The steps involved in prospecting are implied in the statement of the purpose of personal marketing earlier. Personal marketing brings the right products into contact with the right customers and makes certain that ownership transfers take place. There are four steps: (1) formulating prospect definitions, (2) searching out potential accounts, (3) qualifying prospects and determining their probable requirements and, (4) relating company products to each prospect's requirements.

Formulating Prospects Definitions

To be considered prospective customer, or prospects, potential buyers must fulfil certain requirements. They must have the willingness, the financial capacity, and the authority to buy, and they must be available to the marketing-person. Marketing-persons waste valuable time when they attempt to marketing individuals who have neither need for the product nor money to pay for it. Marketing-person's efforts are similarly wasted if they try to sell to the wrong persons; so it important to ascertain which individual in each firm has the authority to buy which of the marketing-person's products. And although individuals may qualify as prospects in all the preceding respects, they may be completely inaccessible to the marketing-person. The president of a large corporation, for example, may need insurance, and be willing and able to pay for it; but a particular marketing-person may have no way to make the contact.

In addition to the above requirements, there are others unique to each company's customers and, before one can prospect effectively, these must be identified. Starting with data on the profitability of present accounts, any characteristics typical of profitable accounts but not shared by unprofitable accounts should be detected. These identifying characteristics ideally should be ones easily recognisable from information appearing in directories or lists. Prospects in many categories of business and professions, for instance, may be readily identified from the classified listings in telephone and city

In understanding the marketing-person-client relation, it is helpful to separate the economic aspects from the strictly social features. The marketing-person wishes to sell a product, and the buyer wishes to buy it-these are the economic features of the relationship. Each participant also places a value and cost upon the strictly social feature. Behaviour convening these features of the relationship can be called sentiments, or expressions of different degrees of liking or social approval. Marketing-persons attempt to get more or less valuable reward (reinforcement) either is sentiment or economic activity, which they do by changing their own behaviour or by getting buyers to change theirs.

Marketing-person's Influence Process

The process by which the marketing-person influences the buyer can be explained in terms of the behavioural equation (B = P × D × K × V). The marketing-person can probably influence P, (predisposition) directly, for example, through interacting with the buyer in ways that are rewarding to the buyer. The greatest affect on P, however, is thought to be the reinforcement that comes from using the brand. There is little doubt that the marketing-person can exert influence through D (amount of motivation), such influence being especially strong when the buyer seeks information primarily in terms of informational cues. If the ends to be served through satisfying a drive or a need are not clearly defined, by helping to clarify these, the buyer's goals, the marketing-person again exerts influence through D. When the buyer has stopped learning—when the buyer's buying behavioural consists solely of automatic responses—the marketing-person influences D by providing triggering cues. When the buyer has narrowed down the choices to a few marketing from whom to make purchase, the marketing-person, by communicating the merits of the company brand, can cause it to appear relatively better, and, thus, affect K (its potential satisfaction for the buyer). Finally, the marketing-person can vary the intensity of his or her effort, so making the difference in V (the intensity of all cues).

Marketing-person's Role in Reducing Buyer Dissonance

According to Festinger's theory of cognitive dissonance, when individuals choose between two more alternatives, anxiety or dissonance will almost always occur because they know that the decision made has certain unattractive features in addition to its attractive features. After making decisions, people therefore tend, according to this theory, to expose themselves to information that they perceive as likely to support their choices, and to avoid information that is likely to favour rejected alternatives. Although Festinger evidently meant his theory to apply only to situations involving post decision anxiety, it seems reasonable that the theory should also hold for situations involving predecision anxiety. Hauk, for instance, writes that a buyer may panic or reaching the point of decision, and rush into the purchase as an escape from the problem, or put it off because of the difficulty of deciding among alternative. It would appear, then, that a buyer may experience either predecision anxiety or dissonance, or both. Howard notes that the reduction of both pre-and post-decision anxiety or dissonance is an important function of the marketing-persons. Recognising that the buyer's dissonance varies both according to whether the product is an established or a new one, and whether the marketing-person-client relation is an ongoing one or new. Howard considers the following four main types of cases involving the nature of the marketing-person's role in dissonance reduction:

(1) An established product—an ongoing marketing-person client relation. Unless the market is unsitable, the buyer tends towards automatic response behaviour, in which no learning is involved, and thus experience little, if any, dissonance, but insofar as this does occur, the marketing-person would presumably be effective because the marketing-person would be trusted by the buyer.

(2) An established product—a new marketing-person client relation. The marketing-person, being new, would presumably be less effective in reducing dissonance.

(3) A new product—an ongoing marketing-person-client relation. Unless the buyer generalises heavily from personal experience with an established similar product, the buyer would experience dissonance, especially if it were an important product. Because of the established relationship with the buyer, the marketing-person would be capable of reducing dissonance.

(4) A new product—a new marketing-person-client relation. The buyer would need dissonance reduction, and the marketing-person would be less capable of providing it.

How can a marketing-person facilitate the buyer's dissonance reduction? Zaltman,

(1) *Drives* are strong internal stimuli that impel the buyer's response.

There are two kinds of drives:

(a) Innate drives: The physiological needs, such as hunger, thirst, pain, cold, and sex.

(b) Learned drives: Learned drives, such as striving for status or social approval, are acquired when paired with the satisfying of innate drives, and represent elaborations of the innate drives, serving as a façade behind which the functioning of the innate drives in hidden. Insofar as marketing is concerned, the learned drives are probably dominant in economically advanced societies.

(2) *Cues* are weak stimuli, as distinguished from the storing stimuli that underlie drives. Cues determine when the buyer will respond:

(a) Triggering cues serve as activators of the decision process for any given purchase.

(b) Nontriggering cues influence the decision process but do not activate it, and may operate at any time even though the buyer is not contemplating a purchase at the moment.

There are two kinds:

(i) Product cues are external stimuli received from the product directly, for example, colour of the package, weight, or price.

(ii) Informational cues refer to external stimuli that provide the buyer with information of a symbolic nature about the product. Such stimuli may come from advertising, conversations with other people (including marketing-personnel), etc.

(c) Specific product and information cues may sometimes also function as triggering cues. This may happen when price triggers the buyers decision.

(3) *Response* is what the buyer does.

(4) A *reinforcement* is any event that strengthens the tendency for a buyers to make a particular response.

Howard incorporates these four essential elements into a behavioural equation, stated in its simplest form as follows:

$$B = P \times D \times K \times V$$

Where

B = response or the internal response tendency, that is, the act of purchasing a brand or patronising a supplier.

P = predisposition or the inward response tendency, which is strength of habit.

D = present drive level (amount of motivation)

K = 'incentive potential,' that is, the value of the product to the buyer or its potential satisfaction to him or her

V = intensity of all cues: triggering, informational, or product.

Notice that Howard believes the relation among the variable to be multiplicative rather than additive. Thus, if any independent variable has zero value, B will also be zero and there will be no response. No matter how much P there may be, for example, if the individual as the moments is totally unmotivated (D = 0), there will be no response.

Furthermore, each time there is a response—a purchase—in which the satisfaction (K) received from the response is sufficient to yield a reward, predisposition (P) will increase in values as a result of the rewarded response. In other words, when the satisfaction received yields a reward, reinforcement occurs and, technically, what is reinforced is the tendency to make a response in the future to the cue that immediately preceded the rewarded response. After such reinforcement, the probability increases that the buyers will buy product (or patronise the supplier) the next time the cue appears—in other words, the buyer has learned.

Buyer-Marketing Dyad and Reinforcement

To the extent that a marketing-person and a buyer interact, each can display a type of behaviour that is rewarding is reinforcing to the other. The marketing-person provides the buyer with a product (and the necessary information about it and its uses) that the buyer needs; this satisfaction of the need is rewarding to the buyers, who in turn, can reward the marketing-person by buying the product. Each can also reward the other by another type of behaviour, that of providing social approval. The marketing-person gives social approval to a buyer by displaying high regard for the buyer with friendly greetings, warm conversation, praise, and the like.

directories. Significant characteristics that identify profitable accounts are assembled into description of the various classes of customers, and these serve as prospect definitions.

If the firm has a good marketing analysis system, the formulation of prospect definitions is comparatively easy. Most of the needed information on customer traits is already part of the system and requires only assembling. In the even that the marketing-analysis system is inadequate, or fails to yield sufficient customer data, it is worthwhile spending the time and effort required for gathering, organising, and processing the needed information. Once a company has a good marketing-analysis system, it also has an information source of formulating definitions of the different categories or prospects.

Searching Out Potential Accounts

Using the prospect definitions, the marketing-person should comb all available information sources to search out the names of probable prospects, or 'suspects,' as they are called. Source of prospect information include: directories of all kinds, news and notes in trade papers and business magazines, credit reports, membership lists for such groups as chambers of commerce and trade and manufacturer's associations, lists purchased from list brokers, and records of services requests. Other sources include: responses to company advertising, marketing-personnel of noncompeting firms falling on the same general classes of trade, conventions and meeting, bankers and other 'centres of influence,' and the marketing-person's own observations. Marketing-people marketing services, such as insurance and mutual funds, find personal contacts among their acquaintances; members of their professional, religious, and social organisations; and from the referrals of friends. Another source of prospects for such marketing-people is the 'continuous chain-referral method'—satisfied customers often suggest, voluntarily or on request, other leads to the marketing-person who served them.

Qualifying Prospects and Determining their Probable Requirements

Names on the tentative prospect list are next subjected or more intensive investigation. With the assembling of more information, it becomes progressively easier to detect bonafide prospects and to eliminate those who are not. As the 'picture' of each prospect develops, estimates are made concerning the extent to which each uses products similar to those of company. Prospects with requirements too small to represent profitable business are removed from further consideration, unless their growth possibilities appear to show significant promise. Even after tapping all readily available information sources, additional information often is required before qualifying certain prospects. In cases of this sort, personal visits by marketing-persons may be the only way to obtain it. Although such visits may not result in marketing, time is saved over the long run, since prospects are separated for nonprospects.

Relating Company Products to Each Prospect's Requirements

The final step is to plan the strategy to use approaching each prospect. From the information assembled, it is usually possible to determine, more or less accurately, the nature of the likely needs of each. From what the marketing-person knows about the company's products, their uses and applications, he or she selects those that seem most appropriate for the particular prospect. The marketing-person has now finished most of the work preliminary to making the marketing calls.

The marketing-person's presentation should now be easy to construct, and it can be tailored rather precisely to extent strong influence upon the prospect. The marketing-person should have rather clear ideas in advance of the specific objections the prospect may raise, and other obstacles to the marketing that may be encountered. The marketing-person is now ready to make actual contact with the prospect, the only tasks remaining being those of making an appointment, deciding how to open the presentation, and determining how best to influence the prospect to become a customer.

Marketing Resistance

To succeed in converting prospects into customers, the marketing-person needs skill in analysing and overcoming marketing resistance. Prospects show marketing resistance by pointing cut real or imagined obstacles to the marketing, and by voicing objections, sincere or insincere. In analysing marketing resistance, skill in the accurate and rapid appraisal of people and their motivations is essential. A prospect's expressed marketing resistance should be identified as either an obstacle or an objection. An obstacle must be classified as real or unreal; an objection, as sincere or insincere. After sizing up marketing resistance in this manner, the marketing-person is in good s rategic position to select the next moves.

marketing manager's main contribution to marketing programme's success generally is to get results through company marketing-personnel, further emphasising the critical nature of this executive's relations with subordinates. Whereas the marketing-person's primary working relationship is with customers, the marketing manager's is with the marketing force.

It is generally easier to maintain good relations with marketing-people if satisfactory relations exist with other employees; and important difference is that marketing-person's interests are frequently more akin to those of executives than to those of other company personnel. Because marketing-personnel operate without personal supervision much of the time, more trust and confidence necessarily must be placed in them. Perhaps that is why the marketing force so often serves as a providing ground for future executives and why some managements tend to develop paternalistic relationship with the marketing staff. But paternalism should be avoided, and democratic administration should be more than just an ideal in the marketing force: it should be customary practice. Close personal relations should exist among marketing executives and marketing-personnel, and individuals in both groups should clearly understand the interest of the other. But favouring certain marketing-people at the expense of others can have only adverse effects upon overall marketing-force morale.

Job satisfaction and a feeling that what he or she is doing is worthwhile are key factors in motivating a marketing-person to stay in a company's employ. Therefore, it is important for management not only to recognise each marketing-person's contribution to company success but to let them know that management knows and appreciates the contributions they are making. All members of marketing force should be made keenly aware of their individual contributions to the good of the company. Although it is impossible to prescribe all the other conditions necessary for building and maintaining satisfactory relations with marketing-people, it is possible to tell when a company has achieved them. When marketing personnel have pride, loyalty, and enthusiasm concerning the company, its products, its policies, and the executives who plan and direct their work, relations with marketing-people are excellent.

Why Marketing Personnel Require Additional Stimulation

Why are some marketing-people more successful than other? What in other words, accounts for variations in marketing success? The answer lies in the differing motivational patterns of individual marketing-persons and the resulting relative amounts and types of efforts they exert in performing their jobs. The analysis leading to this conclusion will be examined later, first we must review three aspects of the marketing-person's job that affect the quality of its performance. Each aspect is also an important reason why most marketing-people require additional stimulation to reach and maintain high productivity.

The first aspect concerns the nature of the marketing-person's job itself. Generally, it is a succession of ups and downs, a series of experiences resulting in alternating feelings of exhilaration and depression. In the course of a day's work, marketing-persons call on many pleasant and courteous people; but they encounter some who are unpleasant and rude, with whom, it is difficult to deal. They are frequently frustrated, particularly when aggressive competing marketing-people are vying for the same business and they meet numerous 'turndown.' Furthermore, marketing-persons must spend not only working time but also considerable 'after-hours' time away from home, causing them to miss many of the beat parts of family life. These conditions can easily cause a person to become discouraged, to achieve performance levels lower than might otherwise be possible, or even to seek a nonmarketing position. The nature of the marketing-person's job being what it is, then, additional stimulation often is required to assure effective job performance.

The second aspect concerns the natural tendency of some marketing-personnel to become apathetic, 'to get into a rut.' Marketing-person who, year after year, cover the same territory and virtually the same customers, tend to lose enthusiasm. Gradually their marketing calls degenerate into routine order taking. Because they feel they know the customers so well, they come to believe that good marketing is no longer necessary. Their approach to a customer typically becomes: "Do you need anything today, Joe?" They fail to recognise that friendship with customers in no way obviates the necessity for creative marketing, and that it is unusual for customers to sell themselves on new products and applications the customer's response, as often as not, is: "Nothing today, Bill." later a competing marketing-person calls on the same account, uses good marketing techniques, and gets an order. Many marketing-people require additional stimulation to maintain continuing enthusiasm for their work or to generate renewed interest in it.

agreement has already been reached, and the prospect is ready to react favourably to the marketing-person's proposal.

But even after an excellent presentation, and in spite of the thoroughness of the prospecting, some prospects refrain from positive commitemnts. The natural tendency of many people is to let inertia guide their reactions—many are perfectly happy to leave things as they are, and marketing-persons leave empty-handed unless they somehow manage to jolt such prospects into buying. In some situations, the skilled closer gives the extra push that triggers a buying response. But it need emphasising again that failures to get an order as much the result of poor prospecting and inept presentations as they are of ineffective-ness in closing.

When an attempt at a close fails, the marketing-person should normally try again. The marketing-person should not be too easily discouraged, because a refusal does not necessary imply an unwillingness to buy; it may simply indicate the prospects; need for addition information, or for clarification of some point. Some marketing executives recommend that their marketing-personnel attempt as many as five closes before abandoning a given effort. Early attempts at a close should be so expressed that the prospect's refusal will not cut off continuation of the presentation. A marketing-person must learn to judge the sincerity of a prospect's refusal surrendering gracefully when it becomes obvious that no marketing will be made.

In most situations, the marketing-person should first try an indirect close; that is, attempt to get the order without actually asking for. It the marketing-person may ask the prospectors to state his preference from among a limited number of choices (as to models, delivery dates, order size, or the like), so phrasing the question that all possible responses are in the marketing-person's favour expect for one - 'None at all.' Or the marketing-person may proceed to summarise, emphasising features that have visibly impressed the prospect showing how the reasons for the purchase outweigh those opposed. Then the marketing-person pauses for the product's which is expected to be, 'Go ahead and write the order.' Sometimes, the extra push may be a concession that makes the purchase appear sufficiently more attractive to affect completing the marketing. Or the marketing-person simply may assume that the marketing has already made, writing out the order and handing it to the prospect for approval—if the prospect balks, the issue becomes clearer. Perhaps one last objection is voiced; but after it is satisfactorily answered, the marketing is made. Many other indirect closes are in common use, and books on marketing contain numerous examples.

When one or more attempts at an indirect close fail, the above-average marketing-person uses the direct approach. Suprisingly few genuine prospects respond negatively to a frank request for an order. In fact, many persons, especially those who are themselves engaged in marketing, do not buy unless the order is asked for directly. Some evidence indicates that a high proportion of marketing-personnel fail to ask for the order directly, one study showing that more than 50 per cent failed in this respect. But those who asked for the order averaged 300 per cent more marketing than those who did not.

Motivating the Individual Marketing-Person

Many a "star marketing-person require little external incentive in climbing the ladder or marketing success." To such people, marketing is the world's most fascinating occupation, and they constantly challenge themselves to improve upon their marketing performance. Unfortunately, however, such self-starters are all too scare in marketing. As a matter of fact, most marketing-personnel do not maintain consistency high levels of marketing performance unless marketing management provides additional stimulation. High productivity in a marketing force comes about neither naturally nor accidentally; it develops through intelligent handling of relationships with marketing-people and the timely use of appropriate incentives. This dissussion focuses on the motivation of marketing-persons and individuals.

The Company and Its Relations with Marketing Personnel

It is possible, although unusual, for a company to have rather poor relations with certain employee groups and still enjoy a good public reputation. But it is essential to have satisfactory relations with marketing-personnel. In so far as customers are concerned, the marketing staff is the company, and the image they project is strongly influenced by the nature of their relations with marketing executives. Marketing territories cover a wide area; and the opinion of the company's marketing force are carried to, and affect the opinion of, distributors, dealers, and customers generally, as well as other groups. Hence, good public relations begin inside the company, and for the marketing department, this means with the marketing force. Moreover, the

Obstacles to Marketing

Obstacles are real or apparent reasons that the prospect has for not buying. If the obstacle is real, it precludes the consummation of the marketing. But if it is only apparent, the marketing-person can find a way of circumventing it. A prospect may say that he cannot buy—because of a temporary shortage of cash—an obstacle, not an objection -- and the marketing-person may help the prospect circumvent it by explaining a methods for financing the purchase. Some obstacles can be circumvented, others cannot. When marketing-persons perceive that an obstacle to a marketing exists, they should determine at once whether or not there is a way to get around it. If they are sufficiently experienced to recognise the specific obstacle and know a way to circumvent it, the next move is to present their solution to the prospect's problem.

Marketing Objections

Objection call for different treatment. They are almost never good reasons for failing to complete the safe, but they nearly always divert the marketing-person's presentation from its main course. At best, an objection requires a short and satisfactory answer; at worst; it blocks the marketing entirely. Adroitness in handling objections is an important difference between effective and ineffective marketing-people.

Sincere objections often trace to incompleteness, inaccuracy, or vagueness in the marketing-person's presentation. Prospects may not recognise the nature of their needs; or they may have real doubts about the appropriateness of the product to fulfil them, be confused in some respect, or may even react unfavourable to the marketing-person's personality. Except when personality conflict is irresolvable (which case would be classifies as a real obstacle, rather than as an objection), sincere objections ordinarily can be overcome by patient and thorough explanations.

Insincere objection are more difficult to handle, for prospects use them to discourage marketing-persons, to get rid of them, to test their competence, or to furnish false excuses for not buying. When marketing-persons sense that an objection is insincere, they should muster their persuasive powers and regain the offensive as soon as they can. Under no circumstances should they permit an insincere objection to provoke an argument—that is one of the surest way to lose a marketing.

Some marketing executives feel that every objection, no matter how trivial or insincere, should be treated with the utmost courtesy and answered as well as possible. Others believe that insignificant objections should be ignored. One things is clear—when the prospect raises an objection, the marketing-person should try to use it to introduce additional reasons for buying. The best defensive strategy for a marketing-person, as for a defending army, often is the strong counterattack, and the marketing-person should seek to region the initiative as soon as he or she can gracefully do so.

Closing Marketing

The tactics of marketing followed during the presentation affect the ease of closing the marketing. Generally, low-pressure marketing are closed more easily than high-pressure ones. In low-pressure marketing to the extent that prospects are made to feel that they are reaching the buying decisions themselves, and primarily through rational processes of thought, there is less need for extra push by the marketing-persons just before the marketing are consummated. By contrast, in high-pressure marketing, the man trust of the appeal is to prospects' emotions, marketing-persons attempt to propel prospects into buying decisions. Often the prospect suddenly regains normal perspective as the marketing nears its climax and; if this happens the marketing-person needs truly unusual powers of persuasion to close the marketing.

Nearly every marketing-person approaches certain closing with considerable apprehension. At this point, either the marketing-person sells the prospect an order, or the prospect sells the marketing-person on a 'no marketing.' But this point also provides the marketing-person with an opportunity to register tangible proof of marketing skill. Occasionally even the best marketing-person has done inadequate prospecting, or made a below-par presentation; on these occasions, he or she must rely upon closing skills.

Prospecting, if well done, should put the marketing-person in the proper frame of mind for the close. He or she should feel that a real service is being performed for the prospect, not that 'a bill of goods is being marketed.' If the prospecting has been thorough, the marketing-person should have little doubt that the product is the best solution to the prospect's problems.

When the marketing presentation has been complete and clear, little difficulty should be met in closing the marketing. All obstacles to the marketing and all objections have been removed, to the prospect's entire satisfaction. Under these conditions, basic

The third aspect is related to the previous two. It concerns both the nature of the marketing job and the natural tendency for job enthusiasm to decline. The marketing-person, working alone for the most part, finds it difficult to maintain a feeling of group identity with other company marketing-people. Team spirit, if present at all, tends to be weak. Thus, the contagious enthusiasm so necessary to improvement of the entire group's performance fails to develop. If marketing management, by providing appropriate added stimulation, success in developing and maintaining teams spirit, individual marketing-people strive very hard to meet group performance standards.

Few people, who consider themselves full-fledged members of the 'marketing team' want to appear as poor performers in the eyes of fellow marketing-persons. Providing a working atmosphere in which the entire marketing force feels they are participating in a cooperative endeavour is not easy; nevertheless, marketing management must strive continuously to achieve and maintain it.

Marketing-personnel, then, need additional stimulation both as individuals and as groups members. Marketing-persons who become discouraged or apathetic are prime targets for personalised, informal efforts at motivation on the part of their superiors. Marketing forces whose member have little feeling of groups identity are ripe for more formal efforts by marketing management directed towards welding them into effective marketing teams.

Handling Relations with Marketing Personnel

Effective handling of relations with marketing-people is a skill not easily attained. Experience, maturity, and commonsense are necessary attributes and, although these cannot be gained through study alone, a few generalisations can be made. Marketing executives should treat all marketing-persons fairly, particularly with regard to assignments, promotions, and changes in pay. They should commend marketing-people for jobs well done; but if performances are not up to par, they should privately call that to their subordinates' attention. When marketing executives find it necessary to discuss a marketing-person's weakness, they should also make it clear that they are aware of the individual's strong points. Before making changes, particular ones affecting marketing-people's jobs or their performance, marketing executives should consult the marketing-personnel affected; this helps to prevent the damaging impact of rumors upon morale. The marketing force should be convinced, individually and collectively, that when sight is on their side, the marketing executive can be depended upon, if the need arises, to carry their case to top management. And, above all else, marketing executives must not lose sight of the fact that they are managing the marketing staff. While encouraging the marketing force's participation in decision, ultimately the marketing executive must be certain that they are 'sole' on plans, policy changes, and anything else that affects them. Real marketing-personnel are all the more sold on their jobs when marketing executives habitually apply good marketing techniques in their relations with them.

Communications and Motivating Individual Marketing People

Communications, simply defined, consists of the transmission and interchange of facts, ideas, feeling, and course of action. In marketing management, it is critically important that good communications exist between each marketing-person and his or her superior – unless it does, there will be depressed morale and low productivity. The marketing-person with pent-up grievances, real or imagined, is likely to display both low morale and unsatisfactory performance. Similarly, the marketing-person, like everyone else, occasionally comes up against personal problems, such as sickness in the family, inability to pay overdue bills, or marital troubles, all of which can affect morale and performance. Thus, the systems of two-way communications between the marketing-person and the superior should allow for free discussion of all business problems connected with the marketing-person's job and, to the extent needed, of any personal problems that, left unsolved, may hurt job performance. For the marketing-person, the existence of good communications represents freedom of self-expression – freedom to talk over problems, business and personal, with the superior in a friendly atmosphere. For the superior, it represents the responsibility for finding occasions and means for talking with the marketing-person not only to determine what, if anything, is 'bothering him,' but also to provide assistance in solving any problems that come to light.

Communication and Role Conflict

Nowhere else in the business organisation are two-way channels of communication more important than in the marketing department. The nature of the marketing-person's job is that of a link between at least four different groups: (1) the marketing-management group, (2) the balance of the organisation who must be depended upon for fulfilment of orders, (3) the customers, and (4) other marketing-personnel, within the company and elsewhere. Each group imposes certain behavioural expectations on the marketing-person and, in performing these different roles, the marketing-person faces specific role conflicts. J.A. Belasco describes three such conflicts.

(1) **Conflict of Identification:** Arises out of the multigroup membership of the marketing-person. As the marketing-person works with the customer, it is reasonable to expect identification with the customer rather than the company. However, on returning to the company, the marketing-person must drop the identification with the customer and identify with the company.

(2) **Advocacy Conflict:** Arises when the marketing-person has identified with the customer, it is logical to expect that he will seek to aid the customer by advocating the customer's position to the other groups with which is linked. Although this function may be every important and may be actually encouraged by the marketing-person's superiors, it places the advocator in a very difficult position.

(3) **Conflict Inherent in the Marketing-person's Dual Role as an Advocate:** Such conflicts are inherent for both the customer and the company, and the marketing-person's pecuniary interest as entrepreneur. As an entrepreneur paid on the marketing volume, he has a decided interest in marketing as much as possible in the shortest possible time. However, he may uncover facts overlooked or unknown to the customer, indicating that difficulties in the customer's organisation will limit the product's usefulness. If the marketing-person informs the customer of these observations and that, in all probability, the product will not fully meet the customer's needs, obviously the marketing-person runs the risk of losing the marketing and the income that goes with it. Existence of potential or actual role conflicts traceable to the marketing-person's linkage with groups that often have divergent interests explains why the roots of misunderstandings, grievances, poor morale, and even lack of productivity so often are found in communications breakdown.

Compounding the communication problem is the fact that marketing executives and marketing-persons usually work at a distance from each other, often not only throughout most of the workday but over extended periods; and most communications must be by mail and telephone. Despite this, however, marketing executives should do some things to assure that communications are as affective as possible. They should make a point of meeting with their people as practicable, both at the office and in the field. To avoid faulty transmissions, they should speak and write in language that marketing-personal understand—this does not mean that they should 'talk own' to them but rather that they should gear their communications with them to level. They should be certain that their marketing forces understand them and that they understand their marketing-personnel. In all verbal communications, it is to the marketing executive's advantage to be a good listener. By devoting close attention and analysis to marketing-people's remarks, marketing executives can learn a great deal about their subordinates. Similarly, the marketing executives should look for hidden as well react as apparent meanings in marketing-person's written messages. Thus, the marketing executive may gain insights that should go far in explaining why marketing-personnel act and react as they do. This knowledge is invaluable in directing marketing-people's activities and in providing additional motivation.

Interpersonal Contact

Interpersonal contact is the preferred way to communicate with and thereby to stimulate marketing-personnel. Through such contacts, management should make probing and comprehensive evaluations of individual marketing-peoples' moral. Interpersonal contacts provide management's best opportunity for learning of financial, family, or other personal worries that can have important impacts upon marketing-person's overall efficiency.

Marketing executives at all levels, from immediate supervisor to chief marketing executive, should have personal contacts with the marketing staff. Particularly at the higher levels of marketing management, however, face-to-face visits with marketing-people tend to be confined to conventions and marketing meetings. For the most part, then, most of the individual marketing-person's interpersonal contact with management is with the immediate supervisor. Although supervisors have other important functions to perform, such as training, evaluation, and control, they should be made fully aware of their responsibilities for maintaining communications with the people under them. They should, in other words, use their visits with marketing-persons for detecting personal or business problems, and for inspiration and stimulation, in addition to discharging other supervisory responsibilities.

Even though the immediate supervisor is the administrator in closest contact with individual marketing-people, marketing executive at all levels should reserve some time for observing and conferring with marketing-personnel. District managers should allocate time in which to visit each marketing-person on the job in the assigned marketing territory. It may be impractical, especially in the large national marketing organisation, for the top marketing executive to visit personally all territories or even all marketing districts; however, there are other ways from him to maintain personal contact with marketing-personal. One is to arrange individual conferences between marketing-people and the top marketing executive during regional or national meetings – the opportunity to visit with the 'big boss' can provide strong stimulation for individual marketing-persons.

Although interpersonal contact generally is the best way to keep in touch with the marketing staff, there are times when other communications media must be used. Not only is it physically impossible to be in close contact with all marketing-personnel all of the time, but, unfortunately, too often the least-valuable marketing-people demand the lion's share of the personal attention. When this happens, executive contact with the better marketing-people tends to be largely through written means. Confronted with this situation, many marketing executives prefer to keep in touch with their better people, not through letters, but through regular telephone calls, this being particularly appropriate when the staff in the field are far from the home office and visit it only infrequently.

Several instances can be cited in which the executive should contact marketing-people personally, or possibly telephone them, rather than communicate by letter. A drop in a marketing-person's efficiency that the executive suspects was caused by family discord is not only difficult but awkward to discuss in writing. Similarly, when a reprimand is thought necessary, a face-to-face meeting with the marketing-person unquestionably is better than dispatching a letter that could lead to further complications. Personal and disciplinary problems, then, are best handled by interpersonal contact and not through the mail. In exceptional cases, it may be possible through a clear and carefully phrased letter to avoid misinterpretations and misunderstanding, but the executive is still eternally well advised to follow up all such letters with personal contacts.

It is difficult for a marketing executive, particularly for one who supervises marketing-personnel directly, to motivate a marketing-person whom he or she knows only casually. The marketing executive must taken a special efforts to know each marketing-person well, and to learn what is important to each marketing-person—he or she needs this knowledge is subsequent efforts to encourage improves performance are to be at all productive. Marketing executives with direct supervisory responsibilities, then, must develop empathy with their subordinates and carefully plan the time spend in individual communications with their marketing-personnel.

Motivational Interviews

A recent trend, especially in more progressive companies, has been to toward establishing planned 'informational' goals for the executive to keep in mind during personal visits with individual marketing-personnel. A 'motivation interview form,' such as that prepared by Marketing and Marketing Executives-International, is designed to assist marketing executives in organising their efforts to gather motivational data on individual marketing-people. Using such a plan, the executive attempts to find out as much as possible about marketing-people's patterns of need fulfilment and the order of priority assigned to each category of need. Thus, insights are gained on individuals, motivational patterns, and guidance is furnished management in choosing appropriate incentive. Of course, it is unlikely that a single interview could be used to gather all this information; but after many interviews, the executives should be able to assemble the information needed to put together a comprehensive picture. The motivational interview technique provides a way to gather information bit by bit according to some plan of which the marketing-personnel need not, probably should not, be aware.

Written Communications

Supplementing personal contacts with marketing-people, the marketing executive attempts to keep them informed through letters, announcements, bulletins and other mailed pieces. Unfortunately, however, handling written communications tends to become routine and deadening-increase in volume and frequency of mailings often destroy their value. It is ironic, too, that some marketing executives who think nothing of spending hours planning every detail to ensure the effectiveness of marketing meeting almost wholly neglect any attempt to appraise the probable motivational impact of their correspondence. It is true, of course, that no single letter or bulletin is likely to have as strong a motivational effects as a marketing meeting; yet the total impact of written communication, effectively used, can be much great than the occasional formal marketing meeting.

The executive writing personal letters and bulletin to marketing-people should avoid using generalities and concentrate upon helpful suggestions. A letter to marketing-person Brown, reporting that marketing-person Jones wrote a $20,000 order last week, and instructing Brown to go out and do the same provides little real motivation. Describing how Jones succeeded in promoting a new use for the product to a certain kind of customer furnishes much stronger motivation. Writing letters especially those designed to cheer up and spur on marketing-people in the field, is an art, and marketing executives should do their best to master it.

One instance in which a letter is superior to interpersonal contact may be cited. It concerns the executive who wishes to compliment a marketing-person for a piece of particularly good work. A letter provides the marketing-person with lasting evidence that his or her performance has been recognised. Such letters can have a prolonged beneficial effect on the marketing-person's morale, but, of course, they are poor substitutes for deserved promotions or compensations increases. Furthermore, a commendation letter should be supported, whenever possible, by a personal expansion to the effect that management recognise, and is pleased with, the marketing-person's performance.

Concepts from the Behavioural Sciences Useful in Understanding Motivation

The concepts of need gratification and interdependence, developed by behavioural scientists, assist in understanding the nature of the problem involved in motivating marketing-persons as individuals. Marketing executives can use these concepts to construct their own models for motivating the behaviour of individual marketing-people, and this should result in more effective motivational effort.

Need Gratification

Psychological studies shown that human activity—including the marketing-person's behaviour on the job—is directed toward satisfying certain needs. Patterns of individual behaviour differ because individuals seek to fulfil these needs in different ways. How a particular individual behaves depends upon the nature of his or her unfulfilled needs modified by the environmental and social background. The motives lying behind any specific action derive from tensions built up to satisfy certain needs, some of which may be beneath the threshold of conciseness. Any action taken has the goal of reducing these tensions.

To understand motivation, then, we must first understand the nature of human needs. Needs may be grouped as either primary or secondary. Primary needs are the inborn of physiological needs for food, water, rest, sleep, air to breathe, and so forth, the fulfilment of which is basic to life itself. Until primary needs are satisfied, other needs have little motivational influence. Secondary needs, arising from an individual's interaction with the environment, are not inborn but develop with maturity. Secondary needs include those for safety and security, belongingness and social relations, esteem and self-respects, achievement, knowledge and understanding, and beauty.

A.H Maslow, a distinguished psychologist, asserts that as individual seeks to fulfil personal needs according to some hierarchy of importance. He suggests the general priority of need fulfilment shown in Fig. 1. As this figure shows, Maslow suggests that after a person has gratified basic physiological needs, he or she generally proceeds to strive to fulfil safety and security needs, then belongingness and social relations needs, and so on—his or her level of aspiration rising as needs on higher levels are satisfied. Not every individual and certainly not every marketing-person, of course, would establish the order of priority of need fulfilment, suggested by Maslow. Some marketing-people, for instance, definitely appear to assign earlier priority to filing the need for self-respect than they do to filling the need for social relations within a group.

After basic physiological needs have been met, it probably is impossible for most individuals to satisfy fully their needs on any higher level—need seem to multiply along with efforts to satisfy them. As a particular need is satisfied, it loses its potency as a motivator of behaviour; but other unfulfilled needs, some of them new, gain in potency. Individuals continually try to fulfil ever-larger portions of their need structures, and the unsatisfied portions exert the strongest motivational pull.

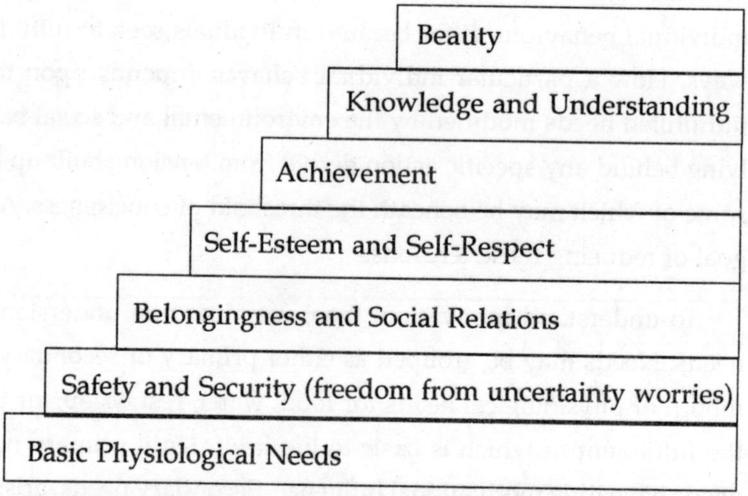

Fig. 1 Hierarchy of Human Needs

What, then, motivates marketing-people in their work? Using the concept of need gratification, we can say that marketing-person's motives for working vary according to the nature and potency of the unsatisfied portion of individual need structures. We must also recognise, however, that some of the marketing-people's needs are filled off the job as well as on it. One marketing-person works because of the need for money to feed a family; another because she views her job a means for gainning esteem of others; still another because of a need to achieve to the maximum of his abilities, seeing his job performance as a means to that end.

If marketing management knew the makeup of the unsatisfied portion of a marketing-person's structure at a particular time, it would be able to determine the best incentive to use in motivating his or her performance along desired lines. The fact that an individual has needs causes him or her, consciously or not, to formulate goals in terms of them. If management can succeed in harmonising the individual's goals with those of the organisation, then individual behaviour can be channelled along lines aimed at achieving both sets of goals. For a marketing-person worried about providing for a child's education, an important individual goal becomes that of obtaining more money to remove the uncertainty. If management sees how furnishing the marketing-person with an opportunity to earn more money will also further the attainment of organisational goals (perhaps that of increasing the size of orders), then offering the marketing-person the chance to earn more money for obtaining larger orders would be a powerful incentive.

Money, however, rapidly loses its power as an incentive once an individual has gratified physiological needs and most or her safety and security needs. Other incentives (for example, a chance for promotion to a position of higher status, which is one way to fulfil esteem and self-respect needs) become increasingly effective. The promise of more money becomes progressively weaker as an incentive the further up in the hierarchy a particular individual's unfulfilled needs are pushed. Whatever power it retains probably is related most closely to the individual's unfulfilled esteem and achievement needs insofar as a large income can gratify them. Of course, too, the threat or likelihood of receiving a lower income, a form of negative incentive, endangers the fulfilled part of an individual's need structure; and to the extent that this threat exists, money continues to have power as an incentive. Notice that whereas motives are internal to the individual, incentives are external. Marketing management can influence the behavioural patterns of individual marketing-people only indirectly through the incentives that it chooses to dangle before them.

Interdependence

In the formal organisational plan, each marketing-person reports to someone higher up in the structure, perhaps to a marketing supervisor, a district marketing manager, or as in most small companies, directly to the chief marketing executive. According to traditional organisational theory, the superior has the authority to require that the marketing-person take action, and the marketing-person is obligated to carry out the superior's orders and directions. The difficulty with this theory is that it assumes, tactly if not explicitly, that authority ("the formal right to require action of others") can be equated with power ("the ability to get things done"). Practical marketing managers long have recognised that issuing an order to a marketing-person or suggesting how he or she should act (that is, change his or her pattern of behaviour) does not necessarily mean that henceforth the marketing-person will be changed. On many occasions, of course, there is little problem in having orders and directions put into effect—as long as they are clearly stated and apply to simple tasks that can be done quickly. However, if orders and directions require significant modification in the marketing-person's behaviour over an extended period, perhaps permanently, then the marketing-person's acceptance of the desired change becomes a great deal more unpredictable.

Whether or not orders and directions are accepted hinges upon the nature of the relations between the marketing-person and the superior. In analysing this relationship, the concept of interdependence, which seeks to explain how the appropriateness of authority varies as a function of dependence, is highly useful. At one extreme, a marketing-person may regard himself or herself as wholly dependent upon the superior, in which case he or she would consider that superior's exercise of authority as fully appropriate; this situation, amounting to build obedience, is rarely found in business. At the opposite extreme, the marketing-person and the superior may be fully interdependent; that is, there is equal dependence both ways. Such a relationship is comparable to that between close friends, and authority is useless as a means of control. Although this situation is also rare, it seems highly desirable—in effect, the marketing-person would be dependent on the superior for reaching his or her individual goals, and the superior would dependent on the marketing-person for help in reaching organisational goals. Thus, full integration of individual and organisational goals would be possible.

However, the usual situation in marketing force-superior relationships is one of partial dependence. The marketing-person feels partially dependent upon the superior and regards the latter's exercise of authority as appropriate in some circumstances and not in other; the superior feels partially dependent upon the marketing-person for help in reaching the organisational goals for which he or she is held responsible by higher management. Each marketing-person, then, has a 'zone of acceptance,' a range over which he or she will accept directions from the superiors; and each superior has a similar zone over which he or she will honour requests from the marketing-person. Within their respective zones of acceptance, too, both the marketing-person and the superior exhibit a 'degree of acceptance' that varies according to the exact circumstances from 'grudging acquiescence' to 'enthusiastic cooperation.'

The marketing manager should try to widen the zone and increase the degree of acceptance of each marketing-person; but accomplishing this also means widening his or her own zone and increasing his or her own degree of acceptance. Actually this is only a very fancy way of saying that effective supervision is prerequisite to improved performance. Through effective supervision, the marketing manager can satisfy many of the marketing-person's needs and, at the same time, obtain fuller cooperation from them in striving for organisational goals. By giving due credit for good work, by convincing each marketing-person of his or her job's importance, by earning the marketing-personnel's confidence in his or her leadership, and by following other enlightened supervisory practices, the marketing executive motivates his or her people to improved performance. Marketing-personnel under this sort of supervision work harder to earn praise and recognition and the resulting social approval, esteem, and self-respect. Good supervision means, above all else, that marketing-people are treated as human beings, as individuals in their own right, and not as mere cogs in an impersonal industrial machine.

❑❑❑

6

Marketing Meetings, Compensations and Marketing Contests

Introduction

The motivation of people as individuals only partially determines their total pattern of behaviour. Many aspects of their total behaviour are strongly influenced by individuals, interactions with others in groups with which they are identified. Particularly important in influencing many of an individual marketing-person's job related actions is the peer group made up of his or her fellows. For the newly recruited marketing-person, for example, perhaps one of the strongest motives for learning, how to perform the job is the desire to demonstrate to fellow workers that the recruit has attained an acceptable level of skill. Similarly, experienced marketing-persons find strong motivation to improve their performance in their desire to show other marketing-people that they are star performers.

Discussion is concerned with motivating marketing-person as members of groups. The two main means for motivating marketing-people as members of group are through marketing meetings and contests or incentive campaigns.

Marketing meetings are necessary both for purposes of communication and motivation. When marketing personnel work on the road away from their employer's premises without the day-to-day opportunity for employer communication and supervision, periodic group meetings provide important occasions for exchanging information and ideas. These meetings also provide appropriate occasions for motivating individual marketing persons through the exertion of group pressures to achieve certain minimal levels of performance acceptable to the group.

Many marketing executives regard contests as a highly effective means of motivating marketing-people as members of groups, but some companies, as a matter of policy, do not use marketing contests. Some executives are firm in their belief that marketing personnel should not be rewarded a second time of doing what they are already being paid to do. Other contend that the beneficial effects of marketing contests on marketing performance are only temporary and do not result in lasting improvements of job performance. However, the experience of most companies indicate that when used properly marketing contests contribute significantly to the improvement of the performance of most marketing-people participating in them.

Marketing Meetings

From time to time most companies assemble their inter marketing force, or small regional or local groups of marketing-people, for formal meetings. The ostensible purpose of such meetings is communication—to provide members of the marketing force with needed information about new products, changes in marketing policies, forthcoming promotional campaigns, and the like. In addition, an underlying, although sometimes well-hidden, purpose of all such meetings is to provide occasion for motivating individual marketing person and for strengthening group identity.

National Marketing Meetings

The national marketing meetings is one in which the entire marketing-force converges upon a central location. Although the costs of bringing all the marketing-people to the convention site are substantial, national meetings are appropriate in certain situations. If, for example, comprehensive changes in marketing or marketing policies are being made, a national meetings makes it possible to introduce these changes rapidly and uniformly, providing the occasion for standardised explanations and clarification of questions. Moreover, major executives whose time is limited may be able to attend a national meeting but not a series of decentralised meetings—and their actual attendance provides more stimulation than their written or recorded messages at decentralised meetings.

There are other advantages in holding a national marketing meetings rather than a series of decentralised meetings. Each marketing-person has the chance to meet informally with his or her counterparts from elsewhere, and there is much to be learned from the inevitable interchanges of experience. On finding that others face and solve similar problems, the marketing-person is encourages to find his or her own solutions. Because of the opportunity provided for marketing-people to meet home office personnel with whom they have been corresponding, better coordination between the office and the field should result. The very size of the national meeting, coupled with strengthening to team spirit, tends to generate contagious enthusiasm, which marketing-people carry back to the field. Management spends much money and time in planning and staging the national meeting and brings in marketing-people from great distances; and these obvious factors accentuate the meeting's importance to all who attend. If the meeting is held at or near factory, there is opportunity to give marketing personnel further product training, and to acquaint them with technical manufacturing details.

The national marketing meeting also has it drawbacks. The expense of bringing in marketing-people from all over the country is substantial. It is difficult to find a convenient time for all marketing personnel to attend, unless the product line is seasonal. Often, too, company routine is disrupted and aggressive promotion by competitors may make in-roads into company marketing while marketing-people are away from their territories. However, most national marketing meetings are so brief that little chance exists of lasting adverse effects on a company's competitive position; and the meeting's stimulative effect upon marketing-people constitutes a counterbalancing benefits. A temporary lapse in marketing coverage should be more than compensated for by the more aggressive marketing that results.

Some executives oppose national marketing meetings on other grounds. A few object to the large amount of advance planning and organising work required. This objection is of doubtful validity unless the only alternative is no meeting at all—the combined effort necessary to plan and organise a series of regional or local meetings is much greater than for one national meeting. Others object that the programme for a national meeting must be general in nature, emphasising problems faced on a nationwide basis. This objection, however, may be easily removed by breaking down a few sessions at the national meeting into smaller regional groups for purposes of discussing local problems.

Regional Marketing Meetings

There is a trend away from the national and toward the regional marketing meeting system, under which a series of smaller meetings is staged at decentralised points. The reasons are several. Instead of the field force converging upon the central office, headquarters marketing executives and personnel attend the decentralised meetings, thereby reducing total travel costs and lowering the loss of productive marketing time. Headquarters executives are bought into direct contact with field personnel, learning about current problems at first hand; most such executives otherwise have a difficult time scheduling personal visits to the field. Although attending a regional meeting is not equivalent to a planned inspection trip, it is better than no visit at all. Each regional meeting may have a programme designed to emphasise unique problems of that region. Because of the smaller attendance at regional meetings, participation time per person should be greater and the resulting discussion more meaningful. Then, too, in contrast to the attitude held by certain marketing personnel toward national meeting, salesmen are inclined to regard district marketing meetings as serious work sessions, not paid vacations.

The system of holding regional marketing meeting also has its disadvantages. The demands on executive time may be excessive; executives may have to be away from the home office for several weeks at a stretch. Consequently, a tendency exists for the top marketing executives to rotate attendance among themselves at regional meetings, rather than for all to attend each meeting. Thus, the smaller percentage of the 'top brass' in attendance tends to depreciate the meeting's importance in the eyes of the marketing staff and, because total attendance is also smaller, it is more difficult to develop a spirit of contagious enthusiasm. The stimulating effect is reduced further by the pressure to economise. The costs of conducting a series of district meetings, for example, preclude using the top-flight speakers and entertainers so often featured at national meetings. Furthermore, the total costs of holding several district meetings may well equal or exceed those a single large national meeting because, in the final analysis, much planning and organisational expense is not fixed but is incurred separately for each meeting.

National versus Regional Marketing Meeting

Both national and regional marketing meetings, as the above discussion indicates, have important advantages and disadvantages. No generalisation can be readily drawn as to which alternative, if either, is best for all companies. Each firm should select the type that best fits its own situation at the particular time. The regional meeting systems is often the best where product demand is not seasonal and when strong competition exists. Where the market in force is small and widely dispersed and the marketing personnel are of high calibre, the national meeting usually is the more appropriate choice.

Executive Opposition to National and Regional Marketing Meetings

Many marketing executives are opposed to both national and regional marketing meeting. Some say that the potential results do not justify the expected costs; but they admit that many of the benefits, such as the effect on the morale of the marketing force, cannot readily be measured in monetary terms. Other executives, especially those whose companies operate in industries without slack marketing seasons, contend that they can ill afford to have marketing-people away from the field, even for a week. Still others base their opposition on the executive demands on their own at sites away from the home office; but even meetings held at the home office require much planning, organising, and coordinating effort by major executives. In a few cases, marketing executives are reluctant to hold national or regional marketing meetings because of a low state of morale in their marketing forces. They fear that marketing personnel will use the meeting as an occasion to compare each other's complaints and to strengthen their convictions that the company is an unsatisfactory employer.

Local Marketing Meetings

Local, or branch, marketing meetings should be an integral part of the programme for motivating the marketing force. The periodic national or regional meeting should supplement, not substitute for, frequent local marketing meetings. Some marketing executives, in fact, believe that larger meetings can be dispensed with if local meeting are held regularly and handled effectively. Local marketing meetings generally are conducted every week or two by district marketing managers or their assistants and, depending upon the frequency, last from 15 minutes to several hours. Although such gatherings are considered formal meetings, the great strength of the effectively handled local marketing meetings is its informality, each marketing-person having ample opportunity to pose questions and to state personnel views. Of course, the system also provides frequent occasions for marketing personnel to get together, become better acquainted. And thus strengthen their feelings of group identity.

Remote-control and Travelling Marketing Meeting

Certain forms of marketing meetings seek to retain the national marketing meeting's advantage while reducing its disadvantages in terms of cost and time expenditures. Among these forms are meetings conducted by closed-circuit television, marketing meetings by telephone, marketing meetings at home, and the travelling marketing meetings.

Closed-circuit Television

Closed-circuit television enables a company to hold a number of marketing meetings-simultaneously. The programme is 'live' at only one meeting site but is telecast to the others, thus retaining much of the inspirational value of the live show/ without incurring costs and losses of productive marketing time comparable to those involved in a national meeting. Televised marketing meetings are especially appropriate for companies with very large marketing forces or large dealer organisation. Many companies use television marketing meetings to introduce new products or to launch marketing campaigns nationally. Large-screen projectors make it possible to gather a large group at each theatre, under which condition the programme can be seen and heard better than in the ordinary meeting room. Users report that their messages receive a high degree of attention.

Marketing Meetings by Telephone

Open-circuit telephone conference calls are used effectively for small group meetings and discussions. For maximum impact, users say the group should be no larger than 20. The meeting itself is conducted in a manner similar to other small group meetings. Usually the marketing manager begins by welcoming the group and presenting the subject for discussion. The open discussion that follows is guided by two rules; only one individual may talk at a time, and all speakers must identify themselves and their cities. At the end of the conference call, the marketing executives given a brief summary. Companies using, the telephone marketing meeting report that marketing personnel have a strong feeling of participation and are enthusiastic about such meetings. Compared to a centralised gathering of the same peo| le, the telephone marketing meeting affords significant savings in time and money, and, of course, marketing-people lose little, if any, time from their marketing activitie s. An obvious shortcoming, however, is the absence of visual stimulation, which is ı nportant, for example, in introducing a new product.

Marketing Meetings at Home

Seeking to reduce the time and costs of marketing meetings, some companies mail recording or printed materials to marketing-people at their homes. One format is to record a conference or meeting of executives and to provide mar.‹eting personnel with copies of the tape. Another is to print an illustrated script of a home office meeting for distribution to marketing-people. Marketing executives using these usual formats point to three advantages: (1) marketing personnel receive the information at their homes, free from distractions; (2) they can review the information as many times as they please; and (3) there are substantial savings in time and many. Objectively, however, one must conclude that formats such as these, because of the absence of group dynamics, are most useful as supplementary motivational devices rather than as substitutes for periodic marketing meetings except, of course, for companies where for one reason or another it is not feasible to hold formal meetings.

Travelling Marketing Meetings

Certain meetings require numerous physical props. For instance, a manufacturer introducing a new product line may want to display and demonstrate each new product. It is difficult in such cases to stage regional meetings because the displays must be transported to, moved, in, and set up at each of a succession of meeting sites. Some companies overcome this difficulty by outfitting one or more motorised vans and trailers with product displays and conference rooms. Thus, the marketing meeting moves from city to city, and at each stop marketing-people and/or dealers come abroad.

Planning and Staging Marketing Meetings

Objectives

In planning any marketing meeting, well-defined objectives are important. The underlying goals are to motivate individual marketing-persons and to strengthen group identity. But more specific goals, sometimes jokingly called 'excuses for holding a meeting,' are required. When marketing start to lag, for instance, a marketing meeting may be held 'to give marketing volume a shot in the arm.' Other specific goals served by marketing meetings include: to provide refresher training; to correct marketing faults; to introduce new products, models, and services; to explain changes in company policies and systems; to improve the quality of marketing-force reports; to orient marketing personnel regarding the advertising programme and show how they can best tie in their efforts with it; and to increase the effectiveness with which marketing-people use their time. In setting a meeting's specific objectives, the executives should answer such questions as: Are these objectives clear and attainable? Are they realistic in terms of time, audience, and other conditions? Will the probable results justify the estimated cost?

Ones specific objectives of the meeting are set, plans are made for achieving them. The means chosen should provide the maximum motivational impact upon the marketing-people. With this in mind, training aids are assembled, speakers obtained, meeting materials (including a carefully through-out agenda) prepared, facilities secured. In addition, plans are made for whatever entertainment is thought necessary. If spouses are to attend, arrangements are made for dances, sightseeing tours, or similar events.

Staging the Meeting

For maximum motivational impact, a marketing meeting should generate enthusiasm among the participants. To arouse their audience, speakers must make genuinely enthusiastic presentations. To maintain this pitch of interest, a rigid time schedule should be adhered to throughout the programme. When a speaker runs overtime, participants frequently lose interest; this, in turn, may cause later speakers to fall behind schedule, whereupon any enthusaism that has been built up tends to disappear.

Time should be set aside on the meeting schedule for group discussion. Marketing personnel must be allowed time to criticise new programme, raise questions, put forth ideas, and air their complaints. Since the large marketing meeting affords little time for widespread participation, the large group should be broken down, for a few sessions at least. This sets the stage for effective interpersonal reactions on such topics at the technical details of new product, new applications, and new marketing arguments. Precautions, however, should be taken to ensure that group leaders are capable of preventing overly talkative individuals from monopolising the discussion.

The setting of the meeting and the nature of planned activities are controversial subjects among marketing executives. Some argue that any marketing meeting, particularly a national one, should be made up entirely of work sessions, covering as much as 12 hours per day. They contend that more is accomplished in such a working atmosphere. Other believe that participants learn more and are more highly motivated in a relaxed setting in which some time is reserved for recreation. They prefer attractive resort areas as meeting sites and provide organised entertainment as part of the programme. The strength of each side of this argument appears to hinge upon the duration of the meeting and management's estimate of the state of marketing-person morale. In many instances a compromise position is the most satisfactory. A 100 per cent working atmosphere, for example, is more palatable for the participants if the surroundings are pleasant and comfortable. In almost every case, frequent breaks from working sessions are desirable—the marketing-person's ability to concentrate tends to decline progressively as the length of the session increase.

Marketing Contests

Essentially, a marketing contest is a special marketing campaign offering marketing personnel incentives in the form of prizes or awards above and beyond those regularly provided by the compensation plan. There are four main reasons for using marketing contests: (1) they provide a mechanism for developing team spirit among marketing-people or distributors who generally have little direct contact with each other; (2) they assist in boosting morale, counteracting the tendency of some marketing-people to become apathetic, bored with their jobs, and depressed; (3) they are capable of stimulating marketing-people to strive harder to better their usual performances; and (4) by pointing marketing efforts toward accomplishment of important tasks, they assist in reaching predetermined marketing and profit goals. These four reasons suggest the basic objective underlying marketing contests—to so motivate the marketing force that they are caused to produce increased and/or more profitable marketing volume.

Specific Objectives

The definition of specific objectives for each marketing contest is necessary to concentrate marketing efforts on the most promising areas. A study by Harrying and Myers at the Indian University School of Business uncovered the list of specific contest objectives in Table-1. The first and third most frequently mentioned, finding new customers and getting better territory coverage, are aimed at motivating marketing-people to tap more of the untouched market potential. The second, obtaining greater volume per call, is pointed toward upgrading marketing performance with present customers. The fourth, promoting special items, is used to motivate marketing personnel to exert greater effort is pushing slow-moving items, high-margin goods, or new products.

Table- 1

Objectives of Marketing Contests

Objective	Rank Order	Number of Mentions
Find new customers	1	273
Obtain greater volume per call	2	208
Get better territory coverage	3	189
Promote special items	4	175
Overcome seasonal marketing slump	5	165
Get better balance of marketing	6	124
Get renewal of business from former customer	7	115
Introduce a new product or line	8	114
Strop or slow a marketing decline	9	108
Develop new marketing skills	10	95
Ease an unfavourable inventory position	11	91
Lower marketing costs	12	67
Sell higher-quality products	13	62
Improve marketing service to customers	14	61
Build better product displays	15	50
Get better marketing reports	16	37
Reduce marketing time	17	24
Eliminate returns and mistakes	18	13
All other	–	26

In formulative specific contest objectives, and later in designing the marketing contest, the executive-in-charge of contest planning should keep in mind the underlying objective—to so motivate the marketing staff that they will produce increased or more profitable marketing volume. One formula for marketing contest planning defines three prime requirements for a successful marketing contest: (1) the contest must make greater marketing effort pay off in terms of greater reward both for marketing-people and the company; (2) it must motivate the marketing force to expend effort; and (3) it must assist marketing-people to pattern their efforts along the most productive lines. Notice that these requirements simply elaborate on what must be done to achieve underlying contest objectives.

Contest Formats

Although the variety of marketing contests is legion, each is built around a theme that provides the basis for the competition. The theme may be, either a straightforward or a novelty type. In contests using own past records, and at other ties with one another, in accomplishing certain tasks or goals. Some users believe that a marketing contest is made not only more interesting but more effective if it is designed to tie in with a current event, sport, or similar novelty, theme. They say that the theme should not only serve as a common denominator but he appealing to all participants. Other uses contend that a theme describing the actual specific objectives, such as lower marketing costs and promoting special items should be used. They believe that novelty themes are insults to nature man and contend that it is not only possible, but less difficult to motivate marketing-people through the use of straightforward, or direct themes.

Most successful novelty themes share certain common characteristics. Experience indicates that the theme should be timely, and its effectiveness is enhanced if it coincides with an activity in the news. An analogous relation should exist between the theme and the product line or some other aspect of the company's marketing setup. The theme should be one that will intensify interest as the contest proceeds; in this regard, the best themes appear to be those in which the marketing-people share a common interest. Finally, the theme should lend itself naturally to contest promotion both before and during the contest period. Many hundreds of themes have been used, but most fall into one or another of the ten general categories shown in Table-2.

Table-2

General Categories of Marketing-Contest Themes

(1) **Games:**

(a) **Team type:** football, baseball, basketball, blowing, tennis doubles, tug-of-war, soccer, etc.

(b) **Individual type:** tennis singles, golf, boxing, wrestling, archery, fencing, broad jump, high jump, pole vault, hummer throw, discus throw, shooting match, javelin throw, bull fight, climbing the greased pole, etc.

(2) **Races:**

(a) **Team type:** crew, cross-country, relay, bobsled, yacht, etc.

(b) **Individual type:** horse race, dog race, air race, soap-box derby, auto race, hurdles, dashes, marathons, dog sled, trotting race, swimming races, speedboat races, etc.

(3) **Card games**: poker, pinochle, bridge, black jack, etc.

(4) **Hunting of fishing:** treasure hunt, big-game hunt, uranium rush, gold rush, land rush, fishing derby, trapping contest, etc.

(5) **Travel:** trip around the world, to Miami, to New York, to Hollywood, to Waikiki, to the moon, to space, etc.

(6) **Climbing:** ladders, stairs, mountains, cliff scaling, ascent to the stratosphere, etc.

(7) The rising thermometer, pressure, gauge, etc.

(8) **Building contests:** skyscraper, other new building, tower, smokestack, etc.

(9) **Military:** naval battles, artillery engagements, bombing runs, invasions, interplanetary wars, etc.

(10) **Clothing contents:** (in one contest of this type, the marketing persons earns one items of clothing at a time and is required to appear at marketing meetings clad only in those items that he or she has earned up to that point).

Promoting the Contest

If a marketing contest is to succeed, it must be effectively merchandised. To most marketing-persons there is nothing new about the idea of a contest. A clever new theme and attractive prizes may help arouse interest, but a planned barrage of promotional material develops the enthusiasm needed to make the contest a success. A teaser campaign sometimes precedes the formal contest announcement; at other times, the announcement itself comes as a complete and dramatic surprise to participants. As the contest progresses, other methods are used to hold and intensify interest. Results and standings are reported at marketing meetings at frequent intervals or by daily or weekly bulletins. The marketing manager may despatch telegrams carrying news of important developments or changes in relative standings. At intervals, new or special prizes may be announced.

Management may encourage individual marketing-persons and various groups to compete against each other, reports of relative standings may be addressed to the marketing-person's spouse. If the prizes are so selected as to arouse the spouses, interest, continuing enthusiasm for the contest is generated in the home. The contest administrator should not wait for a long in contest interest before injecting new life into it. From the start regular news flashes on comparative standing should be sent out and, if the initial incentives provided by the contest do not appear to be producing the desired results, the administrator should add the stimuli needed to make the contest a success.

The duration of the contest is an important factor in maintaining participants' interest. Marketing executives' opinions differ as to the ideal length. Contests are run for periods as short as a week and as long as a year, but most last from one to four months. One executives claims that 13 weeks is the ideal length; another states that no contest should last for more than a month; still another points to a successful contest lasting six months. There are no set guides. Each case is controlled by such factors as the length of time the marketing-person's interest and enthusiasm can be maintained, the period over which the theme can be kept timely, and the interval needed to accomplish the contest objectives.

One effective way to promote continuing and widespread interest in the contest is to make it possible for every marketing-person to win something. The basis for awards should take into account the marketing people's present performance levels and, in order to motivate the average or inexperienced marketing-person along with the star performer, the basis of award should be for important rather than for total performance. Hence, total marketing volume is less effective as the basis for award than, for example, per cent of quota achieved or per cent of improvement in quota achievement. Many successful contests offer prizes for all persons showing improvement, but the worth of individual prizes varies with the amount of improvement. Offering only a few large prizes restricts the motivational force of such contests – because only a few people can win them, sooner or later, most marketing-people become discouraged and stop trying.

Contest Prizes

The majority of contest prizes may be classified under four general headings: cash awards, merchandise prizes, travel, and special honour or privilege awards. Surveys among marketing executives show that cash and merchandise are the most widely used. A growing number of marking contests feature more than one type of award (for example, travel for the large awards and merchandise for lesser awards), and some give winners the option of accepting one type rather than another.

Cash

One would think that a cash prize would be attractive to all marketing personnel, but the potency of money as an incentive weakens the further up in an individual's need hierarchy his or her unfulfilled needs are pushed. Once basic physiological needs and most safety and security needs are satisfied, whatever potency money retains and an incentive is related most closely to unfulfilled esteem and achievement needs; and, of course, noncash prizes are capable of filling these needs at least as well, perhaps better, than cash.

Assuming that the regular compensation plan provides marketing personnel with sufficient income to meet their basic physiological needs and most safety and security needs, an opportunity to win a cash prize is a weak incentive unless a substantial sum is involved; some marketing executives say that this amount must represent from 10 to 25 per cent of the marketing-person's regular annual income. A cash prize of, say Rs. 500 means very little to most marketing-people and they exert only token efforts to win it. However, in many marketing contests small cash prizes are awarded at frequent intervals, tending, users say, to keep interest at a higher pitch than might otherwise be possible. Another important objection, applicable even to large cash prizes, is that winners mix the money with other income, and, thus, are left without any permanent identifiable evidence of their achievement.

Merchandise

The merchandise award is an incentive superior to the cash prize in several respects. Winners have more permanent evidence of their achievement and should continue to be motivated for a longer period. Because the merchandise prize normally is obtained at the wholesale cost, a value large than the equivalent cash prize can be offered. For the same total outlay, too, merchandise prizes than cash awards can be offered; hence, the contest rules can provide for more winners. Nevertheless, merchandise prizes must be selected carefully to assure that items offered are truly desired by marketing-persons and their families. One way to sidestep problems in this area is to allow winners to select their own prizes from a variety of offering provided for each class of winner. This is effective from the psychological standpoint, too, since people generally are happier if they are permitted to assert their individuality and take their choice. A number of 'merchandise incentive agencies,' some of them providing a complete marketing-contest planning service, specialise in furnishing prized. Most of these agencies issue catalogues with 'prices' generally stated in 'points' rather than in money.

Travel

Travel awards are growing in popularity as contest incentives. Few things can be glamorised quite as effectively as a trip to a luxury resort or an exotic land. The lure of a 'trip of a lifetime' is a strong incentive, especially for the marketing-person, who longs for a chance to 'escape' the job's routine, at least temporarily. Travel awards generally provide trips for both winners and their spouses, this being advisable both to obtain the entire family's motivational support and to avoid the family's opposition to encouraging solo vacation trips by the marketing-person. The chief objection to the prize trips is that winners, frequently the better marketing personnel, are taken away from their territories while collecting their awards; however, this objection is easily overcome by providing that prize trips will be taken during regularly scheduled vacation periods.

Special Honours or Privileges

This types of award can take many forms. It may be a letter from a top executives formally recognising the contest winner's superior performance; it may be a loving cup, a special trip to a home-office meetings attended by a restricted few, or membership in a special group or club that enjoys certain privileges. Winners, in addition, generally receive publicity through house organs and in their hometown newspapers. Such awards frequently appear to provide strong incentives, as, for example, in the case of life insurance marketing-person who push themselves to the limit to earn membership in 'the million dollar club.'

The special honour or privilege award is used mainly by firms employing marketing personnel who are almost 'independent entrepreneurs.' Such awards, however, are appropriate incentive wherever management desires to strengthen group identity and build team spirit among the better marketing-people. Note that this type of award appeals to the marketing-person's belongingness and social-relations needs, which, according to Maslow, an individual generally strive to satisfy after he has taken care of basic physiological needs and most safety and security needs.

Managerial Evaluation of Contests

It is sound practice to evaluate each marketing contest both before it is launched and after it is concluded. By sizing up a proposed contest in advance, weaknesses are detected and corrected, having an appraisal afterwards provides insights helpful in improving future contests. In both pre- and post-evaluations, questions similar to the following should be considered.

Is the Contest Well-designed?

Overall, the prizes must provide sufficient motivation of cause the marketing staff to exert the desired efforts, yet the gross margin earned on marketing volume must be increased at the every least by enough to pay contest costs. The theme, whether straight forward or novel, should not only tie in directly with specific objectives but also result in easy-to-understand and fair contest rules. The theme should also lend itself readily to contest promotion.

Will Marketing-people Consider the Contest Fair?

At the time that the contest is announced, every marketing-person should feel that the proposition is one that gives everyone a fair chance of winning the more attractive prizes. As long as the contest lasts, all members of the marketing force should continue to fell that they have real chances to win something. To secure and maintain marketing-people's cooperation in achieving contest objectives, all marketing personnel must be convinced of the contest's basic fairness.

What is the Likely Long-run Effect?

The contest should bring in new business; it is not a success if it merely borrows marketing from preceding and succeeding months. Well-designed contests, too, help to inculcate desirable marketing habits that marketing-people retain long after the contest ends. The contest should boot marketing-people's spirits while it is on, and provide a beneficial carryover effect upon marketing-force morale.

What will be the Effect on Team Spirit?

A good marketing contest should result in improved team spirit. If the contest is conducted in an overly competitive way (for example, if marketing-people are encouraged to engage in personal rivalries to too great an extent), then it may have the counter-productive effect of creating jealousy and antagonism among the marketing force. Even if marketing-people are competing for individual awards, generally it is advisable to organise teams, and to place emphasis on competition among groups for recognition rather than among individual for personal gain.

Are there Better Alternative to the Contest?

It may be that the contest will provide no more benefit than a temporary shot-in-the-arm type of improvement, especially if other aspects of marketing-force management have serious defects. Deficiencies in marketing performance caused by an inappropriate compensation plan, incompetent supervision, or ineffective training are not likely to permanently overcome by a marketing contest. Other avenues to improvement of marketing efficiency should, therefore, be explored at the same time that a marketing contest is being considered.

Objections to Marketing Contests

Marketing contests are used by less than one-fourth of all marketing departments, so it is worth while to note the reasons for nonusage. Among the standard objections voiced by marketing executive are the following:

(1) Marketing-people are paid for their work under the provision of the basic compensation plan, and there is no reason to reward further for performing regular duties.

(2) Higher-calibre and more experienced marketing personnel look upon marketing contests as juvenile and silly.

(3) Contests often had to unanticipated and undesirable results, such as increased returns and adjustments, higher credit losses, and overstocking of dealers.

(4) Contests cause marketing-people to bunch their marketing during the competition, and marketing slumps occur both before and after the contest.

(5) The disappointment suffered by contest losses causes a general decline in marketing-force morale.

(6) Contest are temporary motivating devices and, if used too frequently, have a narcotic effect. No greater results in the aggregate are obtained with contests than without them.

(7) The competitive atmosphere generated by a marketing contest weakens team spirit.

The first reason indicates a fundamental misunderstanding of both personnel motivation and contest design, and the second reason may or may not be true in individuals situations. The reader should note, however, that all the other objections may be overcome through appropriate contest design, intelligent contest administration, and proper handling of other aspects of marketing-force management. Assuming that marketing management is competent in other respects, thorough planning and effective administration of a contest can produce lasting benefits for both the marketing-people and the company. Only if a marketing contest is used as a substitute for good management it is likely to have bad results.

Under some circumstances, nevertheless, marketing contests are ill advised, at least for purposed of stimulating marketing volume. If a firm's products are in short supply, for instance, it is ridiculous to use a marketing contest to stimulate orders; but the same firm might find a contest appropriate to use as part of an effort to achieve such objectives as lowering marketing expense or improving marketing-person's reports. Nor do companies distributing industrial goods (That is, raw materials, fabricating materials and parts, installations, accessory equipment, and operating supplies) normally find marketing contests appropriate for purposes of stimulating marketing—except, of course, in cases where it is possible to take accounts and marketing away from competitors. But, again, contests might be appropriately used along with other efforts directed towards reducing marketing costs, improving marketing-people's reports, and improving service to customers. Similarly, where the product is highly technical and is sold only after much spadework and long negotiation, as is the case with many industrial goods, marketing contests conducted for purposes of stimulating marketing volume are usually inappropriate.

Relative Value of Various Incentives

The relative value of various incentive varies not only for individual marketing-persons but for different groups and different companies, each with its own unique set of incentives. There is little doubt, however, that the most important incentive of all is the basic compensation plan. Without a sound basic compensation plan on which to build, other types of incentives are unlikely to produce desired results. Several years ago, the Indiana University School of Business surveyed marketing executives about the relative values of different incentives in motivating *the average marketing person to do a better job than usual.* The survey results showed that, after the basic compensation plan itself, which ranked first, marketing contests were most important, with a second-place ranking, marketing-persons-supervisor relations ranked third, honour awards and recognition fourth, and marketing meetings fifth.

Marketing-Personnel Compensation Plans

Good marketing-compensation plans assist in channeling the efforts of marketing personnel toward the most productive activities, and they help in attaining the objectives of the marketing organisation. Such plans are drafted to fit a company's special needs and problems, and from them greater returns should for the company and for the marketing-people. Marketing and growth goals should be reached at less cost, and profits should be proportionately higher. Marketing-people should be rewarded for greater productivity with commensurately higher pay. Improved esprit de corps among the marketing force is the chief intangible benefit, since individual productivity and job satisfaction generally go hand in hand.

Compensation plans should be viewed as aids to, rather than substitutes for, good marketing-force management. Unless the quality and skill of the management are of high order, even excellent compensation plans do not guarantee the significant benefits mentioned above. And many compensation plans are less than excellent. They may be based on a very simple and naïve hypothesis that marketing personnel are purely mercenary. Many compensation plans conflict with what may be important motives— to conform, to be like others, to belong, to be likely by one's peers. A big earner may be branded as an apple polisher. As important as the basic appropriateness of the compensation plans themselves are the ways in which they are implemented and administered. Indeed, fundamentally poor compensation plans often work satisfactorily enough when a skilled executive is charged with their administration.

In established companies it is rarely necessary to design completely new marketing-compensation plans, and marketing executives are concerned mainly with revising plans already in effect. Most changes are minor, usually instituted to bring the plan and marketing objectives into closer alignment. If, for example, additional marketing effort is needed for the factory to operate at optimum capacity, and adjustment in the compensation plan may bring forth the extra effort required. This adjustment could involve paying bonuses on marketing over the quota, paying additional compensation for larger orders or for securing new accounts, or simply commission rate schedules. Any such change, of course, could be either temporary or permanent.

Because of possible adverse effects upon morale, it is wise to avoid drastic changes in the compensation scheme. Like most people, marketing personnel tend to resist sweeping changes, particularly when they have to alter accustomed ways of doing things to adjust to a new plan. When a firm decides to switch from paying straight salaries to straight commissions, for instance, some people find it exceedingly difficult to adjust their living and spending habits accordingly. Opinions vary as to how far-reaching changes, when required, should be implemented. Some executives think that to introduce them gradually minimises interference with established habits and elicits far less resistance from the personnel affected. Others claim that such changes should be made quickly, because continual changes often have a deteriorative effect upon marketing-people's morale. Although explanation of impending changes is always important, a careful programme of orientation should precede the introduction of sweeping changes. Whether a change should be made in one step or in many depends upon the specific circumstances surrounding the particular situation, and no easy generalisation on this points is possible.

Two situations involving established companies in which complete overhauling of compensation plans are in order should be mentioned. One involves the company whose marketing force already has low morale, perhaps because of the compensation plan in effect. If the compensation plan is at the root of the morale problem, then drastic change is appropriate. Complete revamping of marketing-compensation plans may also be appropriate in firms anticipating the cultivation of new and different markets. The problems resemble those of the newly organised company, which must build its marketing-compensation plan from scratch—in both cases management must consider many factors, the nature and number of which vary with the company and the situation, but usually including: the types of customers, the marketing channels, characteristics of the product, intensity of competition, extent of the market, and complexity of the marketing task.

Requirement of a Good Marketing-compensation Plan

Although a marketing-compensation plan should be tailored to fit a particular company's needs, any plan should meet six main requirements. First, it should be as simple as possible, so that marketing personnel will easily understand it. Second, it should be fair-no plan should cause marketing-persons to be penalised because of factors beyond their control. Within limits of seniority and other special privileges, marketing-people should receive equal for equal results. Third, the plan should provide a living wage, preferably in the form of a guaranteed income. The person, who is worried about money matters cannot concentrate on doing a good marketing job. Fourth, administration of the plan should provide for easy adjustments of pay of changes in performance. Fifth, the plan should be easy and economic to administer. Although highly complex plans may provide greater refinements in stimulation and reward, often their higher costs of administration are not offset by improvements in performance. Sixth, the plan should help in attaining the objectives of the marketing organisation. Not every compensation plan, of course, will meet all six requirements fully. In designing new plans or improving old ones, however, management should compare the prototypes under discussion with these requirements and make evaluations accordingly.

Devising a Marketing Compensation Plan

Whether contemplating major or minor changes or drafting a completely new marketing-compensation plan, the executives should approach the project systematically. Good compensation plans are built on sound foundations, and a systematic approach is the best assurance that no essential step will be overlooked. The following discussion analyses these steps in some detail.

Define the Marketing-person's Job

In designing a marketing-compensation plan, the first step is to determine, or re-examine, the nature of the marketing-person's job. Up-to-date written descriptions furnish the logical place to start. If the job descriptions are outdated, or if they do not constitute accurate and complete descriptions of the marketing job objectives and work, revision is in order. The marketing executive should ask: Does this description convey a realistic picture of what the marketing-person is supposed to accomplish and to do? If there are no written marketing job descriptions, they should be prepared. Other aspects of company marketing operations should be considered in relation to their impact upon the marketing-person's job. First, the objectives of the marketing department should be analysed for their effect on the marketing-person's job. Marketing volume objective, for instance, whether in terms of rupees, units of product, or number of dealers and distributors, are translated ultimately into what is expected of the marketing personnel, as a group and individually. Second, the impact on the marketing-person's job of various policies should be determined. The particular distribution policies that a firm chooses to follow, its credit policies, its price policies, and policies in many other areas all affect the marketing-person's job. Third, the nature and extent of current and proposed advertising and marketing promotional programmes should be evaluated with respect of their significance for the marketing-person and his duties. This review of company objective, policies, and promotional programmes should throw new light on the information contained in the job description. The precise nature of the marketing-person's goals, duties and activities should now be clear.

Consider General Compensation Structure of the Company

The next step is examine the general compensation structure of the company. Most large companies, and many smaller ones, have systems of job evaluation that are used for determining the relative value of individual jobs. Although job-evaluation techniques do not provide precise quantitative measurements, they do give an indication of the relative value on different jobs. The procedure is not scientific; it is an orderly approach based on judgement. If focus only on the jobs themselves, without considering the ability of the particular employees who do the work. The purpose of job evaluation is to arrive at fair compensation relationships among various company jobs. Therefore, the job-evaluation programme should provide the data needed to fix equitable compensation differentials among jobs requiring varying degrees of: education and experience, mental and physical skills, responsibility, monotonous repetition of tasks, supervision given and received, exposure to unfavourable and hazardous working conditions, and similar job characteristics. There are three basic methods of job evaluation.

Classification Method

The classification method starts with the various job descriptions and ranks all jobs from top to bottom in order of estimated relative importance. The ranked list is then subdivided into several compensation classes, so that jobs of similar comparable rank fall into the same class. This method is used by the U.S. Civil Service Commission and was widely adopted by American companies during and after World War II. It is easier to apply than other methods, but it gives less precise results and involves a greater element of judgement.

Point System

The point systems is the most widely used job-evaluation method. It involves establishing and defining the several factors common to most jobs that represent the chief elements of value inherent in all jobs. The specific factors chosen differ from one company to another and should be selected with a firm's operating problems in mind. They usually include mental and physical skills, responsibility, supervision given and received, personality requirements, and minimum education required. Each factors is assigned a maximum number of points, different ranges being assigned in line with relative importance of the factors. Next, each job is appraised for its requirements against the several factor scales, and individual factor scores are combined into a total point value for the job.

Finally, bands of points and decided upon and become the different compensation classes. Less arbitrary judgement is required under the point system than under the classification method; but an even more attractive feature is that the use of point values makes it possible to determine the gap, or distance, between ranks.

Factor Comparison Method

The factor comparison method somewhat resembles the point system, but it is more complex than either the point systems or the classification method. Except for its greater complexity, it has all the advantages of the first two methods; furthermore, it utilises a scheme of ranking and cross-comparisons that tends to minimise error arising from faulty judgement. In a process similar to that used in the point systems, this method employs certain selected factors and evaluation scales. However, the scale values are in rupees and paise rather than in points, and no upper limit exists to the valuation that can be assigned to any one factor. A selected number of 'key' jobs, fairly typical of similar jobs throughout the company, are then evaluated, factor by factor. This is done by arranging them in rank order, from highest to lowest for each factor. As a check against this judgmental evaluation, the compensation dollars actually paid for each job are allocated to the various factors; the allocation automatically establishes the relationship among jobs for each factor. The judgement ranking and the ranking by allocation of compensation are compared and differences are reconciled, or the jobs are removed from the key list. On the basis of the dollar amounts assigned to the several factors making up key jobs, additional jobs are evaluated and their monetary values for each factor interpolated into the scale. This procedure is repeated until all jobs are evaluated.

Job Evaluation and Marketing Positions

Considerable progress has been made in the field of job evaluation in recent years, but the evaluation of marketing positions is still in the experimental stage. Many marketing executives oppose the extension of job evaluation or marketing positions on the grounds that compensation levels for marketing personnel are more closely related to external supply-and-demand factors than to conditions within the company. Marketing-people enjoy greater job mobility than most other employees, and they are often in everyday contact with potential employers. One things is certain—if a job-evaluation programme in which marketing personnel are included is in operation, there should be marketing department representation on the committee that arrives at quantitative evaluations for the various factors. If a company does not use job evaluation, or if it uses evaluation but does not apply the system to marketing, jobs, the marketing executives should establish, as best he or she can, the relative value of the marketing-person's job to jobs elsewhere in the organisation. This precaution is needed to assure that the monetary attractiveness of marketing positions is no less than it is for comparable jobs in other departments. Furthermore, if the marketing executives keeps informed on the relative differences of marketing jobs and other company jobs, he or she is preparing for the day, which is probably inevitable, when most marketing positions will be regarded as proper subjects for job evaluation.

Consider Compensation Picture in the Community and Industry

Because marketing-person's compensation levels are often closely related to external supply and demand factors, attention should be directed toward the pattern of marketing-people's compensation in the community and industry. Often, the actual amounts of the employee's pay is not as significant as how much they believe they should be paid. This belief depends on whom they compare themselves with. Management needs answers to several key questions: (1) What compensation systems are being used? (2) What is the average compensation for similar positions? (3) How do other companies seem to be doing with their plans? (4) Would it be wise to department from industry or community practice? (5) Should industry or community practice be followed as a matter of policy? The answers to these and related questions, and the degree of significance of the responses, differ with the individual company and industry. But whenever a change in the marketing personnel's compensation plan is under consideration, such matters should be discussed.

If there is a company wide job evaluation and salary administration programme, it should take into account the going rates for similar positions in the community and industry. A salary administration programme used for setting marketing-people's compensation can be sound only, if it considers the relation of external compensation practices to those of the company. Marketing executives should maintain constant vigilance against the possibility that marketing-people's pay will get out of line with what is being paid for similar jobs in the community or industry.

Determine Compensation Level

One of the most fundamental steps is that of determining the amount of compensation, a marketing-person should receive on the average. Although this level might be set through bargaining between the marketing-person and the marketing manager, or on a more-or-less arbitrary-judgement basis, neither expedient is recommended. Before setting the compensation level, management should consider several pertinent factors. Management should ascertain whether the calibre of the present marketing force measures up to what the company would like to have. If the present calibre is too low, if it is decided that the company should have lower-grade people than those currently employed, research should be undertaken to determine the market value of marketing-people of the desired grade. This requires further investigation of the compensation patterns of other companies. Management should also, weigh the worth of individual person to the company, but this assumes the availability of accruable productivity measures. Only a handful of firms have such measures, so as a substitute, management should estimate the number of marketing and profit rupees that the company would lose if particular marketing-people resigned. Still another consideration is the amount the company can afford to pay for the compensation of marketing personnel; this depends, of course, upon a host of other matters. The result of examining these factors, as well as other pertinent to the situation of the individual firm, is a series of estimates for the total cost of marketing-people's compensation. To shed additional light on this problem, it is excellent practice to plot each cost estimate on a breakeven-style chart. When the several plots are compared with the company's cost goals, the marketing volume needed to break even at each compensation level is revealed. Furthermore, the compensation level for individual marketing-people under the proposed plan also should be plotted in break-even style. It is equally evident that similar analysis can be applied to the determination of individual marketing quotas.

In some firms, company-wide job evaluation and salary administration programmes are used to set the compensation levels for marketing positions. In such instances, the procedure recommended above should be used as a check on the compensation levels prescribed through job evaluations. Any discrepancies found must be reconciled, or further studies must be made. When the salary administration programme is sound, there should be few, if any, discrepancies.

Much confusion exists about the appropriate income levels for marketing personnel. It is not unusual to find that two companies operate under similar marketing conditions but with different levels. In other words, marketing-people in one company earn more than marketing-people who do essentially the same work in another company. Relatively speaking, the first group of marketing-people is overcompensated. What explains such situntions? Sometimes, management does not know, or is uncertain of the true worth of individual marketing-persons. In other cases, management is afraid that some marketing-people are indispensable, or managerial inertia prevents the adjustment of the marketing-person's compensation level in accord with changed marketing conditions. In still other cases, marketing managers are biased in favour of high compensation for marketing jobs.

Provide for the Various Compensation Elements

A marketing-compensation plan may contain as many as four basic elements: (1) a fixed element, either a salary or a drawing account, which is intended to provide some stability of income; (2) a variable element (for example, a commission, bonus, or profit sharing arrangement), designed to serve as an incentive to productity; (3) an element providing for reimbursement of expenses of payment of expense allowances; and (4) an element covering the fringe benefits or 'plus factors,' such as paid vacations, sickness and accident benefit, life insurance, pensions, and the like. Each of these elements is considered later in greater detail. Planners must decide which elements should be included and what proportion each should bear to the marketing-person's total income. Not every company wants to, or should, include all four elements. Management should select the combination of elements that best fits the requirements of the firm's marketing situation. The proportions of the total that different elements should comprise also varies with the particular marketing situation. However, current practice indicates that most firms favour marketing about 80 per cent of the marketing-person's total income fixed and allocating the remaining 20 per cent among other elements.

Consider Special Company Needs and Problems

Special company needs and problems should be considered and the plan designed so that it will meet as many of these needs as possible, either eliminating or reducing the seriousness of the problems. Although a marketing-person's compensation plan is no panacea for management's marketing ills, it is often practical to construct a plan that increase the effectiveness of other management policies. If a company's earnings are depressed because marketing personnel overemphasise low-margin items and neglect more profitable products, it may be possible, despite the existence of other managerial alternatives, to adjustment the compensation plan to cause marketing-people to sell better-balanced orders. Specifically, provision might be made for variable commission rates on different products, with the higher rates applying to previously neglected products.

Or, to use another example, a firm might have a 'small order' problem. It is possible to design compensation plans that operate to encourage marketing-person to write larger orders. Commission rates can be graduated so that higher rates apply to larger orders. However, in this instance, to realise maximum benefit, the revised compensation plan probably should be supplemented by a customer classification and call scheduling system, enabling management to vary the call frequency with the account size.

As still another illustration, a company may desire to obtain more displays or local advertising by retailers. With the rise of self-service merchandising, many manufacturers are well aware that the presence or absence of point-of-purchase displays can spell the difference between marketing success or failure. Under such conditions, securing retail displays of company products is highly important, and the task is often assigned to the marketing-people. This is a task that marketing personnel may neglect, especially if they are paid a commission based on marketing volume. To overcome this tendency, an incentive payment for each retail display obtained is often incorporated in the compensation plan.

The three situations above by no means exhaust the possibilities for using the compensation plan as a vehicle to help solve special company problems. Plan may be designed to assist in securing new customers and new business, improving the quality of marketing-people's reports, controlling expenses of handling complaints and adjustments, eliminating price shading by the marketing staff, reducing travelling and other expenses, and making collections and gathering credit information. Management, however, should recognise that other means exist for dealing with such problems, the frequently transitory nature of which dictates that the company should not resort to changes in the marketing-compensation plan. Repeated tampering with the marketing-compensation plan in the effort to solve many and varied management problems all too frequently results in overly complex and difficult-to-administer plans.

Consult the Present Marketing Force

To refine the plan further, management should consult the present marketing personnel. Many grievances have their roots in the compensation plan. Marketing-people should be asked what they like and dislike about the plan and what improvements they would suggest. Their criticisms and suggestions should be appraised relative to the plan or plans management is considering. But at this point again, management should compare the calibre of the present marketing force with that of the people whom it would like to have. If the present marketing-people are not of the grade that the company wishes to attract, their criticisms and suggestions may be of limited usefulness. Since, however, nearly every marketing force has some people of the desired calibre, more weight can be attached to their opinions than to those of people falling outside the designated classification.

Reduce Tentative Plan to Writing and Pretest It

If the preceding suggestions have been followed, the plan should be taking shape rapidly. For clarification, and to eliminate any inconsistencies that may have crept in, the tentative plan should be put in writing. Then it should be pretested. The amount of testing required depends upon the extent to which the new plan differs from the one in use. The greater the difference, the more thorough should be the testing.

Pretest of compensation plans are almost always mathematical and have become increasingly computerised. Past payrolls, for perhaps a year or two, are reworked to check the operation of the proposed plan against experience under the old system. Analysts compare what happened with what would have happened had the new plan been in effect. If the marketing pattern has shown considerable fluctuation, calculation should be made for periods representative of average, good, and poor business. Then a look should be taken into the future. Utilising data from the marketing forecast, new and old plans can be applied to future periods. The plan should be tested for the marketing force as a group and for individual marketing-people faced with different marketing conditions. Conclusions drawn from these tests should reveal whether the plan permits earnings in line with the desired compensation level. If deficiencies show up, management should recognise that the plan may not be at fault. Apparent weakness can be traced to the way in which territorial assignments have been made or to inaccuracies in marketing forecasts, budgets, or quotas.

It is often advisable to conduct a pilot test. Several territories representative of different types of marketing conditions are selected, and the proposed plan applied in each one sufficiently long to detect how it works under current operating conditions. Pilot tests are invaluable for spotting possible sources of trouble and in uncovering and correcting other apparent deficiencies before the plan is put into effect.

Revise the Plan

After the test results have been thoroughly analysed, the plan should be revised to eliminate trouble spots or deficiencies. If extensive alterations are made, it is wise to put the changed plan through further pretests and perhaps even another pilot test. But if there have been only minor changes, it is merely necessary to edit the revised plan.

Install the Plan and Provide for Follow-up

At last, the plan is ready for implementation. Opinion varies as to whether the plan should be submitted to marketing personnel for approval before the actual installation; in any event, management should make a strong effort to convince them of its basic fairness and logic. Marketing-people should made to understand what management hopes to accomplish through the plan and just how this is to be done. Details of changes from the previous plan, and their significance, should be carefully explained. All marketing-persons should be given copies of the plan, and they should be taught to compute their own earnings. Written examples of the proper method for calculating earnings should be provided. Inadequate understanding of the compensation plan is a common cause of marketing-people's dissatisfaction. Too often, management fails to realise that the marketing compensation plan may require painstaking explanation. When marketing-persons do not fully understand the purposes of such features of a plan as quotas and variable commission bases, they are prone to think that unfair advantage is being taken of them. Provisions should be made for periodic checkups, to determine whether the plan is working out in practice. From such checkups, the need for further adjustments can be detected. Management has much to gain from an appropriate marketing-force compensation plan and much to lose from a defective one. Periodic checks provide evidence of the plan's accomplishments, and they help to detect areas of weakness if things are noi working out as anticipated.

Basic Types of Compensation Plans

The four elements of compensation may be combined into literally hundred of different marketing-force pay plans, each of which is more or less unique. If the 'expense reimbursement' and 'fringe benefits' elements are excluded from consideration—as is entirely reasonable, since they are never used alone—there are three basis types of compensation plans: straight salary, straight commission, and a combination of salary and one or more variable elements.

Straight Salary Plan

The straight salary is the simplest compensation plan. Under it, marketing-person receive fixed at regular intervals (usually each week or month but sometimes every two weeks), representing total payments for their services. In addition, they may receive an amount to defray all or part of the expenses incurred in performance of their duties. The straight salary was once the most popular marketing-compensation plan, but it has been declining in importance since the early 1920s. A recent study by American Management Association shows that just under 25 per cent of all marketing organisations operate exclusively on a straight-salary basis. Such plans are considerably more common in companies marketing industrial foods than they are in ones marketing consumer products. Firms that formerly used the straight salary have tended to combine a basic salary with an additional variable element—that is, they have switched to combination plans.

In spite of the trend away from its use, the straight-salary plans is still appropriate in certain situations. It is often the best way to compensate marketing personnel when the marketing job requires extensive missionary or educational work, when marketing-people service the product or give technical and engineering advice to prospects or users, or when marketing-people do considerable marketing promotion work. Thus, if nonmarketing tasks bulk large in the marketing-person's total time expenditure, the straight salary plan is worthy of management's serious consideration.

Straight-salary plans are used for compensating marketing-people engaged in more or less routine marketing. These jobs, in which marketing often is reduced to mere order taking, abound in the wholesale and manufacturing fields, where consumer necessities are distributed directly to retailers. Quite frequently, too, the straight-salary method is used for paying driver-marketing-persons marketing liquor and beverages, milk and bread, and similarly distributed products.

From management's standpoint, the straight-salary plan has important advantages. By its nature it provides strong financial control over marketing personnel, and management secures maximum power to direct their activities along lines that are potentially the most productive. Component tasks making up marketing-person's jobs can be recast with minimum opposition from the people affected. Consequently, greater flexibility is obtained in adjusting field marketing work to changes in the marketing. If marketing personnel are required to prepare detailed reports, follow up on a large number of leads, or perform other time-consuming tasks, they tend to cooperate more fully if paid straight salaries rather than commissions. Straight-salary plans are also economical to administer, since their basic simplicity requires few mathematical manipulations and, compared with straight-commission plans, accounting costs are significantly lower.

From the marketing-person's standpoint, the chief attraction of the straight-salary plan is that the stability of income frees him or her from the financial uncertainty inherent in plans that contain variable elements. Additionally, because salaried marketing-person expect to receive detailed instructions, they are relieved of much of the burden of planning their activities. Finally, because of the basic simplicity of the straight-salary plan, marketing-people usually find it easy to understand.

The straight-salary plan has several market weaknesses. Because there are no direct monetary incentives, many marketing-people do only an average marketing job rather than an outstanding one. They may be inclined to pass up promising opportunities for increased business, at least until management becomes aware of them and orders the taking of required actions. Unless the plan is skilfully administered, there is a tendency to under-compensate good marketing-people and to over-compensate poor ones. If such inequities exist for long, the turnover rate rises; and it is often the most productive people who leave the company first. Situations of this type inevitably result in increased expenditures for recruiting, selecting, and training. Other problems are encountered in maintaining morale, in as much as arguments occur on such matters as pay adjustments for ability, rising living costs, and length of service. Because all the marketing expensed is fixed, the company finds it difficult to adjust to changing economic conditions—a particularly knotty problem during business downswings, when marketing expenses can be reduced only by cutting salaries or releasing personnel. Moreover, during business upturn, the company may experience difficulty in securing its normal share of rising industry volume, because marketing-people paid straight salaries commonly are not disposed to exceed previous marketing records by any large amount. The reader should recognise, however, that many of these weaknesses of the straight-salary plan can be avoided or minimised through intelligent administration.

In administering a straight-salary plan, individual marketing-people should be paid, insofar as possible, according to their relative performance. The difficulty in achieving this ideal is in validly measuring performance. Before performance can be measured, management needs to define what it means by 'performance' and what constitutes good, average, and poor performances. When management has these definitions and develops methods of performance measurements, salaries of individual marketing-persons can be set fairly and intelligently. Users of the salary plan should define performance as total job-performance, not merely success in securing marketing volume or in performing some other aspect of the job—and this definition is theoretically correct, because the payers of salaries assume that they will be able to exercise maximum direction and control over the way salary receivers perform all aspects of the jobs. Some salary plan users, recognising that it is illogical to use success in securing marketing volume as the sole criterion, attempt instead the measure performance by relating total marketing expense incurred by an individual marketing-person (including his or her salary) to his or her total marketing. Although it is desirable to hold marketing expenses within reasonable bounds, to use the expense-to-marketing ratio as sole criterion of performance is to overemphasise the importance of cost control.

In the absence of well-defined quantitative performance standards, and few companies have them, the marketing job description, if up-to date and complete, is the staring point from which to appraise marketing performance. All marketing-persons should be rated not only on their success in achieving marketing and cost goals but on their performance of each assigned duty. The total evaluation of an individual is a composite of the several ratings, weighed according to relative importance. Persons rated as average should be paid average salaries. Salaries of below-average and above-average marketing-people should be scaled to reflect the extent to which their performances vary from the average. Each marketing-person's performance should be regularly reviewed and upward adjustments made for people, who have registered improvement, and, to the extent possible, reductions should be made for those whose performance have deteriorated.

Straight-commission Plan

The theory supporting the straight-commission plan is that marketing personnel should be paid strictly according to their individual productivity. The assumption underlying most straight-commission plans is that marketing volume is the best measure of productivity and can, therefore, be used as its sole measure. This is highly questionable assumption, as was brought out in the preceding discussion of the straight-salary plan.

Although the straight-commission plan, at least in its present form, is almost as simple as the straight-salary plan. Many commission systems develop into rather complex arrangements. Some provide for progressive or regressive changes in commission rates as marketing volume rises to different levels. Others provide for differential commission rates for marketing of different products, to different categories of customers, or during marketing seasons. Such refinements tend to make straight-commission plans more complex to operate than most straight-salary plans.

According to one source, the majority of straight-commission plans falls into one of the two broad classification:

(1) Straight commission at a gross or inclusive rate with no defrayment of expenses by the employer. Marketing-people, therefore, pay their expenses. Advances may or may not be made against earnings.

(2) Straight commission at a net rate in which the employer pays the travel expenses, again with or without advances against commission earnings.

There has been a general trend away from the straight-commission plan, and today probably no more than 6 or 7 per cent of all companies have such plans in use. However, the plan is used in situation where the marketing-person's non-marketing duties are relatively unimportant and management wants to emphasise getting orders. Straight-commission plans are common in the clothing, textile, and shoe industries and drug and hardware wholesaling. Firms marketing intangibles, such as insurance and investment securities, often employ this method exclusively. It is also used extensively by manufacturers of furniture, office equipment, and business machines.

The straight-commission plan has several outstanding advantages. Probably, the greatest is that it provides maximum direct monetary incentive for the marketing-person to strive for high-level volume. The star marketing-person is paid more than he or she would be under most salary plans, and low producers are not likely to be overcompensated. When a commission system is first installed, there is some tendency for the marketing-force turnover rate to accelerate, but analysis usually reveals that the exodus has been mostly among the low producers. Ordinarily, the remaining marketing-people work longer and harder and with more income to show for their efforts, perhaps because of the strong motivation provided such people by a feeling of 'being in business for myself.' Straight-commission plans also provide management with a means for cost control—all direct marketing expenses, except for travelling and miscellaneous expenses (which may be reimbursable in plans of the second classification noted above), fluctuate directly with marketing-volume changes and, in contrast to straight-salary plans, marketing compensation become virtually all variable expense. The straight-commission plan also is characterised by great flexibility, making it readily adjustable to deal with particular company problems. By revising the commission rates applying to different products, for instance, it is often possible to stimulate marketing personnel to give increased emphasis to marketing the items with the highest gross margins.

However, the straight-commision method has certain weaknesses. The greatest is that it provides for little financial control over marketing-people's activities, a weakness further compounded when they pay their own expenses. Marketing-persons on straight commission tend to feel that they are discharging their full responsibilities by continuing to send in customer's orders. They are careless about transmitting reports and other requested information, often neglect to follow up leads provided by the home office, resists proposed reductions in the size of marketing territories, consider individual accounts their private property, are tempted to shade prices to make marketing, and may resort to high-pressure tactics with consequent loss of customer goodwill. Moreover, unless differential commission rates are provided, some marketing-people push the easiest-to-sell low-margin items and neglect the harder-to-sell high-margin items; if management seeks to correct this situation through using differential commission rates, increased record-keeping expenses are incurred. Under any straight-commission plan, in fact, the costs of checking and auditing marketing-people's reports and of calculating payrolls are almost certain to be higher than under straight-salary method. Finally, some marketing-person's efficiency may decline because of worries caused by income uncertainties. If a marketing force has many such worried marketing-people, management may have to invest considerable time, effort, and money in the task of buying up the spirits of downhearted persons. Since new marketing-people, in particular, have difficulties in adjustment to fluctuating incomes, it is wise policy to pay recruits straight salaries until they gain marketing skill sufficient to enable them consistently to earn more on commission.

One comprehensive study of marketing compensation concluded that certain of the following conditions are present in all successful application of the straight-commission plan:

(1) The need for strong incentive to secure the requisite intensive marketing effort.

(2) The desire to reduce fixed salary or other fixed marketing expense to a minimum

(3) The need to make limited finances go further by reducing marketing requirements for working capital.

(4) The desire to fix definite cost ratios for personal marketing so that accounting statements and price estimates can be made more accurate.

(5) Inability or unwillingness, for financial or other reasons, to provide sufficient supervision to supplement lack of incentive of salary of other plans. Sometimes, the thinness of the market and the need for marketing over large and widely scattered areas renders self supervision the only solution.

(6) Straight commission is the accepted and desired method of compensation in the industry.

(7) Personal marketing is the primary and frequently the only means of marketing. Advertising is secondary and supplementary. Consumer advertising is limited in amount.

(8) Commission may be the only feasible plan of compensation when the marketing-person works in a part-time basis or when he sells a number of products of lines for two or more employers or principal. Side-line marketing-people, independent constructor marketing-people, and others fall into this group.

Determining Commission Base

An important aspect of designing a straight-commission system is that of determining the base on which to pay commission. Usually, selection of the base depends upon the individual company's particular marketing policies and problems. If obtaining volume is the main concern, then total marketing probably should be the base. If marketing personnel are required to make collections on marketing, it may be appropriate to base commission in collections. If a firm is confronted with excessive order cancellations, it sometimes is wise to base commissions on shipments, billings, or payments. To control price cutting by marketing personnel, some companies base commissions on gross margins. A sizable number of organisations use net profits as the commission base, thereby seeking simultaneously to control price cutting, marketing expenses, and net profit.

Drawing Accounts

An important modification of the straight-commission plan is known as the drawing-account method, under which the employer establishes separate accounts for each marketing-person, to which commissions are credited regularly and against which they make periodic withdrawal. In practice, drawing accounts tend to resemble salaries, since marketing-people commonly are allowed to overdraw against future earnings. If a marketing-person becomes greatly overdrawn, he or she may lose incentive to produce, because some portion of the earned commission will be used to reduce the indebtedness. What is probably more important, the marketing-person may become so discouraged with the prospects of paying back the overdrawn amount that he or she will quit the company.

To forestall the possibility that overdrawn marketing-people may quit their jobs, some firms use 'guaranteed' drawing-account plans that do not require the paying back of overdrawals. Marketing executives in these firms must exercise considerable care and judgement in setting the size of drawing accounts for different people, for guaranteed drawing accounts are really combination salary and commission plans under a different name. However, the guaranteed drawing account provides a stronger incentive than combination salary and commission, because the rate of commission on each rupee of marketing is higher. Commonly, these plans include a provision in the person's contact that covers the possibility of overdrafts. Legally, in most situations, as overdraft cannot be collected unless the marketing-person specifically agrees that it will be repaid, unless it is really a personal loan or unless he or she given a note acknowledging its receipt. Without a formal undertaking of this sort, the court is likely to hold that the relationship between marketing-person and the company was really a partnership in which the company agreed to finance the marketing-person, and that the resulting loss was only a normal risk incurred in doing business. Even, if the company has an ironclad agreement with its marketing personnel on this point, there remains the perplexing problem of collecting money the overdrawn marketing-people do not have.

Combination Salary and Incentive Plan

Salary Plus Commission

Most marketing-compensation plans are combinations of the salary and commission methods. Most developed in an attempt to capture the advantages and offset the disadvantages of both the salary and commission systems. Where the straight-salary method is used, the marketing executives often needs a means of stimulating the marketing-force to greater effort. Where the straight-commission system is used, the executives may be greatly handicapped because of weak financial control over marketing activities. By a judicious blending of the two basic plans, management hopes to obtain both the required control and motivation. But it should not be inferred that these results are always forthcoming, as actual results depend mainly upon management's skills in designing and administering the plan. Unless there is an extremely fine adjustment of the salary and commission elements, weakness evident in the basic systems reappear.

Use of Bonuses

Many companies use bonuses as financial incentives. Technically, bonuses are different from commission—a bonus is an amount paid for accomplishing specific marketing tasks; a commission varies in amount with marketing volume or other commission base. Bonuses may be paid for attaining a certain percentage of the marketing quota, performing given promotional activities, obtaining a specified number of new accounts, following up on a certain number of leads, setting up an assigned quota of displays, or carrying out other assigned tasks. The bonus, in other words, is an additional financial reward paid to the marketing-person for achieving results beyond a predetermined minimum.

Bonuses are never used alone—they always appear in conjunction with one of the three main marketing compensation methods. If used with the straight salary, the resulting compensation plan resembles the combination plan. If used with the straight commission, the result is a combination plan to which has been added an element of managerial control and direction. When used with a combination salary and commission plan, the bonus simply becomes a portion of the incentive income which is calculated in a different way than the commission.

Companies have five principal reasons for adding the bonus feature to their basic compensation plans:

(1) To increase the marketing-person's income and give him or her a share of the profits of a favourable company year.

(2) To provide special payments for reaching particular objective in terms of marketing volume, the volume of marketing of particular products, the number of new customers, and the level of profits.

(3) To provide recognition for special tasks or special attainments of value to the employer which are not reflected in the usual measures of performance or which have not yet had time to demonstrate their value in marketing or profit results; for instance, the acquisition of product knowledge, complaints or compliments from customers, cooperation in reducing surpluses or overstocks, and diligence and dependability in correspondence and reporting.

(4) To develop tea work and group action in marketing, and in maintaining customers within a branch, district, or other territory.

(5) To provide incentive payments without the unearned windfalls incident to salary and commission incentive plans or without adopting cutoff or other maximum earning features.

Several administrative actions are crucial to success when a bonus feature is included in the compensation plan. At the outset, the bonus conditions should be thoroughly explained and, to minimise later misunderstandings, management must make certain that marketing personnel understand them. Provision must be made for setting up and maintaining the necessary records. Procedures should be established to keep marketing-people of their current standings relative to the goals that qualify them for bonuses. In addition, any misunder-standing or grievances arising as a result of operation of the bonus feature should be dealt with fairly and with the utmost tact and diplomacy.

Strengths and Weaknesses of Combination Plans

If a combination plan is well designed and administered, significant benefits are gained. The marketing-people have both the security of stable incomes and the stimulus of direct financial incentive. Management has both financial control over marketing activities and the apparatus to motivate marketing efforts in desired direction. Marketing costs are composed of fixed and variable elements; thus, greater flexibility for adjustment to changing business conditions exists than under the straight-salary method but still less than under the commission method. Nevertheless, marketing costs, to some extent at least, now fluctuate with the volume of business produced. There also may be beneficial now effects upon personnel morale. Disagreements on such problems as salary increases and territorial changes should be much less violent than under a straight commission plan. Further, if marketing-people are made to realise that the company is sharing their financial risks, a more cooperative spirit should develop between them and the company.

The combination plan, however, is not without disadvantages. Clerical costs of operating a combination plan are likely to be higher than for either a salary or a commission system. More records have to be maintained, and these involve greater detail. Thus, there are risks that the plan will become too complicated and that the marketing-people will not fully understand it. Sometimes a company seeking to provide adequate salaries and at the same time desiring to keep marketing costs down must use such low commission rates that the incentive feature is insufficient to elicit grater effort by the marketing-people. On the other hand, if the incentive portion is increased to a larger percentage of the total income, marketing-people may neglect activities for which they are not directly paid. Therefore, the rations that the base salary and the incentive portion bear to the total compensation are critical factors. As mentioned earlier, the most common distribution of payments in combination plans is 80 per cent salary and 20 per cent incentive and other elements.

Reimbursement of Marketing Expenses: Policies and Practices

With respect to reimbursement of marketing expenses, the two general policy alternatives are: (1) to require personnel to pay their own expenses, or (2) to reimburse marketing-people for all or part of the expenses incurred in performing their jobs. Although the first alternative is the simpler by far, few companies choose it. Those that do are organisation, by and large, that regard marketing personnel as independent business people – an overwhelming majority of these organisations also use the straight-commission compensation method. The main advantage of this policy, from management's standpoint, is that no special expense records are necessary inasmuch as the marketing personnel, rather than the company, are the ones whose desire to control expenses is stimulated. But in successful applications, the level of other compensation reflects the fact that they bear their own expense. It is essential that their regular commission be sufficient to permit them to further the company's best interests. Even when the compensation level takes into account marketing-people's probable expenses, some persons still skimp on expenses, to the company's detriment. To increase their earnings, they stay in second and third-rate hotels, they economise on meals, dry cleaning, laundry, and other travelling expenses, and they avoid entertaining customers and prospects. Furthermore, they resist or ignore many of management's directions and instructions. Little management control can be exercised over their call and route schedules, especially in regard to accounts located in out-of-the-way places. Most marketing-people who pay their own expenses refuse, or neglect, to perform non-marketing-producing activities – they avoid missionary duties, and follow up on marketing leads only when no additional expenses are involved. They 'high spot,' that is, they call only on large accounts that can be dependent upon to given orders; and they feel justified in adding 'side-lines,' other manufacturers' products sold to the same general classes of trade. Taken all in all, except in the most unusual marketing circumstances, it is unwise to require marketing-people to pay their own expenses.

Most firms choose the second policy alternative – full partial reimbursement of marketing expenses. When all or part of marketing expenses are classified as reimbursable, marketing management must be concerned directly with the amount spent. After all, the funds used to defray marketing expenses represent deductions from gross profits realised on marketing. Although there is considerable variation among companies, the average costs of keeping marketing-personnel on the road are higher than commonly supposed. Many factors, of course, influence the amount of marketing expenses. Some of these are territorial size and characteristics, the calibre of the marketing personnel, the nature and breadth of the product line, managerial efficiency, the intensity of competition, and the mode of travel.

Several commonsense principles guide management in formulating expense-reimbursement policies. Reimbursable expenses should be large enough to permit the performance of assigned duties in the manner expected. Normally, all expensed incurred because marketing personnel are away from their home bases of operation on company business should be reimbursable. Expense-reimbursement policies should take into account the customary standards of living of the marketing-person and of the customers, but greater emphasis should be given the latter. The marketing-person should eat in restaurants and stay at hotels of the class ordinarily patronised by the customers. In some instances, different marketing-people in the same company should be allowed different amounts for expenses, reflecting deviation in customers' standards of living. Another reason for different-sized expense accounts is the fact that actual expenses vary a great deal from one territory to another. Reimbursement policies should operate to keep expenses within a reasonable range; they should not be allowed to cause bad feeling among the marketing staff. It is desirable that these policies be economical to administer; that is, only minimum supervision and record keeping should be required of both the company and marketing personnel, but the desire for economy in administration should not result in adoption of arbitrary or unfair procedures. Above all, both in formulating reimbursement policies and in defining procedures for implementation, management needs to guard against the natural tendency to overeconomise. Under no circumstances should marketing-people be forced to economise to the point of impairing marketing efficiency. Nor should marketing-people have to dip into their own pockets to pay legitimate expenses. Reimbursement policies and procedures should be based upon the reasonable needs of the people incurring the expenses; for enforcement, they should rely largely upon person's inherent honesty.

Method of Controlling and Reimbursing Expenses

Flat-expense-account Plan

The flat-expense-account plan provides each marketing-person with a stipulated sum to cover all expenses for a given period. Allocation of this sum among various expense items is left to the individual's discretion. Apparently, the chief reason for employing the flat expense account is to eliminate the necessity for keeping expense reports and the checking of expense accounts. One advantage of the plan is that, since individual expense accounts are determined in advance, the total amount of marketing expenses can be included in the budget. Periodically, then, at budget-marketing time, management may appraise the reasonableness of total planned marketing expenses relative to total planned marketing. A second advantage is that marketing personnel who are free to spend expense allowances as they see fit should have few grievances and arguments over expense accounts. A third advantage is that the plan's nature is such as to cause marketing-people to control their own expenses and, if guided properly by management, they should do a better job planning route and call schedules in order that each expense of rupees may be spent to the best advantage.

Successful operation of the flat-expense-account plan requires skilled administration. It works best either (1) when the exact amounts of expense accounts do not need changing often, as with companies whose marketing-people have small territories in which to sell staple products, or (2) when an individual marketing-person's expense allowances come up for frequent review and, possible, revision In other words, if the marketing situation is not relatively flexible, the amounts of the expense accounts should have flexibility built into them. If the plan is inflexible in a fluid marketing situation, marketing-people may not capitalise on marketing opportunities requiring expenditures in excess of the flat amounts. Even when marketing circumstances favour the use of this plan, management should regularly apprise each marketing-person's allowance for adequacy and appropriateness.

The weakness of flat-expense-account results from the tendency of some scales personnel to overeconomise. These people come to think of the expense account as a regular addition to salary and are reluctant to spend the entire allowance, preferring to save a portion for personal use. Careful marketing supervision is essential to avoid situation of this sort.

Flexible-expense-account Method

The flexible-expense-account method, sometimes known as the 'exact' plan, is the most common reimbursement method. The salient feature of this plan is that marketing-personnel receive reimbursement for all 'allowable' expenses incurred and reported. If this method is to work successfully, management must (1) know the approximate total amount of marketing personnel's probable expenses (otherwise there is inadequate information for planning and budgeting); (2) classify marketing expenses into 'allowable' and 'non-allowable' categories, and furnish marketing-people with clear descriptions of items included under each heading; (3) set up a system and forms for the marketing staff to use in periodic expense reporting; (4) establish procedures for checking itemised expense reports and for expeditious handling of reimbursements.

The plan has much to recommend it. Inasmuch as expense accounts are flexible, marketing opportunity may be capitalised on fully as they arise. There is a basic fairness about the plan, because, almost automatically, it takes into account and makes payments for differences in territories, marketing conditions, and other important factors. Therefore, management can exercise considerable control over marketing routes and call schedules. Finally, marketing-persons are under obligation to perform all their assigned activities, nonmarketing as well as marketing, with the degree if efficiency expected by management.

The flexible-expense-account plan's unattractive features come out in its administration. Administrative costs are sizable, because of the large amount of clerical and accounting work involved in checking expense reports and making reimbursements. Similarly, clerical and accounting work requires a great deal of the marketing-people's time and many executives contened that good marketing personnel are often poor record keepers. Unless close control is maintained, some marketing-people spend the company's money to generously, this situation being further aggravated by the existence of considerable opportunity for expense-account padding— and many disputes over various expenses items. Hence marketing-force morale and productivity may suffer unless highly competent people administer the plan.

Honour System

Under this system, marketing expenses are fully reimbursed. Marketing personnel are not required to submit detailed, itemised lists of expenses but report only their total expenses for the period. The implication is that management has complete confidence in each marketing-person's honesty, and this should affect marketing-force morale favourable. The honour system is also easy to administer and, compared with alternative reimbursement plans, there are savings in both accounting expenses and time. Arguments over questionable expenditures do not arise, and marketing-people do not envision management as parsimonious. Finally, at least in theory, the funds for territorial development should be adequate; however, both the amounts and the ways in which they are used are left to the marketing-people's discretion.

With the honour system, management's control is characteristically weak, and this may cause certain problems to develop. Some marketing-persons evolve into free spenders, since detailed expense reports are not required. Others incur expenses from which the company has little chance of deriving benefit. Still others go so far as to appropriate company funds for their own use, for the system tends to encourage people to regard expense accounts as sources of additional income. Abuses such as these cause inequities in expense allowances, and this may have bad effect upon morale. To avoid such abuses, management, even though committed to the honour principle, should provide for some control over individual marketing-person's total expenses. One way is to establish maximum ratios of marketing expense to marketing for each marketing-person. It is advisable also to watch the trend of expenses; and sudden and sizable increases in a person's reported expenses, unless accompanied by parallel changes in marketing, should be investigated. If dishonesty in expense reporting is detected, remedial action is definitely advisable. In spite of such problems the philosophy of the honour system lies behind the reimbursement policies and practices of many marketing organisations.

Expenses-quota Plan

The expense-quota plan is a compromise between the flat-expense-account plan and the honour system as well as flexible-expense-account plan. This plan's objectives are to retain considerable control over marketing-person's total expenses over long period but to permit week-by-week variations in the amounts reimbursed. In setting up expense quotas, management first studies the size and characteristics of individual territories and estimates the marketing volume each should provide, then establishes upper limits for each marketing-person's total expense likely to be incurred over a specified period. Under the expense-quota plan, marketing personnel receive prompt and full reimbursement, regardless of how greatly 'allowable' expenses vary from week. The budgeted figures are planned amounts only, and management does not hold rigidly to the upper limits. But because upper limits are established, marketing-people have a strong moral obligation to keep their expenses under control. Thus, there are significant advantages to be gained. The principal drawback is that the burden for controlling expenses is placed, in effect, upon the marketing-people rather than upon management. As is true of all expense reimbursement plans, skilful administration is a necessary condition for successful operation of the expense-quota plan. Furthermore, unless marketing and expense forecasts are accurate, and unless marketing-persons are convinced that the upper limits are estimates only, toward the end of budgetary periods marketing-people may curtail their activities because of low balances left in accounts.

Handling Marketing-person's Automobile Expenses

Companies using either the flexible-expenses-account plan or the expense-quota plan, and whose marketing-people operate their own automobiles (rather than company owned for leased vehicles) must adopt a system for determining the amounts that marketing personnel should be reimbursed for using their automobile on company business. Computation of 'exact' automobile expenses is complicated by the fact that variable, semivariable, and fixed expenses are involved. Certain items, including costs of gasoline, lubricating oil and grease, and tires, vary with the miles travelled. Some items such as insurance coverage, licence fees and inspection fees, are fixed. Other costs, such as charges for depreciation and obsolescence, vary with the automobile's age and its rate of use. Hence, total automobile expenses per mile do not vary at a constant rate as mileage increase, total expenses differ with the automobile make and modal. Moreover, expenses of ownership and operation, even for makes and models, vary substantially from one territory to another. And differences in road and traffic conditions also cause auto expenses to vary from territory to territory. These complications make precise computations of automobile expenses a highly involved and tedious process, and most companies have settled on less-exact procedures. Most studies of companies using marketing-person-owned automobiles show that more than one half use flat mileage rates, about one-fifth use graduated mileage rates, and the rest use standard allowances, combinations of standard allowances and mileage rates, the Runzeimer plan, or other systems. Each of the systems is examined in the following discussion:

Flat Mileage Rates

Firms using the flat-mileage-rate system reimburse automobile expenses at a fixed rate per mile travelled. This is now the most widely used system, but there has been a trend away from it—probably because of management's increasing recognition that flat mileage rates are no better than rough approximations of true expenses. Users of this system must try to set the mileage rate high enough to cover all expenses of automobile ownership and operation, yet low enough to permit the company to buy transportation as cheaply as possible. Operating this system is simple. Marketing personnel report mileage travelled on company business, the flat mileage rate is applied, and reimbursement cheques are issued. The system appears to work satisfactorily when a company's marketing force covers small territories (requiring little automobile travel) all in the same geographical area (incurring very similar expenses amounts), and the mileage rate applied is on the generous side (eliminating arguments over actual and reimbursed expenses). Probably for these reasons, the majority of local and regional wholesalers, among other small companies, favour the flat-mileage-rate system.

For most companies, however, the flat-mileage-rate system has fundamental shortcomings. It is based on the erroneous assumption that automobile expenses per mile vary at a constant rate at all operating levels. It ignores cost differentials arising from the use of variouys makes and models. It similarly ignores very real territorial differences in expenses, for example, in the prices of gasoline, oil tires, insurance coverage, licence and inspection fees, and even the automobiles themselves. Furthermore, in administering the flat-mileage-rate systems, management all too often shows great hesitancy in adjusting the rate, upward as well as downward, in line with changing actual expenses.

Graduated Mileage Rates

Under the system, different mileage rates apply for mileage in different ranges, for example, 5 rupees per mile up to 5,000 miles annually, 4 rupees per mile for 5,000 to 10,000 miles, and 3.50 rupees per mile for over 10,000 miles. Thus, an important weakness of the flat-mileage-rate system is avoided, since mileage rates decline as mileage increases. It appears, then, that companies using this system recognise that the per mile costs of automobile operation are lower for long than for short distances, however, setting the rupees-per-mile rates is difficult, since it is necessary to consider different operating levels in determining the mileages at which rates change. This system takes into account, almost mechanically, differences in marketing territories, such as the length of route and frequency of calls. But, like the flat-mileage-rate systems, it does not consider cost variations resulting from operation of different makes and models, and territorial expense differentials. Graduated-mileage-rate systems are most appropriate for use by companies, whose marketing personnel travel long distances annually but who serve fairly concentrated geographic areas (thus, avoiding significant regional expense differences). The basic defect in all mileage-rate systems, whether flat or graduated is that they consider nothing more than total costs that are assumed to vary only with the miles travelled, when, in fact, some costs are fixed, wholly or partially, regardless of the mileage or use.

Standard Allowance

Some companies simply grant marketing-persons a specified sum for each day, week, month, or other period during which they use either personnel automobiles on company business. Taken all in all standard-allowances systems. It assumes that total automobile expenses vary with duration of use rather than with mileage travelled. At best, the standard allowance can be put a rough estimate of actual costs of automobile ownership and operation. Companies using the system to penalise marketing personnel whose territories are large and require extensive travelling for adequate coverage, and the standard allowance, unless amounts are varied for individual marketing-people fails to reimburse for these differences. If allowances, for all marketing-people are uniform, morale is bound to suffer, because the marketing force will recognise the obvious inequities. Morale is affected adversely, too, by revision in the standard allowances made as costs change, particularly when the revisions are downward. Only when the entire staff faces similar driving conditions, possess comparable makes and models of cars, and have nearly equal-sized territories, each requiring approximately the same marketing coverage, is the standard allowance defensible. Needless to say, it is unusual for all these conditions to be present in the same situation.

Combination of Standard Allowance and Mileage Rate

This system reflects recognition that both fixed and variable expenses are involved in automobile ownership and operation. A fixed periodic payment (intended to cover such fixed and semivariable costs as insurance premium, licence fees, and depreciation) is combined with a mileage allowance (for reimbursing all operating expenses, including the costs of gasoline, oil, and tires.) This plan, is an improvement over both parent systems, because it allows for the fact that some expenses vary with automobile usage and some do not. In contrast to mileage-rates system, it provides for the expenses that do not vary directly with the operating level; in contrast to the standard allowance system, it takes account of cost differentials arising from different operating levels. If all marketing personnel are granted identical standard allowances, this system, like the other, fails to consider territorial expense differentials and cost variations resulting from operation and ownership of different makes and models of automobiles.

Some companies using the combination system accumulate reserves to cover depreciation changes on marketing-person's automobiles and reimburse marketing personnel when they buy new cars. This assures that the marketing-person can buy a new car without resorting to outside financing. Furthermore, this practice makes it unnecessary for the marketing force to request company financial help in buying new cars. It should be noted that these reserves represent, in effect, the withholding of some portion of automobile expenses allowances that otherwise would be paid directly to the marketing staff on a periodic basis. When the withholding, or reserve, feature is not used, marketing-people often delay replacing old cars because of personal financial problems. The withholding feature assures that the marketing staff will not have to drive dlapidated automobiles and hence risk embarrassing the company.

Runzheimer Plan

The plan, originated by the consulting firm of Runzheimer and Company, is basically a combination standard allowance and mileage-rate system. However, the plan is an important over most combination systems in that it takes account of geographical variations in expenses of automobile ownership and operation by dividing the United States into twenty-nine 'auto-use basic cost areas.' Standard allowances are expressed on a per diem basis and include provisions for insurance premium, state licence, title and driver's fees and depreciation. Mileage rates are applied to cover expenses incurred for gasoline, oil, grease, washing, service maintenance, and tyres. In addition, Runzheimer and Company recommends that certain expense items not provided for in the standard allowance be reimbursed as incurred and reported by marketing personnel. Such expense items include local city licence fees, property taxes, daytime parking, overnight parking away from the home city, and toll charges. A further refinement provides that automobile depreciation allowances for marketing-people travelling more than 20,000 miles annually be adjustment, monthly or annually, at the rate of approximately Rs. 600/- per 1,000 miles in excess of the 20,000 miles of average annual travel within each of the 29 cost areas. The purpose of the depreciation adjustment is to enable the high-mileage driver to trade in his car when it reaches the 60,000-total-mileage point. Standard allowances are also computed to allow for the operation of different makes and models of cars. Since the installation of the plan, the service has been greatly extended and refined, it is presently used by several hundred companies.

Fringe Benefits

Marketing-men once almost universally excluded from eligibility for the fringe benefits granted to other employees; today, all but a tiny minority receive such benefits. Marketing-person were regarded in the past either as independent contractors or as part of management, and the thinking was that marketing-people and marketing executives were supposed to arrange their financial affairs to provide for retirement, pay for their own vacations, buy their own insurance, pay their own medical and hospital bills, and so on. Changes in tax laws and rates, enactments of such laws as the Social Security and Medicare acts, and the increasing universality of the desire of fulfil security needs have drastically altered the picture.

Today's marketing personnel normally share in all or most of the fringe benefits enjoyed by other company employees. Most and more marketing executives recognise that most marketing-people regard such benefits as important, necessary, and attractive features of employment. They also recognise that appropriate choices of fringe benefits for marketing personnel can have significant and beneficial influences not only upon marketing-force morale, but upon productivity and the marketing-force turnover rate.

When a company provides fringe benefits for marketing-people, essentially it pays them additional compensation. Fringe benefits represent additional, although sometimes deferred compensation (for example, social security and pension benefits), and, at least in theory, others forms of compensation (such as salaries and commissions) must be lower because of them. The costs of fringe benefits, of course vary with their nature and number, but the proportion of marketing-person's total compensation accounted for by fringe benefits has been steadily rising. Marketing executives say that fringe benefits make up 20 to 25 per cent of their total costs for marketing-force compensation.

❑❑❑

7

Marketing Force Management

Introduction

Marketing force management is a specialised version of personnel management. Yet, there are good reasons why the responsibility for marketing-force management is assigned to marketing executives rather than to personnel executives. While the same set of basic human problems must be dealt with in personnel management of marketing, production, or office workers, each class of problem varies in nature and importance with the work field. In contrast to production and office workers, for example, marketing personnel most often work independently; therefore, close and constant supervision is usually impractical. In further contrast, marketing-people generally work at some distance from their immediate superiors and co-workers, so it is more difficult to develop a spirit of identity with and loyalty to the company and to weld them into a unified team.

Of necessity, then, marketing personnel are given freer rein than most other workers at the comparable organisational level. To a considerable degree they must be relied upon as individual to plan and control their own activities. Despite a growing trend for marketing-people and executives to travel more by air, a marketing-person's visits to the home office are still usually infrequent, and centralised direction of his or her activities continues to be mainly by letter, telegraph, or long-distance telephone. The nature of the marketing-person's job provides only limited opportunity for face-to-face contact and supervision. Indeed, because of this necessary independence, marketing personnel are often described as account administrators.

Still other unique conditions surround the marketing-person's job, often requiring that he or she be away from home and family for extended periods. It involves great dependence upon human actions and reactions. Disheartening order turndowns and dealings with rude customers frequently require the marketing-person to repress natural responses and to suppress a natural tendency to become discouraged. The psychological effects of such condition accentuate the need for marketing management's continual attention to motivational factors.

Similarities to Conventional Personnel Management

Although there are distinctive features of marketing-force management, there are similarities to conventional personnel management. People are still being managed, and substantially the same human relations concepts are applicable. Marketing personnel share feelings resembling those of other employees with respect to job tenure, old age security, guaranteed wages, and equality of opportunity.

The basic steps in general personnel management are equally basic to marketing force management. The starting point in all personnel work is job analysis, to determine the nature of each position in terms of its component tasks. Then, each job is evaluated to ascertain the necessary qualification of employees. Next, there is the recruiting of qualified applications, and the marketing executives must be well informed with respect to prospective source of employees. From the supply of application, it is necessary to select those who meet the job specifications and, through interviewing and testing techniques, to evaluate qualification of applicants. Once a person is hired, marketing-force management focuses attention on training, which ranges from informal instruction to highly organised formal programmes: training may consume a few hours or several years, depending upon the complexity of the marketing job. An additional step is to develop compensation plans, and these range all the way from the straight salary to the straight commission.

Once a marketing-person is assigned to the field, other personnel problems are encountered. The marketing-person must be motivated and encouraged to plan and make productive use of working time. If a marketing-person is to maximise the effectiveness of marketing calls, counselling aimed at improving working habits methods is required. The final step in marketing-force management relates to control, which involves analysis of marketing and other records with the objective of improving the planning and supervising of operations. For example, the marketing-person's work week may be analyse to determine the proportion of time spent in actual marketing. Such information is used to plan territory coverage and to evaluate marketing performance. Each of these aspects of marketing-force management is discussed in greater detail in following pages.

Interrelations of Marketing Force Management Activities

The various activities performed in marketing-force management mesh together and should be thought of as a system. Faulty execution of any part of the system results in complication for other parts. If a substandard job of recruiting and selecting is done, tasks involved in training are magnified, problems of supervision become greater, motivating and controlling marketing-persons is more difficult, and the marketing-force turnover rate is accelerated. If training is inadequate or poorly administered, potentially good people fail to each high productivity, the compensation system does not work as planned, supervision is ineffective, and there is high personnel turnover. Similar difficulties arises in cases of ineffective performance of other activities in the marketing force management system.

Economies of Effective Marketing Force Management

Economies result from effective marketing force management. Assume that Company X has ten marketing-person, each making five calls per day, a total of 50 per day for the company. If, through better management and control of workday activities, each marketing-person increases the number of calls to six per day, the company's total calls per day become 60. This is equivalent to adding two new marketing-people at the old call rate. If marketing personnel are paid wholly, or partially, on a commission basis. Because some costs are related directly to the number of marketing-people, the company's average cost per call is also reduced.

The expenses of maintaining marketing people may be divided into fixed items identical for all marketing personnel regardless of efficiency; and into variable items costing proportionately more for the last effective marketing-people. Fixed expenses include those for transportation and travelling, equipment (automobiles, marketing folios, marketing manuals, and so forth), and advertising used to assist the marketing force. These expensed are essentially the same for every marketing-person. Variable items are those for which the most efficient marketing-people spend less than inefficient marketing-people, and they include expenses for training, motivating, supervising, controlling, and evaluating. For these items a company usually receives it highest return from its best marketing-people.

Fixed and incentive pay are classified separately. From the fixed portion of compensation, the poor marketing-person usually receives more than he or she deserves and the good marketing-person is underpaid. Because the incentive portion of compensation varies with productivity, it is generally true that individuals are paid amounts proportionate to their efficiency. A useful generalisation, which should be kept in mind by marketing executives, is that expenses per unit of product sold tend to vary inversely with effectiveness of the marketing-person.

Reducing the Rate of Personnel Turnover

One measure of the quality marketing-force management is the rate of turnover of the marketing personnel. This is calculated as the ratio of separations per 100 marketing-people. For example, a company employing a marketing force with an average strength of 250 persons and having 20 separations during the year has a rate of turnover of 8 per cent.

The marketing executive should keep the turnover rate at a reasonable figure, because costs of marketing-force management are strongly affected by the turnover rate. Costs of recruiting, advertising, fees to employment agencies, and so forth, often cost in excess of Rs 1000 per recruit. Interviewing costs are also high, because most companies interview several applicants for each selection. If an interview by an executive takes two hours, and executive time is worth Rs 400 per hour, total interviewing costs amount of Rs 24,000 per person hired if 30 people are considered for each vacancy. The costs of travel and time used for preparatory and follow-up training run as high as Rs 20,000 per person.

Some costs are not so readily calculated. For example, new recruits do not usually produce as much as experienced marketing personnel, and the ratio of marketing expenses to marketing for a new person is likely to be excessive for at least the first year. A conservative estimate of these excess costs is at least Rs 1,20,000 per new marketing-person during the first year, and in some companies this cost will be higher because it takes even longer for a marketing-person to get fully into stride.

When costs of breaking in a new marketing-person are totalled, a sizable sum is seen to be at stake. In a survey of member companies, the American Management Association several years ago found that the average cost for replacing a marketing-person was $6,684. Almost one-fourth of the respondents said their costs of turnover were $10,000 or more per marketing-person. A few placed the cost at over $20,000. No recent study is available, but a conservative estimate is that the current average cost of marketing-person replacement exceeds $10,000.

The costs of personnel turnover can account for a significant drain on profits. For example, in a company with a force of 400 and an annual turnover of 25 per cent, if the costs of replacing a single marketing-person come to $10,000, the annual costs of turnover total $ 1 million-and this relates only to out-of-pocket costs. Other important costs are increased expenses for supervision and motivation, lost business, decline in customer goodwill from mistakes of unexperienced marketing-persons, and miscellaneous expenses associated with taking on people who do not succeed. Few companies have accounting systems that permit quantitative measurement of the impact on profit of excessive personnel turnover. But it cannot be denied that profits are lower because inexperienced marketing-people are assigned where turnover has occurred. Profits are not realised from marketing never consummated.

Little comparative information is available on average turnover rates for marketing personnel in various industries. However, the annual turnover of marketing personnel in companies marketing staples and industrial products is usually less than 5 per cent. Companies marketing intangibles, such as insurance, securities, and specialty or luxury items have a higher rate, sometimes 50 per cent per year. Marketing forces of manufacturers generally show a lower rate than those of wholesalers; and firms whose marketing-people call on middlemen and industrial users commonly experiences less turnover than those engaged in door-to-door marketing.

All turnover is not bad, even though it may seem expensive at the time. Many marketing executive report that most marketing-people who leave a company have less than three years of service. In other words, turnover is largely accounted for by relatively new personnel. If a person is providing unsuccessful, and it is likely that he or she will leave eventually, it is desirable that he or she do so immediately. The earlier the unsuccessful person leaves, the better for the marketing-person and the company, both in terms of dollar costs and in terms of effect upon attitudes of other marketing-people. Too low a rate of turnover may indicate that the marketing force is overloaded with veterans who do not produce as much as new personnel might. Where this situation exists, it may be assumed that the entire system of marketing-force management needs re-examining and possible overhauling. Some turnover is desirable. A marketing force with no turnover may be growing stale; prospective new marketing-people are not attracted, and older persons may linger on because of management laxity and the comparatively security of established positions.

The age distribution among marketing personnel should be analysed for its impact on marketing-force turnover. It is usually desirable to have marketing-person's ages spread over a wide range. Otherwise, the productivity curves for all may rise together, with all reaching their peaks and decline together, and all reaching retirement at the same time. Under these circumstances, it is necessary eventually to recruit an entire marketing force almost at once, at considerable loss in market coverage and customer relations. Companies should establish an average length of service, which management considers desirable for marketing personnel, before evaluating the turnover rate. If management decides that the average length of service should be 20 years, then, assuming no errors in selection, the personnel turnover rate should be 5 per cent—one-twentieth of the marketing force should be replaced each year. Because even the best selection procedure is far from perfect, the actual turnover rate would run higher than 5 per cent. In addition, many people do not take marketing jobs with the intention of keeping them forever. A marketing job is often the springboard to higher positions, and a company using its marketing force as a source of managerial talent should anticipate higher turnover.

Awareness of the current turnover rate is alsø necessary for planning the operation of service function. The personnel turnover rate is an important factor in planning recruiting, selection, and training programmes. For example, a company with a turnover rate of 25 per cent is replacing its marketing force every four years. It must organise its service functions to handle an annual volume of new recruits equivalent to one-fourth of its marketing force. The costs and extent of the recruitment selection and training programmes largely depend upon the magnitude of turnover.

The personnel turnover rate should be analysed periodically to determine the causes. Analysis often uncovers areas where improvement is needed. A useful information source is a terminal interview between the departing marketing-person and either a line executive or a personnel consultant. This exit interview provides the marketing executive with an opportunity to identify conditions contributing to personnel turnover. Identification enables management to modify or correct conditions that lie within its control.

Causes of personnel turnover can be separated into two main groupings, as shown in Table-1. Management should take appropriate corrective action when the causes are largely concentrated on the controllable list, particularly when turnover is caused by reasons 1 through 7. Turnover resulting from reason 8 sometimes is unavoidable, and that resulting from 9 and 10 is usually desirable. Managerial action may be called for, even in the cases of some reasons appearing on the 'non-controllable' list, in fact, only reasons 2, 3 and 6 may be regarded as completely unavoidable.

Table-1

Causes to Turnover of Marketing Personnel

Caused by Action Controllable by Company	Caused by Actions Not Controllable by Company
(1) Poor recruiting	(1) Retirement
(2) Improper relation and assignment	(2) Death
(3) Training deficiencies	(3) Illness or physical disability
(4) Inadequate supervision and motivation	(4) Personal and marital difficulties
(5) Breakdown in communications	(5) Dislike for the job – travel, type or work, working conditions, etc.
(6) Unsatisfactory performance customer complaints, etc.	(6) Military duty
(7) Discharged for cause, e.g., alcoholism, conviction of a felony, dishonesty, etc.	(7) Better position elsewhere
(8) Cutback in personnel	
(9) Transfer to another department	
(10) Promotion to a higher position	

Marketing Executive as Leader

Competent marketing executives are leaders, rather than drivers, of people. They earn and retain the voluntary cooperation of their followers, inspiring them to strive willingly toward mutual goals. They coordinate their follower's activities so that efficiency of the group is maintained at a high level; they find ways to overcome difficulties in the application of marketing plans and policies; and the devise methods for dealing with other problems. Development of leadership ability is a matter of great importance.

Contrary to popular belief, leadership ability can be developed. Although some executives may be 'born leaders,' most acquire leadership ability through education, training and experience. It is not possible, of course, for everyone to become a leader; not everyone possesses, or can acquire, the necessary qualifications. As to the exact nature of these qualifications, management writers are divided. Several have constructed lists of leadership traits. Among the items included in such lists are:

(1) The true leader possesses a high degree of self-control and has stable emotions. An executive, who is moody and inconsistent misleads subordinates. If they are unable to judge their superior's reactions, they cease to function as a team.

(2) A leader has a through understanding of how people think and react. By absorbing many points of view-those of superiors, associates, subordinates, competitors, and others—a leader can anticipate their reaction to particular situations.

(3) A leader is decisive—both willing and able to make decisions. The poor administrator makes decisions by default, delaying and hoping that someone else will bring for the solution or that the problem will solve itself. The effective leader decides and then acts. Because the decision is reached after a careful review of the facts, the leader acts with confidence.

(4) The leader readily accepts responsibility. Although the capable executive delegates authority to subordinates according to their abilities, he or she willingly accepts final responsibility for their actions and never shirks responsibilities.

(5) The leader's mental ability is superior to the majority of the followers yet the

leader is not surrounded exclusively with less able people. The leader secures capable subordinates to whom authority can be delegated, and develops the most capable of these as possible successors.

(6) The leader is technically competent, skilled in the discharge of particular administrative tasks. The leader also has some competence in tasks assigned to subordinates; this is a prerequisite to effective training and supervision.

(7) The leader possesses the ability to communicate ideas and thoughts clearly. Subordinates carry out the programme more fully because they understand what is expected. Top management regards the leader more highly because the leader succeeds in communicating plan and needs effectively.

(8) The leader has the ability to teach and to motivate other. The good leader knows people's motivations, desires, and ambitions, and used this knowledge to lead them into the necessary activity—whether it is learning or performing.

(9) The leader enjoys above-average health and energy, and sets the pace for the followers, and physical stamina enables the leader to do his or her own job alertly and enthusiastically.

Beyond possessing leadership traits, the executive leader must use tested management procedures. First, as many problems as possible should be made subjects of group-thinking. People cooperate more willingly in carrying out policies they have helped to make. Subordinates should feel that some plans are their plans, not directives imposed from above; but this does not mean that the administrator should abdicate executive responsibilities. The final decision is still the executive's. After problems have been discussed with subordinates, it is up to the executives to face the issues and decide.

Second, a leader is courteous to subordinates. Courtesy goes beyond mere politeness; it reflects sincere consideration for the ideas and feelings of others, politeness is an outward manifestation of good manners. Courtesy and consideration arise from a genuine interest in others. Subordinates are quick to recognise the difference.

Third, a leader gives credit where it is due. When a subordinate's idea proves successful, recognition should be given. Some executives are too easily tempted to accept credit for subordinates' ideas in order to build personal prestige. In the long run, this discourages the submission of ideas and destroys the executive's effectiveness.

Finally, the leader sets a good example. The 'do as I say, not as I do' approach is not effective in motivating people. The executive works with the same diligence he or she expects of the staff, and the executive leads his or her life as he or she expects them to lead theirs. It is natural for subordinates to emulate the superior. The superior is, or should be, a symbol of success.

Unionisation of Marketing Personnel

The marketing-person has been the target of organising drives by various unions since the Great Depression of the 1930s. Despite such efforts, unions have made only slight inroads in organising marketing personnel as compared with their success elsewhere. There are several reasons. First, in most marketing departments it is difficult to develop strong group identification because each person works alone and sees his or her peers on the marketing force only infrequently. Little opportunity exists for mutual exchange of grievances, and organising is difficult because marketing-people are generally isolated from one another. Second, in contrast to most employee groups, marketing-persons usually think of themselves as independent operators rather than as cogs in large industrial machir.e. Third, managements' working-hour problem is less significant with marketing personnel than with other workers, because most people on the marketing force have some control over their workday and work week. If they work excessive hours, it is often to add to their compensation; but they may occasionally take an afternoon off or start a working day later than usual. There are no time clocks to provide checks on their actions. And finally, higher wages have never served as a string organising incentive for marketing personnel. Rightly or wrongly, marketing personnel have been made to fell that low earnings are the results of personnel ineffectiveness, not of the employer's niggardliness.

It is estimated that only one of ten marketing-persons belongs to a union. When unionisation has occurred, it has usually been because of management failure. Some grievances of marketing personnel are: too many reports, competition of house accounts, inadequate expense allowances, unequal territories, too many people on the marketing force (which results in inadequate territories), and too many non-marketing duties.

Unionisation has made the most headway in industries where marketing-people are paid largely on a straight-salary basis, where they work together on the same premises (retail marketing), and where the marketing job is combined with that of delivery, as in the distribution of beer and soft drink. Unions have made little progress in organising marketing-people who sell directly to industrial users or those who make calls on middlemen. Marketing personnel in these classifications, generally paid in whole or in part on the basis of productivity, almost all oppose union affiliation.

Many marketing executives oppose unionisation of their marketing forces. Their opposition is based chiefly upon the effect that unionisation may have on the control of individual marketing-persons and upon the limitations that union contracts place on aggressive management. Managerial action in important areas be circumscribed by rules laid down in the collective-bargaining agreement, and uses of incentive system of compensation are restricted. Commonly, unions object of marketing contests and other devices for motivating the marketing force; sometimes they insist that all additions to the marketing force be recruited through the union; they discourage the use of quotas and other standard of performance; and a strict systems of seniority is almost always among their demands. Furthermore, marketing executives generally maintain that the organisational structure of existing unions does not harmonise well with the demands of the marketing job, since marketing and marketing management require more flexibility than running a plant or an office. They argue that in the nature of things all marketing-people are called upon at times of extra effort, this being the price a marketing-person pays for comparative freedom from day-to-day supervision.

Federal law prohibits marketing executives from active discouragement of unionisation, and it is wise to take a positive approach. Progressive marketing management has come more and more to recognise that the interests of the marketing force are usually not in conflict with those of the company. Normally, marketing personnel are reasonable people, and usually they regard themselves as members of the management team. The wise marketing executive utilises every opportunity to hammer home the mutuality of interests.

Marketing Manager's Creed

Sales and Marketing Executive—International (SME-I), a professional association with members throughout the world, has long concerned itself with the improvement of relations among marketing personnel and marketing executives. In an effort to apply its members' knowledge of special employee conditions affecting the marketing-person's job to the general problem of employer-employee relations, SME-I has published, and revised from time to time, a code of ethical conduct known as the Marketing Manager's Creed. The most recent revision is reproduced in Table-2. Although not every marketing executive subscribes fully to this creed, all are well advised to study its provision—most are directly or indirectly traceable to company practices and policies that have been frequent causes of unrest among marketing personnel.

Table-2

A Creed

I Subscribe to the Marketing Manager's Creed, Prepared by Marketing and Marketing Executives-International, which I Believe to be in the Best Interests of Business

All marketing-men shall receive fair compensation during their initial or subsequent training periods.	Marketing-men's expense reimbursement policies shall be uniform, after taking all variations of condition into consideration.
While recognising changes in compensation or territory to be functions of marketing management, marketing-men shall be consulted prior to establishing such changes and given reasonable notice of the effective date.	A sharp distinction shall be drawn between salesmen's earnings and expense allowance, and any systems that affords salesmen either a substantial profit or loss on expense accounts shall be corrected.
Earnings of commission or bonus of marketing-men shall be unlimited, unless otherwise specified at the time of their employment. Should basic changes in a business justify modifying this policy, all marketing-men affected shall be advised of the fact a reasonable time prior to establishing such ceilings as become necessary.	Marketing-men shall be given either a contract, agreement, or letter covering those conditions of his employment which might otherwise be the basis of later misunderstandings.
When evaluating the ability of marketing-men, conditions beyond their control, such as differences in the marketing potentials of their territories, shall be given full consideration.	If quotas are used– (a) marketing-men should know how their figures have been determined, and (b) the quotas shall be based on reliable seasonal personal evaluation of accurate and adequate criteria.

Marketing-men shall be offered the same vacation, job or income security, and other employee benefits as are enjoyed by other employees in comparable positions in the same company.

A marketing-men whose health or well-being gives evidence of being prejudiced by the nervous tensions involved in his work, shall be given such relief as may be possible.

The only 'house' or 'no commission' accounts shall be those clearly defined in advance of solicitation.

Pressure to achieve results shall be of a constructive nature, avoiding the use of 'fear' psychology or threatened loss of employment.

The paper work required of marketing-men shall be held down to a minimum and its value clearly justified.

No matter where a marketing-men may be located, he shall be provided with a simple means of stating his grievances, which shall be promptly considered and answered.

Copyrighted by Sales and marketing Executives-International, New York.

Contracts with Marketing Personnel

A marketing employment contract is a formally executed agreement between the employer and the individual marketing-person, outlining condition of employment. Citing the possible avoidance of later misunderstanding as the justification, the Marketing Manager's Creed suggests the use of written agreements ('contract, agreement, or letter') covering employment conditions. Proponents of marketing-person's contracts argue also that some measure of legal protection is provided both parties—the marketing personnel against arbitrary company action, such as cuts in commission rates, and the company against unauthorised action by the marketing-person, such as marketing outside the assigned territory. Table–3 shows a marketing-person's contract of the sort used by insurance companies for their 'agents' (that is, independent marketing-persons) and by some firms manufacturing products sold on a straight-commission basis. The most extensive of contracts is by made companies marketing such 'products' as insurance, securities, other intangibles, and real estate—in all of which marketing compensation is primarily by commission. Some use of contracts is made by firms in other fields where marketing-people are paid wholly or mostly by commission. Otherwise, contracts are little used, the main reason being that

Table–3

Contract Form for Agents Used by the Travellers Insurance Company and the Travellers Indemnity Company

THE TRAVELLERS INSURANCE COMPANY

THE TRAVELLERS INSURANCE COMPANY

of Hartford, Connecticut, hereinafter called the Company, and

----

----

of ____________________________ **hereinafter called the Agent, pursuant to request that the underwriting facilities and other services of the Company be made available to the undersigns as Agent and for the considerations hereinafter expressed, agree together as follows:**

1. This contract shall become effective on the .... day of .... 200.

2. The Agent has full power and authority to solicit applications or proposals for insurance, and to bind the Company and issue policies, for such classes of risks as the Company from time to time may authorised to countersign policies of insurance, renewal receipts, certificates, and endorsements pertaining it such classes of risks; and to collect, receive, and receipt for premiums on such insurance, except for premiums which the company bills directly.

The Agent shall promptly forward applications, proposals or daily reports to the Company's Office at ____

The Agent shall promptly pay over premiums to the Company's Office at ____

3. Commission shall be payable in accordance with the commission schedule adopted by the Company and supplied to the Agent. On business for which premium are collected by the Agent, commissions may be retained by the Agent out of premiums collected, as full compensation for such business. The Company at any time, by written notice to the Agent, may change the commission schedule as to premiums due on and after the date specified in the notice, provided such notice shall be given 60 days in advance of the effective date whenever a material change in commission is involved.

4. It is a condition of this contract that the Agent shall refund ratably to the Company, on business heretofore of hereafter written, commissions on cancelled insurance and on reductions in premiums at the same rate at which such commissions were paid to the Agent.

5. If the Agent notifies the Company within his customary accounting period that an additional premium is uncollectible which was developed by audit or report or values on any account where coverage is no longer in force and the Agent has exhausted his normal collection efforts, the Agent shall be relieved of the responsibility for collection and shall have no commission interest in such premium. This provision shall also apply to uncollectible anniversary premiums on court, probate, licence, permit and other miscellaneous surety bonds.

6. Except as specifically authorised by the Company, the Agent has no authority to make, alter, vary, or discharge any policy contract. To extend the time for payment of premiums, to waive of extend any policy obligation or condition, to incur any liability on behalf of the Company, or to insert any advertisement respecting the Company in any publication.

7. The Company shall not be responsible for agency expenses such as rentals, transportation facilities, clerical help, solicitors' fees, postage, advertising, exchange, personal licence fees, or any other agency expenses whatsoever.

8. The Agent shall be responsible for all risks placed in the books of the Company through his agency by any sub-agents or brokers together with all premiums or moneys collected by them in connection with such risks the same as if they had been produced directly by the Agent.

9. Any Company supplies furnished to the Agent by the Company shall always remain the property of the Company and shall be returned to the Company or its representatives promptly upon demand.

10. The Company shall indemnify and hold the Agent harmless from and against all sums, including costs and expenses of suit defense and settlements, which the Agent shall become legally obligated to pay by reason of liability imposed on him by law for damages sustained by policyholders, caused solely and directly by error or omission of the Company in the preparation and handling of policies, including timely premium notice.

11. All moneys collected or received by the Agent for or on behalf of the Company

shall be held in a fiduciary capacity and shall not be used by the Agent for any purpose whatsoever except as specifically authorised by the Company and shall be paid over to the Company in accordance with the terms of this contract.

12. This contract cancels all previous contracts or agreements whether oral or written between any of The Travellers Companies and the Agent covering the classes of risks referred to herein, This contract may be terminated by either party at any time upon written notice to the other, provided any such notice by the Company shall be given 60 days in advance of the effective date if the Agent has paid all balances due the Company in accordance with the Company's customary arrangements with the Agent.

13. In the event of termination of this contract:

(a) The Agent's records, use and control of expirations, including direct billed business, shall remain his property and be left in his absolute possession.

(b) The Company shall furnish the Agent upon request a record of direct billed policyholders, expiration dates and details of the coverage provided, including the latest rating information recorded.

(c) Paragraphs 3 and 4 of this agreement shall continue to apply to additional or return premiums on policies written prior to the date of termination but expiring subsequent thereto.

The provisions of this paragraph shall apply so long as premiums are remitted in accordance with the Company's customary arrangements with the Agent. If at the time of termination the Agent has failed to pay balances due the Company, this paragraph shall apply only if the Agent shall thereafter pay all collected premiums to the Company immediately.

IN WITNESS WHEREOF, the Company has caused this contract to be signed at the Home office and the Agent has subscribed his name here to this__________day of______200__

Sd/-
President

____

____

Agent

Second Vice-President Casually property Dept.

________ Sd/- ________

Authorised Signature

many marketing executives look upon written job descriptions (covering job objectives, duties and responsibilities, etc.) as a more effective means of avoiding later misunderstandings. Furthermore, unlike contracts, the written job description can be altered without necessarily obtaining the marketing-person's consent.

Several other reasons can be cited for nonuse of contracts. One is that many employers consider them unenforceable, since it is often impractical, unwise, or both, to take marketing personnel into court for nonperformance. When court action is taken and the judgement is favourable to the company, it may be difficult, often impossible, to collect it; yet the company is tied to the contract terms when the marketing-person sues. It is seldom possible to foresee all contingencies at the time the contract is drafted, and changes in conditions may make certain stipulations unworkable. Still another reason for nonuse is that, since contracts generally set forth specific grounds on which marketing-persons can be discharged, the release of incompetents may be made more difficult. Although these problems do not destroy entirely the envisioned purpose of the marketing contract, they do point up the importance of careful preparation and use. If the main role of the marketing contract is that of reducing the seriousness of later misunderstandings on employment terms, its provisions must anticipate matters about which misunderstandings are most likely to arise, and on which it is especially critical to have a clear meeting of minds. The more common matters of this type are: work assignments, working hours, compensation arrangements, and requirements concerning reports and other written records.

Recruiting Marketing Personnel

A prime concern of the marketing manager is to field sufficient marketing-people to service the needs of prospective customers for the company's products. Ultimately, marketing managers must concern themselves with achieving efficient marketing-performance, but they must first find the potential performers. The effectiveness of marketing performance depends both upon the caliber and the number of marketing people at the disposal of marketing management. Spatial problems make the task recruiting and selecting marketing-people more difficult than for other employees. Since a marketing force works over broad geographic areas rather than in restricted plant locations, it is often necessary to recruit marketing personnel in the markets they are to serve, a factor that makes the recruiter's task much more difficult.

From management's standpoint, there are four important steps in recruiting and selecting a marketing force. Step one is, to determine marketing personnel needs, and this requires job analysis and the establishment of job specifications. Step two is, to identify the sources from which marketing-people with good potential might be obtained. Step three is to locate and recruit prospective marketing-people from the identified sources. Step four is to select from among these prospects the ones who have the highest probability of success.

Organisation for Recruiting and Selection

Responsibility for recruitment and selection of marketing personnel is assigned to the marketing manager in some organisations, the personnel manager in others, and to the two executives jointly in still others. There is no one best place for assignment of this responsibility. Company size, executives' personalities, and departmental organisation all affect this decision. Where the marketing manager has a personnel staff assistant, recruiting and selection of a marketing staff usually is handled entirely within the department. In companies with small marketing forces, it sometimes is desirable to have these functions under the control of the personnel manager, but this is unusual. It is more common for the personnel department to handle recruiting and preliminary screening and for the marketing department to make final selections. In all companies, whatever the formal organisation, considerable exchange of information and cancellation takes place between the two departments.

Location of responsibility for recruitment and selection of marketing personnel in concerns with regional marketing offices is another organisational factor that varies from one company to another. These functions tend to be centralised at the home office when the firm requires high calibre marketing personnel. Other factors, for example, size of regional organisations and location of training programmes, make it difficult to draw further generalisations. However, decentralised recruitment and selection generally result in reduced interviewing and time and facilitates the hiring of local applications for marketing work.

Need for the Proper Setting

For recruiting and selection programmes to succeed, they must be installed in a favourable setting. Market exploration must have been carried to the point where management knows: the size of the potential business, identities and locations of customers and prospects, which individuals in customers' organisations influence buying decision, and the best methods for reaching them. Product used and applications must have been identified and the different marketing appeals evaluated as to relative effectiveness. With this foundation of market and product knowledge, management is prepared to determine its marketing-personnel requirements, draft appropriate recruiting and selection programmes, and install them in an environment conducive to success.

Marketing Job Analysis

No matter what position, a company is seeking to fill-marketing-person, file clerk, executive, factory hand, plant guard, or other-the-task is approached, consciously or not, with some preliminary analysis of the job. Even though management may not have recognised this need for job analysis to the extent of marking a formal evaluation, it recognises instinctively the desire to fit the individual to the job. In companies where this need has been recognised, formal system of job analysis have developed. Experience indicates that the formal, systematic approach to job analysis results in a much higher proportion of people being placed in the right job.

Analysing a marketing job is basically a matter of developing the information needed for a job description. It involves asking question to determine the job's objectives and to uncover what the marketing-person does or should do in pursuit of them. The first question, for example, should be. What the purposes of this job? What is the title of the job–marketing-person, marketing representative, marketing counsellor, or what? These questions might be followed by: To whom does this person report? What products does this individual sell? To whom does this person sell? What information should this person gather, and what reports should this person make? The answers might elicit details concerning special skills required, planning responsibilities, relations with customers, service duties, and the like. Such question asking, together with formal arrangement and systematic grouping of the answers, provides the means of analysis and results in a marketing job description. Outlined below is a suggested nine-step procedure for marketing job analysis:

(1) Prepare a questionnaire for marketing personnel, asking them to list the main

objectives of their job, together with the major functions and sub functions performed in doing the job effectively.

(2) Prior to receipt of the completed questionnaires, have all executives interested in marketing activities write down their conceptions of the marketing-person's job objectives and the functions they feel should and should not be performed in achieving them.

(3) Survey customers to find out, what they believe should and should not be the functions of a company marketing-person.

(4) Tabulate the information received.

(5) Reconcile differences revealed by the three viewpoints, write a concise statement of job objectives, and prepare a detailed list of activities that marketing personnel are to perform.

(6) Classify the activities into major functional groups, such as marketing, service, territory management, marketing promotion, executive, and goodwill duties.

(7) Determine, what a marketing-person needs to know, the qualifications necessary to perform designated activities, and the reasons that necessitate performance of each activity assemble this information into a written job description.

(8) Submit the written job description to marketing-persons for discussion and recommendations, and make alternations as required.

(9) Periodically revise the job description, following the preceding eight steps, when changes in products, competition, the economic climate, or customers' demands require a review of job objectives and the activities involved in reaching them.

An alternative approach to marketing job analysis to use checklist itemising the functions and sub-functions generally accepted as comprising the marketing-person's job. One such checklist, organically developed for the U.S. Small Business. Administration is shown in Table-4. The checklist approach is less reliable than the suggested nine-step procedure, as it fails to provide for definition of job objectives; does not focus on the viewpoints of marketing personnel, executives, or customers; and does not require 'reasons' in support of activities eventually written into the job description. However, this approach can be helpful in preparing tentative descriptions of a new marketing job when the time factor is important.

Job Specifications

The duties and responsibilities set forth in the job description should be converted into a set of qualifications that a person should possess in order to perform the job satisfactorily. This set of qualification is called the 'job specification.' If the job description states, for example, that the marketing-person is to train dealers' marketing personnel, then the marketing-person must be qualified to conduct such training. What will the marketing-person have to know about the products and the dealers; customers? About the dealers' operating methods and problems? About training methods? Will this duty require the marketing-person to have a certain amount and kind of experience? Similar sets of questions must be answered with respect to each of duties and responsibilities contained in the job description.

Table–4

Checklist for Use in Analysing Marketing Jobs and Compiling Job Descriptions

Outline for Compiling a Marketing Job Description
Sales:
Make regular calls
Sell the line; demonstrate.
Handle questions and objections.
Check stock; discover possible product uses.
Interpret marketing points of the line to customer.
Estimate customer's potential needs.
Emphasise quality.
Explain company policy on price, delivery, and credit.
Get the order
Service:
Install the product or display.
Report product weaknesses, complaints.
Handle adjustments, returns, and allowances.

Contd. . .

Handle requests for credit.

Handle special orders.

Establish priorities, if any.

Analyse local conditions for customers.

Territory Management:

Arrange route for best coverage.

Balance effort with customer against the potential volume.

Maintain marketing portfolios, samples, kits, etc.

Marketing Promotion:

Develop new prospects and accounts.

Distribute home office literature, catalogues, etc.

Make calls with customer's marketing-people.

Train personnel of wholesalers, jobbers, etc.

Present survey reports, layouts, and proposals.

Executive:

Each night make a daily work plan for the next day.

Organise field activity for minimum travel and maximum calls.

Prepare and submit special reports on trends, competition.

Prepare and submit statistical data requested by home office.

Investigate lost marketing and reason for loss.

Prepare reports on developments, trends, new objectives met, and new ideas on meeting objections.

Attend marketing meetings.

Build a prospect list.

Collect overdue accounts; report on faulty accounts.

Collect credit information.

Goodwill:

Counsel customers on their problems.

Maintain loyalty and respect for the company.

Attend local marketing meetings held by customers.

There are, of course, differences among the qualifications that a new addition to the marketing force may be expected to bring to the job, those that an individual may acquire through training, and those that a person will gain through field marketing experience. It is marketing management's responsibility to decide which qualifications all new recruits should possess, and which should be provided through training. A company specifying somewhat higher entrance qualifications than another can expect, other things being equal, that its training programme will have to accomplish less. But the first company is likely to encounter greater difficulty in finding as many possible recruits as the second company, with its lower entrance qualifications. A trade-off must be made between (1) recruiting persons with many qualifications, which reduces the need for training; and (2) recruiting persons with few qualifications, which increases the need for training.

Marketing job specifications should set forth the personality characteristics required. These the marketing-person must bring to the job, since marketing, training programmes are seldom effective instruments for personality development. All marketing personnel should have certain traits: empathy and the ability to get along well with other; integrity and character; and maturity, in terms of a sensible self-perspective. Motivation is especially important-some marketing jobs require their holders to be routine order takers only, but others serve as proving grounds for future managers. There is a kind of optimum level of motivation for each job. If new marketing-persons are too strongly motivated, they may not be content for long with a routine job or one lacking in advancement opportunities.

Job specifications may stipulate minimum requirements with respect to education and product or technical knowledge, but *legally so only if* the company can prove that such requirements are significantly related to successful job performance. The importance of such requirements, as one would expect, varies widely. Some marketing jobs demand the detailed and highly technical training offered only by colleges of engineering; others require only average ability to read, write, and do simple arithmetic; and there are all gradations in between. Graduation from an educational institution is tangible evidence that the job candidate has a certain level of ability. If a specified amount of formal education is set as an absolute minimum requirement, however, a risk is taken that some otherwise highly qualified applications will be eliminated from consideration. In addition, setting a specified amount of formal education as an absolute minimum requirement is dangerous on legal grounds – EEOC guidelines, for instance, specify that the employer must prove that this requirement is significantly related to successful job performance and does not result in discrimination on the basis of race, colour, religion, sex, or national origin.

Flexibility in defining standards of age and physical appearance is usually desirable. A company that is putting new recruits through a long period of marketing training and internship may well want to recruit younger persons than a company with only a brief training period. Except for this consideration, however, age should be a selection factor only to the extent that it helps or handicaps marketing-persons in their work. The same applies to physical appearance. Short, fat, or ugly marketing-persons may be handicapped in some marketing situations, but they may have an advantage in situation where their appearance increase customer empathy.

Job specifications sometimes provide recruiters with an important device for the conservation of time and energy—the set of minimum requirements or standards to use in weeding out obviously unqualified applicants. This usually takes the form of a list of negative factors, the presence of any of which automatically disqualifies as applicant. Factors such as the following often were included in these lists prior to the passage of the Civil Rights Act of 1964: inability to express one's thoughts clearly; unusually poor language usage; sloppy or dirty clothing or grooming job-hopping-more than a given number of previous jobs, or too frequent job changes, acne or other skin disease, or unusually unattractive teeth. Such a set of minimum requirements, or preliminary screenings standards, should be prepared only after a company analyses its dismissals and should reflect the main reasons why a company's marketing personnel fail. Since 1964, companies have become increasingly careful in setting such minimum requirements or standards because they now must be prepared to prove that each is significantly related to successful job performance and does not result in discrimination on the basis of race, colour, religion, sex, or national origin.

Analysis of the qualifications of a company's marketing personnel helps recruiters determine what they should look for in job applicants and assists in planning the marketing training programme. Guidance to recruiters is provided by studying the qualifications, which the company's successful marketing personnel had when hired, for instance, education, material status, previous experience, and size of savings. Guidance in planning marketing training is furnished by answering such question as: How specialised are the marketing people? How long does it take to become familiar with the line? What were these people doing immediately before they came to the company? After analysing company marketing-person's backgrounds, one marketing manager concluded that:

(1) Marketing personnel who preciously sold competing or related lines learned more rapidly, but not significantly so.

(2) The average marketing-person knew the product line sufficiently well to sell productively in four weeks time.

(3) The new marketing-person's awareness of specialised problem with respect to the product line equaled that of any veteran marketing-person within four months' time.

(4) All successful marketing personnel had previous marketing experience, although the range varied from house-to-house to industrial marketing. This indicated that the ability to sell was transferable to the company's products.

Because no two companies have exactly the same situations, each must construct its own specifications. Questionnaires are helpful in obtaining the necessary information. Marketing-persons, supervisors, and others of the marketing staff can be asked to express their opinions of the qualifications for success. Customers, as well as others, can provide similar information. From the returns of wisely designed questionnaires it should be possible to write a description of physical, mental, and skill requirements.

Source of Marketing Force Recruits

Thus, far we have examined certain factors that marketing management should consider in determining personnel requirements—job analysis comes first and results in job descriptions from which are derived job specifications. These are necessary preliminaries to the next step—the identification of sources of promising recruits.

Recruiting-Source Identification

One approach to the identification of the best source of recruits is to analyse those used in the past. Each source is analysed to determine the total number of recruits produced, and 'successes' and 'failures.' Each source, in other words, is analysed quantitatively and qualitatively. One source may have provided numerous recruits but few successes; a second fewer recruits but a high proportion of successes. Consider the analysis given in Table-5 of 80 marketing-people recruited by one company over a period of five years.

Table-5

Source Analysis of Marketing Personnel Recruited by Electrical-Products Manufacturer

Source	Number of Recruits	Percentage of Total	Number of Successes	Ratio of Successes to Total
Recommendations by own marketing-people	22	27.50	10	0.455
Educational institutions	14	17.50	10	0.715
Marketing personnel for noncompeting firms	12	15.00	2	0.167
Employment agencies	10	12.50	3	0.300
Personnel acquaintances of executives	8	10.00	5	0.625
Customers' employees	6	7.50	1	0.167
Unsolicited applications	5	6.25	2	0.400
Competitors' marketing-people	3	3.75	3	20.670
	80	100.00	35	
Ratio of success of total from all sources				0.437

In the table, the source accounting for the largest number of recruits showed a success ratio only slightly more favourable than the ratio for all source—but is did account for ten of the 35 successes recruited and, for this reason, management might want to continue using it. Three sources had higher-than-average success ratios, and management should explore ways of increasing the number of recruits from them. Three other sources had very low success ratios, and management should use them sparingly in the future. A word of caution: These results indicate the experience of only company, and should not be considered typically of industry in general. Furthermore, the definition of 'success' adopted by a particular management affects this sort of analysis. In the example given, success was defined as "demonstrated ability to meet or exceed quotas in two years out of three." Other managements might well define success differently.

Another word of caution with regard to data of the above type: Its reliability depends upon the size of the group evaluated. More reliable conclusion could be drawn on the worth of a source producing 22 recruits than one producing only three recruits. However, even if, only a small number of cases is available, the data may still serve as a helpful, although necessarily less reliable, guide in identifying promising sources of new marketing-people.

Some frequently used sources of recruits are discussed below. The intent is to describe general source characteristics and to point up significant advantages, disadvantage, and other pertinent information concerning each source.

Source within the Company

Company Marketing Personnel

Individual apply for specific marketing jobs because they know company marketing personnel; and marketing-people's recommendations may constitute an excellent source. Often such applicants already know something about the job and about company policies; and the fact that they apply is an indication of favourable disposition toward the company. Marketing-people fairly typically have wide circles of acquaintances, since both on and off the job they continually meet new people and generally have many friends with similar interests. It is natural, then, that many of their contacts have good potential as marketing personnel – indeed, many now well for other firm. However, some marketing-people are not discriminating in their recommendations, and for this reason such recommendations need careful appraisal. One special recruiting situation in which marketing-people are a particularly useful source of recommendations is when jobs must be filled in remote territories; then marketing personnel in the same or adjacent areas may now considerably more about unique territorial requirements and local sources of personnel than home-office executives.

Company Executives

Recommendations of the marketing manager, the president, and other company executives are another internal source of recruits. Marketing executives' personal contacts may yield top-calibre people because of their own involvement with the marketing field and understanding of the needed qualifications. Other executives' recommendations, by way of contrast, more often are based mainly upon personnel friendships and tend to represent less objective appraisals. Experience is almost the only way to evaluate each executive's worth as a source of new recruits, and the type of analysis shown in Table-5 adapts easily to this purpose.

Internal Transfers

Two additional sources of personnel from within the company are other departments and the non-marketing section of the marketing department. Employees desiring transfer are already familiar with company policies, and the personnel department should have considerable detailed information about them. One factor that limits the recruitment of transfers is that the company usually knows little about their aptitude for marketing work; an offsetting factor is that they often possess excellent product knowledge. Aptitude for marketing, of course, can be tested formally or by 'trial' assignment to the field. Transfers are especially good prospects for marketing positions whenever product knowledge makes up a substantial portion of marketing training, since their background makes it possible to accelerate field assignments.

Sources Outside the Company

Educational Institutions

The source includes colleges and universities, business college, high schools, and night schools. It is reasonable to expect that graduates have attained certain minimum educational levels, the amount depending upon the school. Moreover, many have had training in general business, marketing, and marketing techniques. Schools are a particularly fruitful source of new marketing personnel at graduation time, and some maintain year-round placement services for graduates seeking job changes. Most recent graduates represent net addition to the labour market and, consequently, need not be attracted away from other jobs.

Colleges and universities have become increasingly important sources of marketing and management trainees, and competition is keen for their graduates. Often the graduating senior is in a position to choose from among several attractive job offers. Companies not maintaining close relations with the colleges are at a disadvantage, frequently being unable to obtain appointments on overcrowded campus recruiting schedules, and finding it difficult to attract students away from companies better known to the college. Even better-known companies face stiff competition with each other in hiring the cream of the graduates. A few companies offer marketing-training programmes to outstanding juniors during vacations periods. Thus, the trainee and the company have an opportunity to evaluate each other, and trainees who prove satisfactory are offered jobs upon graduating.

Competitors' Organisations

Marketing personnel recruited from competitors' organisation generally require minimal training because of experience in marketing similar products to similar markets. But this is often a costly source, because a premium must be paid to persuade marketing-persons to regions their present jobs. Some marketing manages are reluctant to hire competitor's ex- marketing-persons because they suspect their loyalty. An individual hired away from one organisation for higher pay may be similar tempted at a future time. An important question to answer is: Why is this person leaving his or her present positions? When the new job does not improve or status for the applicant, his or her desire to change may result from personality conflicts, or instability. Dissatisfaction with the present job is not necessarily the fault of the marketing-person. If good reasons exist for making the change, it may be possible to obtain in first-class person who is ready at once for productive work.

Marketing-people for Noncompeting Companies

Marketing-people working for firms in related and non-related industries constitute a source of recruits. Such recruits may not be fully acquainted with the product line, but they do have marketing-experience. This source provides a channel of advancement for marketing-people in 'dead-end' jobs to those seeking to upgrade their employment.

Marketing-people Making Calls on the Company

The purchasing agent is in daily contact with marketing personnel from other companies and is in a strategic position to evaluate their on-the-job performances. It is not unusual for the purchasing agent to meet high-calibre marketing-people for whom jobs with the company would be attractive financially or in other respects. The purchasing agent should be encouraged to make the appropriate recommendations.

Employees of Customers

Some companies regard their customers as a recruiting source. Customers are asked to recommend able persons in their own organisations who have reached the maximum potential of their existing jobs. Such transfers may have a favourable effect upon morale in customer's organisation. However, since customer good will is of prime importance, a customer's marketing-people should normally the recruited only with the prior approval and recommendation of the customer.

Marketing Executives' Clubs

Many marketing executives' club operate placement services. Marketing-person's seeking new positions submit personal data sheets that are duplicated and forwarded to members. At regular club meetings, the marketing executive has additional opportunity for informal discussion and exchanges of placement information.

Employment Agencies

Many marketing managers traditionally have regarded employment agencies as unpromising sources of recruits. Many use agencies only after other sources are exhausted. Many believe, usually with little evidence, that 'good' marketing-people neither need nor will use an agency's services. Experience, unfortunately, tends to reinforce such attitudes, because too often agency referrals fail to meet marketing job specifications. Sometimes this traceable to agency deficiencies (such as the overzealous desire to receive placement fees); but at least as often the fault is that of the prospective employer, who may be using unrealistically high job specifications, may not make the company's requirement clear, and so on. Unquestionably, an employer would be unwise – as well as unjustified – in generalising from unsatisfactory experiences with one or a few agencies, whether they be privately operated or local offices of state employment services. Experiences with individual agencies should be reviewed periodically, using the pattern of analysis illustrated in Table-5.

Whenever an agency is used, it should receive a clear statement of the job's objectives and a complete rundown of job specifications. If possible, the recruiter should meet with the agency counsellor to assure that pertinent information is furnished and fully understood. Also, agencies need time to learn about an employing firm and its unique requirements, thus, considerable gains accrue from continuing relationships with agencies that perform satisfactorily. Agencies have steadily improved and expanded their services (often they administer tests of various sorts, check references, and perform tasks otherwise done, if at all, by the employer). As the nature of these service becomes better understood by marketing executives, this source should grown in importance. One development of interest to marketing executives is the growing number of agencies that take the initiative in searching out promising job candidates, employed or not, instead of confining themselves to 'volunteer' applicants. Unfortunately, most such agencies recruit only executives and are, therefore, of no use as a source of marketing personnel.

Direct Unsolicited Applications

Most companies receive some unsolicited 'walk-in' and 'write-in' applications of marketing positions. Some marketing managers favour immediate hiring of applicants who take the initiative in seeking marketing jobs, the reasoning being that this may indicate marketing aggressiveness. Others reject direct applications automatically because they believe the proportion of qualified applicants from this source is low. Probably the most logical policy is to treat all volunteer applications the same as solicited applications—applicants not meeting minimum requirements as set forth in job specifications should be eliminated at once; those meeting these requirements should be processed together with other applicants. The selection systems, if it works well, should result in hiring the best-qualified applicants regardless of the sources from which they come. It should be noted that direct unsolicited applications cannot to relied upon to provide a steady flow of applicants; the volume fluctuates markedly with changing business conditions.

Older Persons

In the past many companies, as a matter of policy, refrained from actively recruiting individuals over 40 years of age. As noted earlier, the Age discrimination in Employment Act prohibits discrimination in hiring decisions against persons 40 to 65 years of age.

In spite of the fact that discriminations against persons in this age group is outlawed, such individuals frequently have a difficult time obtaining jobs, so companies willing to consider them many select from a group for which there is little competitive bidding Many people in this age group have years of marketing experience and the maturity that is so valuable in most marketing situations. It is important, of course, to ascertain why an apparently good persons is unemployed, but the reasons are often beyond the control of the individual. When older persons are under consideration for marketing jobs, assuming that their qualification compare favourable with job specifications, hiring decisions may hinge upon the length of the training period needed to bring them up to full productivity.

The Recruiting Effort

The marketing-personnel recruiting effort differs in importance from firm to firm, the differences stemming in part from variations in the calibre of person desired. The higher the caliber desired, the more difficult it is to obtain. The caliber desired, of course, is influenced by the nature of the job, complexity of the product line, problems in serving customers, and so forth. If job specification call for a special talent, such as the ability to apply considerable imagination to the solution of customer's problems, then individuals of high calibre are needed. If job specifications require only order-taking ability, as in the case of many beer and soft drink marketing personnel, then persons of lower caliber will suffice. Similarly, a higher calibre is generally indicated for a product that is technical, complex, or that sells at a high unit price.

The importance – and the scope – of the recruiting effort are also influenced by the number of recruits that must be obtained. Recruiting rises in importance with the number of persons needed, and this, in turn, is affected by such factors as forecasted marketing, promotional and marketing strategy, and the marketing-force turnover rate. Normally, a large business with a large marketing volume needs more marketing-people than does a small business. But two firms of comparable size in the same industry may have significantly different-sized marketing forces, often because one uses a different marketing channel or stresses advertising more in its promotional programme. As might be expected, firms with high marketing-force turnover rates must do much more recruiting than those with lower rates.

It is wise to precede actual recruiting with and analysis of methods currently in use, an evaluation similar to that used in identifying sources of promising recruits. Success, failures, and terminations should be analysed to determine if they are related to specific recruiting methods. Such analysis should aid in choosing the most appropriate methods. There are two basic methods of recruiting – personal recruiting and indirect recruiting.

Personal Recruiting

Personal recruiting is chiefly used for recruiting graduates of schools and colleges. Campus interviewing is often planned as a company-wise affair, because this avoids much duplication of effort. Although representatives of different departments do the interviewing, the personnel department plans and coordinates the recruiting drive. In many efforts of this type, an assistant marketing manager shares with the regional or district marketing manager located nearest the campus responsibility for interviewing students. In other cases, home-offices marketing executives rotate campus interviewing responsibilities among themselves; sometimes each returns annually to the same campus, thus building long-term relationships with individual schools.

College recruiting requires planning well in advance of the campus visit. Statement of trainee requirements should be mailed to college placement officers early, preferably no later than January. The list of colleges, based primarily upon past interviewing experience, is updated, and letters are sent out requesting interview dates. The best months for recruiting graduates are February, March, and April; and March in the most demand. If the visit comes too late in the spring, interviews find that many of the best-qualified graduates have already taken jobs. After visiting dates have been confirmed, college are sent letters specifying such details as salary, desired marital status, and starting data of employment. Some recruiters also send copies of promotional materials, company histories, and applications blanks.

College placement officers schedule a 20 to 30 minutes interview for each student. All interested students are granted interviews – few companies prescreen college applicants. Generally, interviews are the only screening devices used. The most promising candidates are invited to company officers for follow-up interviews. However, many campus interviewers have authority to do hiring if it appears that promising candidates will be lost through delay.

Indirect Recruiting

Advertisements in classified and other sections of newspapers and trade journals have long been used for recruiting marketing personnel. Until recently, however, advertisements were considered useful only for hiring low-grade marketing personnel for routine jobs. Even for this grade of personnel, the proportion of qualified to unqualified respondents to a given advertisement was often small; and it was time consuming and costly to screen all applicants. Furthermore, most marketing executives believed that high calibre people would not seek employment offered in such an impersonal way. Nevertheless, a change in thinking has occurred. Today, city newspapers carry many advertisements publicising openings for marketing personnel and even for marketing executives.

So great is the number of prospective job candidates reached by a single advertisement that companies often must take steps to reduce the volume of applications. If the employer is willing to publish details about the company and job, fewer persons who obviously are not qualified will answer the advertisement. Specific details vary with the company and its situation, and should be in the ad if it is to attract good applicants. Some ads mention the salary range of successful company marketing personnel. Other explain that the person selected is to the replace a regular marketing-person in an established territory with active accounts. Still others specify that only professional marketing-people need apply. Information of this sort helps convince promising applicants that the opening represents a legitimate established job.

Most marketing managers favour 'open' over 'blind' advertisements, although mixed practice exists. The company name, especially if well known and respected, should be prominently featured so as to attract the best applicants. Location of the advertisement in the publication is also important. Newspaper advertisements on sports or financial pages are usually more productive but cost more per insertion than those in classified sections. Display ads on a sports page, for example, not only attract unemployed persons looking for work but employed individuals who are not in the job market but who can be attracted by the lure of better jobs.

Sometimes brochures outlining company marketing-career opportunities are distributed to applicants answering advertisements as well as to those contacted by other methods. The most effective brochures are written from the viewpoint of the prospective marketing recruit.

Besides describing the company and its history, they make clear the qualifications required for marketing jobs, and the marketing-person's duties, responsibilities, and advancement opportunities. It is effective to include short, case histories of those who have been successful marketing-people with the company. Many brochures make liberal use of pictures, charts, diagrams, and other visual presentations.

Direct-to-consumer organisations have a particularly difficult time in recruiting marketing personnel. The type of marketing and the uncertainty of earnings result in high turnover rates among these marketing-people. Fortunately, these companies can rely upon recruiting methods that are satisfactory in obtaining the lower-grade marketing-people they require, although almost useless for recruiting high-grade marketing personnel. Their best source of recruits is recommendations from their own marketing-people, and they often offer bonuses for each new person recruited. When time method proves inadequate, direct-mail recruiting is used, the mailing list often consisting of the names of former marketing people the company hopes to re-employ. In addition, 'help wanted' ads are placed in local newspapers or in publications such as Specially marketingman. As a last resort, direct-marketing companies, especially those with field supervisors use cold canvas recruiting in open territories.

The Selection System

Selection systems range form simple one-step systems consisting of nothing more than a single informal personnel interview, to complex multiple-step systems providing many devices and techniques designed to gather information. It is helpful to visualise a selection system as a set of successive 'screens,' at any of which the applicant may be removed from further consideration. Because some screens are more expensive to administer than others, the system should be designed to incorporate the most inexpensive screens early, thus eliminating unpromising candidates with minimum delay, and economising on money and effort invested. Applicants who survive all screenings are offered positions.

No selection system is infallible; all eliminate some who would have succeeded as a marketing-people and recommend hiring some who fail. A selection system fulfils its main mission if it improves management's ability to estimate success-and-failure probabilities of individual applicants. Every company should design its selection system to fit its own requirements. Each step should be included for a purpose, and each should be eliminated when it no longer makes a worth while contribution. The selection system should be well integrated, with each step contributing needed information for hiring decisions.

Pre-interview Screening

Many companies use an initial screening before the first formal interview to eliminate obviously unqualified applicants and save the time of both interviewers and applicants. This screening may be in two steps: (1) providing the applicant with a job profile and basic data on the company, and (2) gaining initial information about the applicant from an interview application form and perhaps a screening test. The interview application obtains information on the job candidate's basic qualifications. Before routine interviewing and testing are begin, predetermined minimum qualifications regarding such factors as educations, health, and experience must be met. The interview application form, which is at most two pages long, is completed in a few minutes. It should not be confused with the longer, more detailed application form used later in the selection system.

The Interview

The interview is the most widely used selection step, and in some companies, it comprises the entire selection system. Some personnel experts criticise the interview as an unreliable selection tool, but it is an effective way to obtain certain needed information. Not other method, for instance, is quite so satisfactory in judging an individual with respect of such matters as ability in oral communication, personal appearance and manners, attitude toward marketing and life in general, reaction to obstacles presented face to face, and personal impact others.

Importance over the years have operated to increase the reliability of interview results. Newer techniques, such as patterned and nondirective interviewing, are being used with apparent success. Many companies now provide training for all executives and staff members who interview, and scientifically designed rating scales and interview record form help interviewers to guide discussions along orderly lines. The net effect is more reliable interview results that yield more easily to analysis.

Because of the time involved, interviewing is costly. Consequently interviewers should avoid covering the same ground as other selection devices. The interviewer should review the completed application form before the interview in order to refrain from asking questions that have already been answered. Perusal of the completed application should indicate areas that require further questioning. Too often the interviewer appends for too much time in telling the applicant about the company and its policies. Although, it is important to sell the individual on the organisation, particularly when there is a scarcity of marketing personnel, there are more efficient ways of accomplishing this. One is by providing the applicant with a brochure relating important facts about the company and asking that it be read before the interview. Another may be used when several applicants are to be interviewed consecutively, as in college recruiting. The interviewer holds meetings preliminarily with the whole group, and describes general company policies. But even after such orientation, it is necessary to answer additional question during individual interviews. Nevertheless, most of the interview should be used for obtaining information about the applicant. A helpful rule is that, during an interview, the interviewer should do a minimum of the talking.

The job interview can be a trying experience for the applicant. Even for experienced marketing-persons accustomed to marketing themselves and their products daily to strangers, the great importance attached to a job change and the unfamiliarity if the situation may cause nervousness. The interviewer should put the applicant at ease. One way to relieve tension is of the interviewer to begin with questions on the person's family and educational background, subjects about which most people talk freely. The interviewer must remember that the applicant is not the only one marketing himself. It is the interviewer task to persuade the potential employee that the firm is a desirable employer. Far too often, the job interview impresses the applicant as an inquisition so that the applicant's nervousness makes the results less reliable. Throughout the interview, pleasant rapport between interviewer and job applicant should be maintained.

How Many Interviews?

A single interview seldom provides sufficient information to evaluate an individual as a potential marketing-person. At the second interview, additional facts secured may cause a revision of the first impression. Many tensions present in the first interview are reduced, since the applicant no longer is a complete stranger in an unfamiliar situation. The applicant's behaviour should be more nearly normal.

Commonly, the first interview is short, perhaps no more than 20 minutes. Questions about the company and the job are answered while the interviewer determines whether the applicant meets minimum qualifications. If this hurdle is passed and the applicant expresses interest, he or she is asked to fill out a detailed application form, and an appointment is made for the second interview.

Who shall Interview?

In filling most marketing jobs, it is advisable to have several persons interview and evaluate all applicants considered worth hiring. In most large companies, first interviews are conducted by personnel department representatives. Next, promising applicants are invited to the home office or, in a decentralised company, to a regional office. These interviews vary in number and kind with the importance of the opening. One large steel company, which needs persons capable of highly specialised marketing to important accounts, brings applications to Pittsburgh for interviews by two assistant marketing managers, and the general marketing manager, and the marketing vice-president. All four executives must approve a decision to hire an applicant. A manufacturer of office machinery and supplied which required marketing personnel for more routine marketing work hires applicants after two interviews, one by a branch marketing manager and one by an assistant branch marketing manager.

Interviewing the Spouse

Because of the necessity for frequent overnight travel, the majority of outside marketing-people are men. Some employers sound out the attitude of the male applicant's wife. If she objects, for instance, to having her husband out of town several days at a stretch, it is unlikely that he can succeed in a job requiring extended travel. This is the main reason that an interview with the wife is often part of the selection system. Frequently, however, the occasion amounts to nothing more than an imprompty dinner with the applicant and wife, during which the wife's' attitudes can be ascertained.

Interviewing Techniques

The informal, unplanned interview has been giving way in many companies to newer techniques, some of are described below:

(1) Patterned Interview: Here the interviewer uses a prepared outline of questions designed to elicit a basic core of information. The interviewer may work directly from the outline, recording answers as they are given; but this tends to make the conversation stilted and the applicant nervous. Greater spontaneity results when the outline is memorised and the answers recorded after the interview. Interviewers should avoid too many questions that can be answered with a simple 'yes' or 'no'. It is better to use more penetrating questions that reveal the attitudes and thinking of the prospective employee.

(2) Nondirective Interview: Some personnel experts say that a nondirective technique yields maximum insight into an individual's attitudes and interests. In this technique the applicant is encouraged to speak freely about his or her experience, training, and future plans. The interviewer asks few direct questions and says only enough to keep the interviewee talking. The nondirective interview does not provide answers to standard questions, and much time is spent on outwardly irrelevant subjects. Expert interpretation, however, reveals, much about the applicant—often including things of which the individual is not consciously aware. This technique's proponents claim that it is the best method for probing an individual's personality in depth. The main drawback to its use is that administering the interview and interpreting the results demand specialised instruction.

(3) Interaction Interview: The interaction interview simulates the stresses the applicant would meet in actual marketing situations and provides the occasion for observing the applicant's reactions to them. This form of interview requires two interviewers. On uses psychological techniques to set up the simulated situations, and the other, who is present but not an active participant in the interview, observes and records the applicant's reactions. Because of their subtlety, the delicacy involved in application, and the need for exert interpretation interviews should be planned, administered, and interpreted by trained psychologists.

(4) Rating Scales: One widely recognised defect of the personal interview is its tendency to lack objectivity, a defect that can be reduced through rating scales. These are so constructed that interviewer's ratings are channelled into a limited choices of responses. In evaluating an applicant's general appearance, for instance, one much-used form forces an interviewer to choose one of five descriptive phrases; very neat, nicely dressed, presentable, untidy, slovenly. Experience indicates that this results in more comparable ratings of the same individual by different interviews. One drawback of the rating scale is that its very objectivity restricts precise description of many personal qualities. It is good practice, therefore, to encourage interviewers to explain ratings in writing whenever they feel comments are needed. Companies using rating scales as a technique for accessing job suitability must keep in mind—in accordance with the guidelines issued by the EEOC and OFCC—that they also need empirical data to demonstrate that the technique is predictive of or significantly correlated with successful job performance and does not result in discrimination on the basis of race, colour, religion, sex, or national origin.

Formal Application Form

The formal application form serves as a central record for all pertinent information collected during the selection process. When completed, it becomes part of the permanent personnel record of the new employees. As a general rule, a formal application is filled out only after a preliminary interview indicates that a job candidate has promise as a company marketing-person. The application form may be filled out by the applicant personally or by interviewer who records the applicant's response. Practice varies in this respect, but in either case the completed formal application amounts to a standardised written interview, since cost most of the information that it contains could be obtained through one or more conventional and more personal interviews. Sometimes, sections are reserved for later recording of the results of such selection steps as psychological testing, reference checks, and physical examinations standardised application blank is prepared by Marketing Management magazine. One other standard forms are available, but ideally each company should prepare its own. No two companies have precisely the same requirements, and information significant for one may be useless for another. However, if a firm has only a small marketing force, and recruits relatively few people, the time and cost of preparing its own application form may warrant the choice of a standard form. Firms using standard forms simply ignore inappropriate items and obtain needed additional information during interviews.

Certain items of information are almost always needed for selection decisions, and these can be conveniently assembled on the application form. Among these are: present job, dependents, education, employment status, debts, time with last employer, membership in organisations, previous position, records of earning, reasons for leaving last job, networth, living expenses, and length of job hunting period.

Final decisions as to the specific items to include on the form should be based upon analysis of the existing marketing force. The names of marketing personnel should be arranged along a continuum, the best performer at one end and the worst performer at the other. This list is divided into three or more parts; for example, good, average, and poor; if the marketing force is large, finer subdivisions are justified. In measuring current qualification, data are collected from marketing records, supervisors' evaluations, and similar sources. The next step is to compare good and poor performers according to qualifications possessed by each at time of hiring. This should reveal any factors that differentiate the two groups, and these are the items that should be included on the application form. The validity of this basis of evaluation depends upon the size of the several groups studies, and for reliable results no group should be smaller than 30.

Objective Scoring of Personnel-History Items

It the total profile, rather than any single item, that determined the predictive value of personnel-history items. Considered singly, few items have value as selection factors, but individuals with all the personal-history requirements are those most likely to succeed. However, many potentially successful marketing-people do not possess all the requirements. One company, for instance, found that most of its best marketing-people were hired between the ages of 30 and 35 years, yet there were some as young as nineteen and as old as fifty-two. The significance of each personal factor is relative, not absolute. Although 30 to 35 may be the preferred age range, applicants outside this age range should still consideration (since other factors in their backgrounds may more than offset the fact that they are outside the desired age range).

Some firms with large marketing forces establish objective measures for personal-history items. A maximum possible score is assigned for each items, and the points given to a particular individual depend upon proximity to the ideal. In one firm 15 personal-history items are used as selection factors, at a maximum value of ten points each. The maximum score is 150 points, and the cut off score is 120. Successful marketing-persons in this company all scored over 100 when hired, and the company automatically disqualifies all applicants with scores under 100.

Objective personal-history scoring was pioneered by the life insurance companies. Their marketing forces were sufficiently large to permit establishment of reliable standards. It is doubtful practice to set such scoring standards when the marketing force is rather small (say, under 100 people), as the distortion of scores tends to increase in inverse proportion to the size of the marketing force used for setting the standards. Furthermore, with the passage of the Civil Rights Act and the Age Discrimination in Employment Act, a company using objective personal-history scoring must be prepare to prove empirically that the technique does not result in discrimination against applicants on the basis of race, colour, religion, sex, national origin, or age. Further, they must prove that the scores above the cutoff point are predictive of or significantly correlated with important elements of work behaviour which comprise or are relevant to the marketing position for which applicants are being evaluated. Therefore, marketing executive should use objective scoring or personal-history items with great caution, although they may safely use 'cut off scores' to indicate the need for further investigation of an applicant's qualifications.

References and Opinions of Acquaintances

References provided by friends and former employers of the applicant are used to secure information not available from other sources. The value of references denied by some employers, who contend that writers of reference letters generally hesitate to criticise personal friends, or even ex-employees. But the experienced employer 'Reads between the lines' of letters of reference, where, for example, the weak candidate may be damned by faint praise. Personal contact is the best way to obtain information from references, since facial expression and voice intonations can reveal a great deal, and most people are more frank orally than in writing. When a reference is located at a distance, a telephone call may substitute for personal contact. Solicitation of written recommendations is the weakest approach and should be a last resort.

Applicants tend to name as references only those on whom they can rely to speak in their favour. In addition, there is a natural tendency for references to be biased in favour of an applicant. These limitations can be partially offset by contacting persons not listed as references but who know the applicant. Individuals, who know the applicant but who are not specifically listed as references often are excellent source for candid appraisals of the candidate. These acquaintances fall into four classifications:

(1) **Present or Former Employers:** These persons have observed the applicant under actual work conditions. As a matter of practice, however, many marketing executives do not approach the present employer without the applicant's permissions.

(2) **Former Customers:** If applicants have marketing experience, their former customers are in a position to assess their marketing ability. It is advisable to contact these individuals without the applicant's assistance. This helps avoid those who are personal friends of applicants.

(3) **Reputable Citizens:** If references suggested by the applicant are used, it is best first to contact those who are reputable, well-known citizens. Such people do not stake their personal reputations on those in whom they have little confidence.

(4) **Mutual Acquaintances:** Those who know both the applicant and the employer may give frank evaluations. What is even more important is that the employer is better able to judge the reliability of such evaluations.

Physical Examinations

Since good health important to marketing-person's success, most companies require physical examinations of all applicants seriously considered for marketing positions. Because of the relatively high cost of the physical examination, it generally is one of the last steps in the selection system. Even in companies requiring entrance physical examinations, poor health often accounts for separations; but when the examinations are not compulsory, the number is higher. It is advantageous to the applicant as well as to the company to identify physical ailments that may later prevent the attainment of full productivity.

Credit Information

Many companies run credit checks on applicants for marketing positions. Credit files are compiled on most people by local credit bureaus, and special credit reports are obtainable through such organisations as Dun & Bradstreet. When a heavy burden of personal debt is found, it may be indicative of financial worries interfering with productivity, or of a motivating factors serving to spur productivity—to determine which one of these may be true requires, and should be given, further investigation. In analysing the entire credit report the executive should look for the 'danger signals'—chronic lateness in marketing payments, large debts outstanding for long periods, or bankruptcy history—the presence of any of which should signal the need for additional probing of the underlying facts. Financial irresponsibility may or may not be indicative of irresponsibility in meeting job obligations; hence considerable data on all aspects of the applicant's behaviour, nonfinancial as well as financial, must be on hand to warrant whichever conclusion is drawn.

Psychological Tests

Psychological testing provides objective way to measure many traits or characteristics of applicants for marketing positions. Until the mid-1960s the trend was for more and more companies to make some use of psychological tests as one of the last steps in selection system (the tests come toward the end because of their relatively high cost). Since the passage of the Civil Rights Act in 1964 and with the issuance of guidelines by the EEOC and OFCC, there has been tendency for companies to either abandon or rely less upon psychological tests as an aid in making selection decision from among job candidates. Roughly 20 per cent of the complaints filed under Title VII of the Civil Rights Act change that tests have been used in way that result in unfair discrimination against members of minority groups. One reason fewer companies use psychological tests today then previously is the difficult in validating them and in securing the empirical data needed to prove that test results are predictive of or significantly related to successful job performance and, further, that test results are being used in ways that do not result in illegal discrimination.

The task of validating tests is complicated because many situations exist in which different sets of behaviours or attributes can lead to successful job performance. Because of this, separate validity studies should be performed for different ethnic groups. The different cultural experience and exposure of each group may affect the relationship of test scores to job-performance criteria. Results of certain tests may underestimate the true ability of disadvantaged applicants and cause tests that are valid for the advantages to be invalid for the disadvantaged. White marketing personnel, for instance, may make effective use of certain marketing techniques with white customers that are different from the technique black marketing personnel find effective with the same customers. Tests can predict aptitude for using these techniques; but such tests would be appropriate only for white applicants if the tests have not been validated for use with black applicants. In some situations differential validity is found, in others not. Actual research is required in each situation to determine whether or not differential validity exists, and both the EEOC and OFCC emphasise the need to validate test results separately for minority-group members.

Validation of Tests

Because of the increasingly important need for proof that a test is related to job-performance criteria and because of the possibility that differential validity exists (for different groups of applicants), it is important to discuss the validation of tests. The illustrations used relate to validity studies conducted on separate ethnic groups, but the same general approach is used for validity studies conducted on other types of groups, for example, for different age groups or for males and females.

Using psychological tests for selection purposes, then, required considerable sophistication. Not only is there the possibility that certain tests possess differential validity, but the very objectivity of tests leads many users to expect more validity and reliability in predicting marketing success than the tests can offer. Furthermore, it can be said in all fairness that some widely used tests are almost worthless for selection purposes, simply because they were designed for entirely different purposes; others are of questionable value even for measuring what they were intended to measure. Psychological testing is still an experimental field, and every experiment does not succeed. Yet more than a few testing 'failures' are on the market, are even promoted and recommended by the producers, and used by executives unaware of the limitations.

In addition, tests tend to favour conformity rather than individual dynamics—they tend to rule out creative thinkers and imaginative, aggressive individuals who might be ideal for the job being filled.

Nevertheless, there are some useful and reliable tests available, and certain basically weak tests can serve as screening devices as long as their limitations are recognised, but, as brought out earlier, it is increasingly important for test users to perform actual research to determine whether or not differential validity exists. The requirement for doing such research makes it even critical that test users secure the services of trained specialists in psychological testing for purposes of selecting, administering, and interpreting the tests used for any particular company.

Types of Tests

Three types of psychological tests are used in selection systems for marketing personnel; tests of ability, of habitual characteristics, and of achievement. Tests of ability attempt to measure how well a person can perform particular tasks with maximum motivation. They are tests of *best* performance, and they include tests of mental ability ('intelligence' tests) and tests of special abilities, or aptitude tests. Test of habitual characteristics attempt to gauge how prospective employees would act in their daily work normally, i.e., not when they are on their best behaviour. These are tests of typical performance, and they include attitude, personality, and interest tests. Achievement tests are designed to measure how much individuals have learned from their training or education.

Basis for Evaluation of Tests

Before examining the psychological tests used in marketing-person selection, we need some criteria for evaluation. Earlier discussion emphasised the importance of a test having validity—that it measures what it purports to measure—and of detecting differential validity. But even in cases where statistical validity has been demonstrated, it is possible for a test not to be valid in a particular instance. For example, a written intelligence test in English is not a valid measure of the *mental ability* of a Spanish-speaking person with an English-language handicap. A low score does not necessarily indicate low intelligence; it may merely reflect poor understanding of the English language.

Test reliability is also important. Reliability refers to the consistency of test results. If a test has reliability, an individual should receive approximately the same score in subsequent retesting with the same or equivalent tests.

Test objectivity is important, too. If a test has objectivity, it is so administered that the score's opinion does not enter into the test results. Whenever a person giving or scoring the test can affect the test results, it is misleading to compare the results obtained by different testers.

Other factors to consider in selecting tests are cost, time, and ease of administration. Wide variation in cost exists, and even small differentials may be important if testes are given to large groups. Because, there is little relationship between cost and quality, it is sometimes possible to obtain quality tests at low cost. There, is similarly, wide variation in the time required to administer and score tests. Because time frequently is crucial in selection of marketing personnel, the employer must balance the time requirements of alterative tests against their relative effectiveness. If the best available test consumes more time than can be spared, a mediocre test that can be given and scored by persons with little or no special training. Again, employers must balance the gains associated with more complex test against their costs in time and money.

Test of Mental Ability

Mental tests are used satisfactorily in a wide range of areas, and they have higher validity and reliability than most psychological tests. It must be understood, however, that they measure primarily the abilities that make for success in educational or training situations, namely, language usage and comprehensions, and abstract reasoning, or problem-solving ability. They do not measure creativeness, originality, or insight. Therefore, they should be regarded more as measures of mental aptitude than of general intelligence. Because tests of mental ability are 'timed tests,' they provide an innovation of an applicant's ability to learn quickly and to arrive at accurate answers under pressure.

Within these limitations, mental tests are helpful in the marketing personnel selection process. Where there is no other evidence of ability, such as graduation from college, the mental aptitude test serves as a screen to eliminate applicants falling below a predetermined level. A wide variety of mental aptitude tests is available.

Tests of Special Aptitudes

Certain tests are designed to measure special aptitudes, such as: spatial and perceptual abilities, speed and reaction time, steadiness and controlled movement, mechanical comprehension, and artistic abilities. Aptitude tests used individually aid in marketing selection for some industrial jobs, as illustrated, for example, by the use of perception test for selecting clerical personnel. But because marketing requires diverse aptitudes, and marketing job specifications differ even among competing companies, and especially designed battery of aptitude tests is more appropriate for marketing personnel.

The procedure for developing a battery of marketing aptitude tests for a particular company is fairly straightforward. The test expert begins with the job specifications derived, as you will recall, from the job description, checking them to assure that the abilities required for job performance are correctly identified. Then the expert selects existing tests and/or constructs new tests to measure each aptitude. Finally, the tests export develops a scheme for weighting and combining the scores of individual tests. This work of preparing—and later validating—a test battery is time-consuming and costly, and calls for a psychologist's services. Thus, generally only those companies which process large numbers of marketing job applicants annually feel they can afford specially developed test batteries to measure marketing aptitude. Since, unfortunately, batteries not custom tailored for a particular marketing job frequently have little validity, companies with small marketing forces find it impractical to include marketing-aptitude test batteries in their selection systems.

Personality Tests

Personality tests initially were used to identify people with psychotic tendencies—and certain tests have proved useful for this purpose. Subsequently, attempts have been made to use them for measuring personality traits in normal individuals, for which purpose they seem to have little to no validity or reliability. The basic limitation is the lack of uniform definitions for such traits as initiative or aggressiveness, which these tests purport to measure. To the extent that these tests are at all valid measuring normal individuals, validity must be determined by the total score rather than by scores for individual traits. The chief use of the personality test is that of screening device to identify persons with abnormal personalities.

Projective tests, of which the Rorschach is the best known, are a promising technique for personality measurement. However, they must be administered by skilled testers, and their results represent a subjective opinion rather than an objective measure. Further refinements of projective techniques eventually may provide useful personality measurements.

Interest Tests

In using interest tests as selection devices, a basic assumption is that a relationship exists between interest and motivation. Hence, if two persons have equal ability, the one with the greater interest in a particular job should be more successful in that job. A second inherent assumption is that interests are constant, that those of a person at age 40 are essentially the same as they were at 21.

The interest test is useful for vocational guidance, but it is not wholly satisfactory as a selection device. This is because of the opportunity for faking responses-individuals may select answers overstating their real interest in a particular field. Of the two most widely-used interest tests, the Strong and the Kuder, the Strong uses the more indirect and subtle approach and is harder to fake; but because of its greater complexity, it is more expensive to score. The U.S. Air Force, which has experimented with a technique to eliminate faking, uses an information test to measure interest on the theory that persons should be best informed about those field in which they are most interested.

What proof is there of the value of interest tests in predicting marketing success? Unfortunately, very little! Strong demonstrated that there is a positive but low correlation between interest scores and success in insurance marketing. Significant variation has also been found in the interest test scores of successful and unsuccessful marketing-persons of accounting machines. Otherwise, there is little tangible proof of the value of interest tests as devices for predicting marketing success.

Attitude Tests

Attitude tests are more useful as morale-measuring techniques than as selection aids. They are used to ascertain employees' feelings toward working conditions pay, advancement opportunities, and the like. Used as marketing personnel selection devices, they may make limited contributions by identifying abnormal attitudes on such broad subjects as big business, labour unions, and government. Their validity is questionable, since people often profess socially acceptable attitudes they do not actually have. In addition, attitude tests do not measure the intensity with particular attitudes are held.

Achievement Tests

Achievement tests seek to determine how much individuals know about a particular subject. Few standardised test of this type are used by industry, because the special skills involved in each job require different types of knowledge. Tests of clerical and stenographic ability are one exception, and civil service examinations are another. For the employer who has decided that it is worthwhile to custom design an achievement test for marketing applicants, such an instrument can provide as assessment of knowledge applicants possess in such areas as the product, marketing channels, and customers relations; however, as with other psychological tests, such test designing is a job for an expert, not an amateur.

Research has produced some evidence that the existence of two basic qualities, empathy and ego drive, are essential in good marketing-people. Empathy is the ability to fell as others do, to put oneself in another person's shoes. The empathic marketing-person senses the reactions of his or her customers and is able to adjust to these reactions, achieving real interaction with customers. The second basic quality, ego drive, makes the marketing-person want to make the sale in a personal way, not merely for the money to be gained. His feeling is that he has to make the sale. His self-picture improves by virtue of conquest and diminishes with failure. The good marketing-person has a proper balance of these two qualities. The developers of this hypothesis have demonstrated in experiments that measurement of these two qualities alone (through the use of specially developed psychological tests) has greatly improved predication of success or failure in a number of different marketing jobs.

Conclusions on Testing

Besides the legal requirements that tests must not be used for making selection decisions in ways that discriminate unfairly against minority-group applications, there are other important precautions to observe when incorporating psychological tests into a marketing personnel selection system. It is essential to have accurate job specifications, derived from up-to-date and complete job descriptions, to make certain that the specific abilities required of a good marketing-person are known. A qualified expert's services are required in the choice of tests (and in devising new ones when necessary), in determining test validity and in detecting differential validity, in administering the tests themselves, and in interpreting the significance of results. In addition, marketing executives need to recognise the fact that psychological testing, although potentially capable of making a valuable contribution, is but one element in an effective marketing personnel selection system.

Planning and Conducting Marketing Training Programmes

The modern marketing executive's attitude toward marketing training has changed markedly in recent years. Marketing managers typically used to believe in 'sink-or-swim' training—outing new marketing-people into the field with scanty instructions and expecting them to do their best, learning what they could in the hard school of experience. For example, as recently, one of *Fortune* magazine's 500 largest corporations introduced its first formal marketing-training programme in one of its major industrial products division. Prior to that time, this division gave product descriptions, a territory, and an order book to new marketing-force recruits with instructions to 'go out and sell.'

The lack of recognition of the need to train marketing-people reflected an attitude that many marketing managers held toward marketing. The older generation of marketing managers operated on the comfortable—albeit superficial—assumption that good marketing-people were 'born,' not 'made.' Admittedly, then as now there are some 'born' or 'natural' marketing people. But, given appropriate training, the majority of recruits can be 'made' into marketing persons; and both 'born' and 'made' marketing personnel improve with continued marketing training. Modern marketing executives still consider experience the most valuable marketing training but they believe strongly that formally planned and executed marketing-training programmes contribute significantly to the improvement of marketing performance. They regard formalised marketing-training programmes as important supplements to, rather than substitutes for, field marketing experience.

Organisation for Marketing Training

Placement of Training Responsibility

Organisational planners do not agree on the question of where to place primary responsibility for initial marketing training. Some consider it a line function and assign the marketing training responsibility to the chief marketing executive; others consider it a staff function and assign the responsibility to the personnel manager, reserving only an advisory role for marketing management. In most situations, both executives should pay a role in initial marketing training—the marketing executive because he should be an expert on marketing, and the personnel manager because he should be an expert on training. How a particular firm should decide the placement of responsibility for initial marketing training depends upon comparative costs. If much of the initial training of new marketing personnel parallels that given other employees, cost considerations often result in primary responsibility being assigned to the personnel manager. If very little of the initial marketing training parallels other new employee training, then primary responsibility is assigned to the marketing executive.

Once initial marketing training is over, responsibility for continuing training definitely resides with the chief marketing executive. Introduction of new products, adoption of revised marketing policies, perfection of improved marketing techniques, and similar developments call for training action-and logic dictates that top marketing executives should be in the best position to recognise the need. In the well-managed business, marketing training is a never ending process and, regardless of who is responsible for the initial period of indoctrination, the chief marketing executive has continuing responsibility.

Marketing Training Staff

Even though chief executives may be ultimately responsible for both initial and continuing marketing training, they usually delegate actual performance of the function to subordinates. Often large marketing organisations have a full-time marketing-training director, reporting directly to the chief marketing executive. The director might personally conduct some training and coordinate that given on a decentralised (and usually part-time) basis by regional and district marketing managers. In smaller organisations, some chief marketing executives handle part of the training themselves, but in most cases, they rely upon others, such as assistant marketing managers or district managers, to do most of the training. Even companies without marketing training directors often have full-time or part-time marketing trainers, or both. The large marketing organisation generally can make efficient use of a full-time marketing-training director and sometimes even a full-time staff, but the small organisation ordinarily must rely on executives to do marketing training 'in addition to other duties'. Because of specialised knowledge requirements, the tendency is for companies to training their own marketing trainers rather than to recruit outsiders.

Training the Marketing Trainers

No marketing-training programme, however carefully designed, can be more effective than the people, who conduct it. For this reason, a growing number of companies provide special training programmes for marketing trainers. The straining point is the identification of the subjects that trainers should know thoroughly, such as the company and its policies, the products, the customers, and their problems. The marketing-person's job, and marketing techniques. If the potential trainers are not already experienced marketing-people, they should be given field marketing experience to provide a realistic feel for marketing problems. Subjects presented formally should be handled by personnel already skilled as trainers, wherever possible using instructional techniques similar to those trainers will use later.

Not only should marketing trainers have expert and specialised knowledge, they must be effective teachers. Throughout their period of preparation, the theory and mechanics of teaching should be stressed. Trainers should be required to master these, learn how to apply them effectively, preferably through doing practice training themselves. They must also learn to plan and organise teaching material for clear and effective presentation. Although formal training alone will not prepare an individual for effective teaching, a well-planned and executed programme for marketing trainers can certainly help. For the most part, however, marketing trainers must develop their own teaching skills. To emphasise this point, management often reminds them that; "If the trainee hasn't learned, the trainer hasn't taught."

Building Marketing Training Programme

Many companies conduct several types marketing-training programme. Generally, the most comprehensive and longest programme is that for newly recruited personnel. More intensive and usually shorter programmes on specialised topics are presented for experienced marketing-people. In addition, periodic 'refresher' marketing-training programmes are considered desirable in most companies. Some marketing-training programmes in certain forms are designed especially for the development of marketing trainers or for persons whom management believes have potential as marketing executives. Each type of programme serves different purposes, and the scope and content of each should reflect its particular purpose.

There are several sequential steps in integrating marketing training with the operating objectives of the business. First, these objectives should be clearly defined and phrased in terms of the marketing force and its capability with respect to achieving these objectives. Then, it must be determined what marketing training is necessary to close the gap between capabilities and objectives. At this point a minimal system of marketing-training programmes, procedures, and projects can be designed to close the gap.

Building an effective marketing-training programme of any type requires a number of important planning decisions. The purposes to be served by the training must be clearly defined, programme content must be decided, training methods selected, arrangements made for programme execution, and procedures set up to evaluate the results. Some marketing-training specialists refer to these planning decisions as the A-C-M-E decisions—aim, content, method, and execution and evaluation—each of which is considered in the following discussion.

Defining Training Aims

The first step is, to decide what the marketing-training programme should seek to accomplish. Of course, the general aim of all marketing training is to improve marketing performance—both of individual marketing-persons and of the entire marketing force. Improved marketing performance is achieved through measures taken to increase marketing-people's productivity and to control marketing costs. Without training, a marketing-person's productivity tends to increase with experience; hence, if training can substitute for some portion of the needed experience or can usefully supplement it, higher productivity levels should be reached earlier. Marketing costs per unit of products sold decline with rises in marketing productivity, so they also tend to be related to experience. Furthermore, the marketing-force turnover rate for new marketing personnel nearly always is higher than for experienced people—often unexperienced staff members find themselves unprepared to do satisfactory jobs, become discouraged, and leave the company. If marketing training can help marketing-persons to increase their productivity more quickly, the marketing force turnover rate will drop, hiring and training costs should fall, and marketing efficiency will rise. Marketing performance is influenced also by the state of relations with customers and prospects, the marketing force playing a crucial role in moulding and maintaining these relations. Generally, experienced, marketing people make better impressions on prospects and maintain better continuing relations with established accounts. Here, again, marketing training can contribute through accelerating the process of 'learning through experience.' In all these ways, then, marketing training serves to improve marketing performance by providing a mechanism through which the benefits from an 'experienced' marketing force can be realised much earlier and more surely than might otherwise be the case.

It is not sufficient, however, to define only general training aims—specific aims of particular programmes also need to be identified. Although, we may be interested, say, in increasing the marketing force's productivity through training, we need to identify, what must be done to achieve the general aim of increasing productivity. General aims need translating into more specific aims phrased in operational terms before the programme can be planned in detail. These process of specific aim definition begins with a review of general aims and the means currently employed to attain them; however, the process cannot be completed until management actually perceives training needs from which specific training aim derive directly. In the next two sections, discussion focuses on factors that management should consider as it seeks to identify training needs for (1) initial marketing-training programmes, and (2) continuing marketing-training programmes.

Determining Initial Training Needs

Determining the need for, and specific aims of, an initial marketing-training programme requires consideration of three main factors: requirements of the marketing job, prior background and experience of individual of trainees, and company marketing policies.

Job Requirements

Marketing job analysis provides the information required for preparing the job description, which, as you recall, consists of a statement of job objectives and an explanation of essential tasks involved in its performance. Management should study the job description for clues about the points on which new personnel are most likely to need training. But, it is at least as important to consider other information relative to marketing job performance: How should marketing people apportion their time? Which duties require the greatest proportion of marketing time? Which tend to be neglect? Why? Which marketing approaches are most effective? Answers to these and related questions help in formulating the qualifications that a marketing-person should have to fill the job satisfactorily.

Individual Trainees' Prior Background and Experience

Each person in an initial marketing-training programme enters it with a somewhat unique educational background and a highly individualised record of achievement. Conceptually, then, the gap between required job qualifications for a particular trainee and those he or she already has represents the nature and amount of training needed. But in a large organisation with a fully structured and formalised programme, it is not always practical to adjust training precisely to individual differences in background and experience. Time and money may be saved by putting all recruits through identical programmes. Nevertheless, in more flexible training situations, information about trainees' qualifications makes possible to some extent the tailoring of programme to individuals, increasing both trainee satisfaction and programme efficiency. In all companies, large and small, determining recruit's real needs for training is essential to developing initial training programmes of optimum benefit to company and trainee alike.

Company Marketing Policies

A company's particular marketing situations should be analysed in determining the needs to be served by individual marketing training. For instance, marketing a line of machine tools requires emphasis on product information and customer applications whereas marketing simple, nontechnical products demands more emphasis on marketing techniques. Thus, differences in products and markets make for differences in marketing practices and policies, which, in turn, point to needed differences in initial marketing training programme. The same applies to differences in promotion, price, marketing channel, and system of physical distribution – all have implications for the needs that the initial marketing-training programme should serve. In the case of promotion, for example, if advertising is not used or used relatively little, marketing training should prepare marketing personnel to handle considerable promotional work; but, if advertising is used extensively to supplement marketing-people's efforts, there is a need to teach new marketing personnel how to coordinate their efforts with advertising.

Determining Continuing Training Needs

Training a marketing force is a never-ending process. Even though the initial training programme may be excellent, its graduate are soon in need of refresher courses as the company's product lines and markets change and as they become careless in their marketing habits. Although, the concept of continuing instruction for all marketing personnel is still new in a great many companies, it is being rapidly accepted. The experience of the Armour-Dial division of Greyhound Corporation illustrates the value of such training. Armour-Dial ran a study on marketing personnel who had attended a recent session as its Aurora (Illinois) marketing training centre. The result was a boost of 12 per cent in case marketing, 62 per cent in displays sold, and 250 per cent in marketing to direct-buying or chain accounts.

Determining the specific aims to be served by a continuing marketing-training programme also requires perception of specific training needs. Problems arising from forthcoming changes in company policy, procedure, or organisation should be anticipated and studied – they may have implications for needed training. More basic changes in products and markets almost always given rise to a need for additional training. It is also helpful for management, as it seeks to perceive needs for continuing training, to take such actions as: analysing the marketing job description relative to experienced persons' qualifications; surveying marketing personnel for suggestions; scrutinising marketing-person reports for symptoms of training needs; inspecting and analysing marketing records to uncover performance weaknesses; and personally observing marketing-people in action to detect deficiencies. Marketing management must know a great deal about how experienced marketing personnel are doing their jobs in order to define specific aims for their continued training.

Deciding the Content of Marketing Training Programmes

The actual content of a marketing training programmes, whether initial or continuing, should be derived from the specific aims that management, after analysing its training needs, has formulated. Initial programmes generally are characterised by broader scope and coverage than continuing programmes. Initial programmes, must provide instruction covering all important aspects of performing the marketing-person's job; continuing programmes may concentrate more on specific job aspects where management believes experienced persons to have more room for improvement. Therefore, the following discussion mainly relates to determining the content of initial marketing-training programmes.

For an initial marketing-training programme to contribute maximally toward preparing new recruits as marketing personnel, it must cover all important aspects of the marketing-person's job. Content varies considerably from company to company, because of differences in factors such as products, markets, company policies, trainees' ability and experience, organisational size, and executives' training philosophies. No two programmes are, or should be, alike. Different companies tend to cover the same general topics despite the fact that variations always exist in the exact and in the relative time developed to each major topic. But it is possible to generalise to the point of saying that every initial marketing-training programme should devote some time to each of four main areas—product data, marketing techniques, markets for the product, and company information.

Product Data

Some product training is basic to any initial marketing-training programme, even though all companies need not emphasise it. Companies with highly technical products commonly devote more than half of their programmes to product training. But in many situations, especially with standardised products sold routinely, new marketing personnel need receive only a small amount of formal product training. In all cases, however, management must make certain that new marketing-people know enough about the products, their uses, and applications to serve customers' information needs adequately and promptly. Product knowledge is basic to a marketing-person's self-confidence and enthusiastic job performance.

Understanding product uses and applications is especially important. Trainees should receive instruction on customers' problems and requirements and should learn how company products can help solve these problems and meet these requirements. Training should provide them with full appreciation for buyers' viewpoints, perhaps through role-playing instructional techniques. Through such training, new marketing-persons learn to relate company products to the fulfilment of customers requirements, thus equipping themselves not only for effective marketing but for effective handling of marketing resistance met later in the field.

Creative marketing is the name given a marketing approach that places the emphasis buyers' needs. The National Cash Register Company pioneered the use of this technique around 1900. Progressive companies make extensive use of it today. In order to indoctrinate trainees in applying this approach, initial marketing-training programmes often provide a period during which trainees are in direct contact with ultimate users or consumers. Through personal experience, such as in retail marketing or product servicing, trainees gain valuable insights on the ways different users react to company products.

More and more companies require a period of initial marketing training at the factory. This provides trainees with opportunities to observe and study the products during the various manufacturing and testing phases. They have the chance, too, to talk with or even to work alongside factory personnel. The instructional benefits should be more through product knowledge and greater confidence in subsequently demonstrating to otherwise presenting products to customers. Inordinate amounts of time, however, should not be devoted to technical production detail—such detail is important only insofar as it helps the marketing-person in actual marketing situations.

Some training on competitors' products usually is desirable, particularly in highly competitive industries. Marketing-people should not only know the important characteristics of competitor's products but be well posted on their uses and applications in solving customers' problems. They should be thoroughly familiar with how the strengths and weaknesses of competitive products compare with those of their own company's products. Thus informed, marketing-persons to emphasise superior qualities of features of the company's product, and they are well equipped to answer customers' question and to deal with their objections. Training on competitors' products must be continuous, the focus shifting as changes and improvements are made in both competitive and company products.

Marketing Technique

Most new recruits need formal instruction in marketing techniques, and an increasing number of firms provide such training. Some marketing managers still believe, however, that careful selection of marketing personnel and a heavy programme of product training are sufficient to ensure effective personality, good appearance and voice, reasonable intelligence, and knows the product, he will be able to sell it easily. But the predominant view is that new marketing personnel need basic instruction in how to sell. This is reflected in individual company marketing training programmes and in industry-wide programmes offered by such groups as the National Association of Food Manufacturers and the National Association of Machine Tool Builders. In all marketing-training programmes the practical as well as the theoretical side of marketing should be covered. In many companies, as an important adjunct to learning how to sell, new personnel receive training in the development of human-relations skills. In a few exceptional companies, training provides for practical analysis of the psychology of human behaviour and motivation relative to company marketing problems.

Marketing for the Products

It is especially important for the new marketing-person that training provides a comprehensive understanding of the market. The new marketing-person must know, who the customers are, the particular products in which they are interested, their buying habits and motives, their location, and their financial condition. In order to sell, in other words, the marketing-person needs to know not only who buys what but, more important, why and how they buy. When trainees are not given adequate instruction on the market, they may take years to acquire the needed understanding independently. During this period of trial-and-error learning, through no fault of their own, their productivity is lower than it should be. In fact, left to their own devices, some trainees never gain important market information. For instance, a marketing-person who is unaware of certain prospects' potential as buyers may neglect completely to canvass them or even to canvass entire classifications of prospects. Because markets are always changing, training in this area should be continuous, the content changing as significant market changes occur.

Company Information

Certain items of company information are essential to the marketing-person on the job; others, not absolutely essential, contribute to overall effectiveness. The training programme should include coverage of all marketing policies and, preferably, the reasoning that led to their formulation. The marketing-person must know company pricing policy in order to answer customers' questions about it. The marketing-persons also needs to be fully informed on other policies, such as those relating to products services, spare parts and repairs, credit extension, and customers relations.

The initial training programme must equip the marketing-person to perform such tasks as recording and submitting customer's orders for processing and delivery, preparing expense and other required reports, handling inquiries, following up on customers for handling these and similar tasks. If trainees are to perform them properly and efficiently from the very start of their field assignments, the initial marketing-training programme must provide the needed instruction. Otherwise, company systems and procedures are learned, if at all, through a costly and time-consuming process of trial and error.

Another aspects of company information that should be explained in initial marketing-training programmes relate to the marketing department's personal policies. Coverage includes selection procedures, training programmes, compensation and incentive systems, advancement requirements and opportunities, saving and retirement plans, medical and insurance plans, and the like. Having such information improves employee morale and job effectiveness. Not having it shows up in employee uncertainty and needlessly excessive marketing-force turnover rates.

Another ingredient that contributes to the building of morale among new employees might be described as "general company information.' This concerns the company's history, its importance in the industry and economy, and its policies with regard to relations with stockholders, unions, competitors, government, and other groups. Having been briefed on these items, the new recruit's early and natural feelings of strangeness and uneasiness are replaced with some sense of belonging and company loyalty. Knowing something about the personality, or image, of the company also should bolster the confidence of recruits in its products, which they will shortly be trying to sell. It is worthwhile, then, to provide formal training covering selected items of general company information. But it also should be recognised that a common failings of initial marketing-training programmes is that too much time is spent on company background, history, and prestige building. The challenge is to provide sufficient general company information, but no to allocate instructional time disproportionate to its importance in the total programme.

Selecting Training Methods

Having defined specific training aims and determined programme content, management must select appropriate instructional methods. There is a wide variety from which to choose. Professional educators and marketing trainers have re-evaluated and refined time-honoured methods, such as lectures and discussions of different sorts, and, in addition, have developed new ones, such as the business game and role playing. Psychologist have influenced modern instructional methods through their studies of the learning process, motivation, retention, and so forth. From the many instructional methods available, the problems is to choose those that will most effectively and economically achieve programme aims.

Instructional methods can be segregated into two major categories: those requiring group participation and those involving individual training.

Group Instructional Methods

These are used wherever trainees are grouped for instructional purposes. The group instructional methods most frequently used in marketing training are: the lecture, the group discussion, role playing, and the simulation or game.

The Lecture

Lecturing consists of primarily oral presentations, sometimes supplemented with visual aids, by an instructor in a formal classroom situation. This ancient teaching method, in use before the invention of printing, is still widely used in marketing training.

Trainees participate mainly through watching and listening, although some versions of lecturing permit the asking of questions and allow for other interruptions. Generally, however, the lecture involves passive, rather than active, trainee participation, this feature constituting its main weakness—teaching is emphasised more than learning. But a lecture can be effective, provided the lecturer is an able and enthusiastic speaker and makes liberal use of examples, demonstrations, and visual aids. Compared with other group instructional methods, too, the lecture is economical in terms of time required to cover a given topic.

Many professional business teachers, perhaps most, regard lecturing as the last effective group instructional methods. Professional marketing trainers seem, by and large, to agree with this evaluation. Estimates are that the average trainee can immediately recall less than 10 per cent of what he hears in a non-illustrated lecture, and no more than half of what he sees and hears in a lecture using visual aids. Furthermore, because of the absence in a lecture participant feedback, no lecturer has any immediate or objective means for gauging the effectiveness of a lecturer, but must rely on a personal appraisal of its reception, or on volunteered (and generally unreliable) comments by participants.

Even with its limitations, some lecturing in marketing training is often a practical necessity. If formal training is brief, for instance, lecturing may be the only way to cover major portions of the desired content. It may also be the only practical way to handle instruction when the training group is too large to permit constructive audience participation. Given longer training period and smaller training groups, however, lecturing is probably most appropriate for introductory and orientation sessions and for proving summaries of major topics taught mainly through methods such as case discussion and role playing. It also is used extensively, and in most instances appropriately, in continuing marketing-training programmes for providing new information about the company, its policies, products, markets, and marketing programmes. Recent Research learning process can be considerably improved by using a carefully planned multimedia approach. In this approach the lecture room is equipped with two to six projectors and screens, and the entire lecture is projected visually on succeeding screens across the front of the room.

Further lecture support is provided by projecting illustrations, charts, and graphs, and through the provision of sound effects, where appropriate. Tests have shown that this version of the lecture method significantly increases attention, comprehension, and retention.

The Group Discussion

Group discussion differs from lecturing in several important respects. The instructor or discussion leader assumes a less dominant role, the trainees are active rather than passive participants, learning receives more emphasis than teaching, and the instructional atmosphere generally is much more informal and relaxed. Considerable flexibility is possible, too, in instructional format, the two main variations being the impromptu discussion and the case discussion. Because of these important advantages, and with the increasing sophistication of marketing trainers, group discussion methods are not only being used more extensively, they are being incorporated into an ever-growing number of marketing-training programmes.

In the impromptu discussion, often called a marketing seminar or conference, the instructor, group leader, or some member makes a brief oral presentation on a problem faced by marketing-force members in their everyday work. This is followed by general give-and-take discussion. Group members gain a meaningful application for and understanding of many problems that otherwise might be acquired, if at all, only through long personal experience. Many complexities and implications that might go uneducated by individuals are revealed to all; and trainees may learn an even more valuable lesson—fixed marketing rules and principles are often less important than careful analysis and handling of specific problem situation. Experience shows, in other words, that impromptu group discussion of problems improves the marketing-person's ability in handling those problems, and others arising in connection with the job.

The case discussion involves individual and sometimes group study of write-ups of actual marketing and other problems encountered on the job. Group analysis and discussion follows. This format, originated by professional business educators with a view toward providing a partial substitute for learning by experience, has been widely adapted for marketing-training purposes. Each case should either describe a real marketing or administrative problem, or be developed around a situation sufficiently real to stimulate emotional as well as objective involvement by trainees. Participants should be required to identify the issue(s), marshal the relevant facts, devise specific alternatives, and choose the one they consider most appropriate. Most users believe that securing a through grasp of the problem situation is more essential to learning than the rapid production of solutions. To derive maximum benefit from case decision, each session should provide for the drawing of generalisations of 'lessons learned.'

Group-discussion methods are effective in training either new or experienced marketing-people, but certain conditions must be met to achieve maximum benefits. Because discussion easily can drift into extraneous subjects or become sterile, an effective discussion leader or moderator is essential. The discussion leader must command the participants' respect, be skilled in dealing with people, and be extremely well informed not only on the subjects under discussion but on the marketing-person's job and its problems. If advance assignments are made, as in case discussion, it is absolutely imperative that the participants be prepared – otherwise valuable instructional time is wasted. It is important, too, to realise that group discussion requires considerable instructional time to be effective. If the aim is to maximise trainee learning of specific points in depth, and not to provide a broad general survey, group discussion is an appropriate instructional method.

Role Playing

The role playing method requires trainees to act out parts in contrived problems situations. As used in training on marketing techniques, the role playing session begins with the instructor describing the situation and the different personalities involved. The instructor provides all needed props, then designates trainees to play the roles of marketing-person, prospect, and other characters. Each plays his or her assigned role and afterwards they, together with other group members and the instructor, appraise each role plays effectiveness and suggest how each might have improves his performance.

In another version of role playing, one of the group is given a bit of information on, for example, a buyer's objection to a particular product, and then is asked by the instructor to extemporise a solution. Sometimes called a 'sweat session,' this provides individual trainees a chance to apply what they have learned. 'Post-mortem' critiques afford opportunities to reinforce what has been learned through participating in, or viewing, the role playing.

Role playing, as an instructional method, presents comparatively few problems. But there are some. Those playing assigned roles must become not only actively but emotionally identified with the characters they portray; audience interest must be maintained throughout, even through spontaneous reactions should be suppressed. Achieving these conditions is not easy. It becomes even more difficult when role players 'ham it up' or there is laughter or other involuntary audience reaction. Nonparticipants' comments should be saved for later, usually until the role playing is completed (although occasionally during 'cuts' called by the instructor). If note-taking is permitted as the play unfolds, some players tend to be distracted. This tendency, however, is overcome with repeated use of the method. These and similar problems can be minimised, provided that trainees are thoroughly briefed on what is and is not permissible, the group is limited in size (perhaps to no more than ten to twelve trainees), the instructor exercises discipline and control throughout, and role-playing assignments are realistic enough to make their learning potentials clear to all.

More than offsetting the few administrative problems are the many raining benefits flowing from successful use of this instructional method. It provides realistic practice in applying what has been learned in other formal training or by experience. It is highly flexible training method in that there is extreme diversity in role-playing situations. Experience shows, too, that role playing instruction lends itself to easy adjustment for training new personnel, experienced marketing-people, or even mixed groups. Among other benefits incidental to or derived from role playing instruction are the following:

(1) Most persons learn to accept criticism from others, and the group soon recognises that sound suggestions benefit everyone.

(2) When a person criticises another's performance, that person has an incentive not to perform similarly later.

(3) Role players practice introspection through participating in the appraisal of their own performances. The increasing use of tape-recording and playback equipment makes self-criticism even more beneficial and objective.

(4) The 'free-wheeling' nature of role playing is highly conductive to the generation of new ideas and approaches. Defects inherent in many stereotyped and 'school' solutions soon become apparent.

(5) In role playing sessions for mixed groups, junior people have a chance to learn

valuable 'tricks of the trade,' and experienced personnel are 'kept on their toes' as a matter of personal pride.

(6) Role players gain acting experience, which may be of great value to them later in handling difficult marketing situations.

The Simulation or Game

This instructional method, which somewhat resembles role playing, uses highly structured contrived situations, based on reality, in which players assume decision-making roles through successive rounds of play. A unique feature is that players have the benefits of information feedback. Trainees may play the roles of decision makers in customers, organisations, using data ordinarily available to make decision on the timing and size of orders, managing marketing forces and advertising efforts, and so on. The 'results' of these decision then are calculated by referees (sometimes using electronic computers) and feed back for the players to use in their next round of decisions.

Thus far, simulations or games used in marketing-training programmes have tended to be restricted to groups being prepared for management positions; but no insurmountable reason exists for not using them in other types of programmes. Perhaps, the main reason for not using games more extensively is the initial difficulty of preparing them. Preparation requires considerable research to dig out the needed facts, expert skill in incorporating these into a game model, development of detailed instructions for players and referees and the writing of a computer programme. Expertness and substantial investments in time and money, then, are required; but partially offsetting this is the fact that, once prepared, a game may see repeated use in many training programmes.

The game or simulation has several attractive advantages as an instructional method. Among the more important are the following: (1) participants learn easily because they involve themselves enthusiastically in game play; (2) players develop skill in identifying key factors influencing decisions; (3) games readily lend themselves to demonstrations of the uses and values of such analytical techniques as inventory and other planning models; and (4) in contrast to other instructional methods, games, with their built-in information feedback features, are highly effective in emphasising the dynamic nature of problem situations and their interrelationships.

Among the main instructional limitations of the game are the following: (1) some minimum time is required for playing, usually at least three or four hours, to generate sufficient decision 'rounds' to provide the desired learning experience; (2) since game designs generally are based on ordinary decision-making processes, their rules often prevent payoffs on unusual or novel approaches; and (3) players may learn some things that 'aren't so,' a limitation applying especially to carelessly prepared and/or poorly designed games. Most of these and other limitations may be partly or wholly overcome through careful game design and administration. Thus the game, or simulation instructional method, possesses great potential for marketing-training purposes.

Individual Instructional Methods

Some methods are used for training marketing-people on an individualised, one-person-at-a-time, basis. These techniques are used by large companies and are particularly appropriate for those with small marketing forces, low personnel turnover, and small numbers of trainees. The more important individual methods are discussed below:

On-the-Job Training

The method, sometimes known as coach-and-pupil training, is a combination of telling, showing, practising, and evaluating. The coach, who may be a professional marketing trainer but is more often a seasoned marketing-person, begins by describing to the trainee particular marketing situations; explaining various techniques and approaches that might be used effectively. Next, accompanied by the pupil, the coach makes a number of actual marketing calls, discussing each with the trainee afterwards. Then, under the coach's supervision, the trainee makes marketing calls, each one being followed by discussion and appraisal. Gradually, the trainee works more and more on his or her own, but with continuing, although increasingly less frequent, coaching sessions.

The instructional effectiveness of this method depends mainly upon the coach's qualifications. Given a qualified coach, the trainee starts off on the right foot, using marketing techniques that the company wants used. Early deficiencies are corrected before they harden into difficult to change. If, however, the coach is not qualified, the trainee probably will learn the coach's bad habits as well as skills. Furthermore, many seasoned marketing-people, otherwise well qualified for coaching, are unwilling to devote the necessary time and effort. This is especially true in companies whose marketing personnel are paid commissions on marketing. The problem of recruiting competent coaches, nevertheless, can be resolved through such means as paying bonuses for each person coached, or 'overriding' commissions on pupils' marketing for a certain period.

On-the-job training should form an important part of every initial marketing-training programme. There is no more effective way of learning about a job than by actually doing it. This method is uniquely appropriate for developing trainees' skills in making marketing presentations, answering objectives, and closing marketing. Training in these aspects of marketing requires practice, and this method provides expertly supervised practice.

Personal Conferences

The potential of this instructional method commonly goes unrecognised probably because many marketing executives assume that learning occurs only in structured situation. Psychological research, however, has demonstrated repeatedly that learning may occur in structured and unstructured, formal and informal situations. In personal conference instruction, the trainer (often a marketing executive) and trainee jointly analyse problems of mutual concern, such as effective use of marketing time, route planning and call scheduling, and handling unusual marketing problems. Because such training is expensive in terms of the trainer's time, idle chit-chat and purely personal conversation should be minimised. Maximum advantage should be taken of available time for instructional purposes.

Correspondence Courses

This instructional method is used both in initial and continuing marketing-training programmes. In the insurance field, for instance, it is used to acquaint new marketing-people with industry fundamentals and for instruction in basic marketing techniques. In companies with highly technical products and small but widely deployed marketing forces, correspondence course sometimes are use to acquaint experienced marketing-people with new product developments and applications. Occasionally, too, this method is used for training non-company marketing personnel, such as distributors' marketing-persons, with a view toward improving their knowledge of the manufacturer's product line and marketing techniques. But, despite these varied applications, effective marketing training is difficult to achieve solely through correspondence, and few companies use the method exclusively.

For most companies, correspondence training is most appropriate as an interim method of instruction when trainees are scattered geographically, but groups are assembled periodically at central points for lectures, seminars, role playing, and other instructions. Initial marketing training, for example, might be by correspondence course begin at different times and places; continuing, or follow up, training might come later through group instructional methods at a central location. Preparing a standardised correspondence course covering technical product data, general company information, marketing techniques, and markets presents few difficulties other than those of choosing, organising, and writing up the material.

Successful use of the correspondence method of instruction requires considerable administrative skills. The greatest problem is that of providing motivation to trainees to complete assignments on schedule. Not only are enrollees engaged in full-time work requiring that correspondence lesson lessons be completed after hours, but few people have sufficient self-discipline to study without some direct supervision. Usually it is necessary to provide regularly scheduled examinations, prizes for completing work by given dates, or other incentives. Nor does this instructional method provide answers to individual enrollees' question; hence, the most successful users arrange for periodic face-to-face discussions. Similar problems are met in processing trainees' completed assignments, in evaluating their work, and in correcting errors. If these and related administrative problems are solved, correspondence instruction servers as a useful supplement to other marketing-training methods.

Programmed Instruction

This instructional method represents a considerable advance over the correspondence course. It involves breaking down subject matter into numbered instructional units called 'frames,' which are then incorporated into a book. Each frame contains an explanation of a specific point, plus a question or problem for the trainee to use in testing his or her understanding. Trainees check their answers by referring to another designated frame. If answer is correct, the trainee is directed to new material; if it is incorrect, additional explanation is provided, and the trainee is retested on the point before going on to new material. Thus, trainees check their own progress as they work through the materials and may move through them at their own speed. Companies using programmed instruction, however, generally regard formal examinations as necessary incentives for the trainees.

To date, programmed instruction has not been widely adopted for marketing training purposes. Most applications have been aimed at providing needed information. The Schering Corporation, for instance, provides programmed instruction on the clinical and pharmacological background of its drug products. This method is not used widely for training in marketing techniques and market information because of difficulties in preparing appropriate programmed instructional materials. Preparation requires expert skills and thorough grounding in the psychology of learning. One ready-made programmed instructional course focusing on marketing techniques, however, is available-prepared by Jack Schiff of Pace College, for Marketing and Marketing Executives-International.

Balancing Group versus Individual Instruction

Generally group instruction is used in formal training programmes, and individual instruction is given in the field. Both have contributions to make to the overall training programme, so management must decide the role and the timing of each.

When there are large numbers of new personnel, group instructions is the most practical way to provide marketing training at the least cost per person. In planning the curriculum content of the marketing school, however, management must also determine the content that should and can be taught in the field-group instruction is often more effective when supplemented by individualised field training. To minimise needless overlap, and to maximise instructional results, careful attention must be paid to integration of what is taught by group methods in marketing schools: product data, company information, market information, and the theoretical and practical fundamentals of marketing. Advanced instruction in marketing technique usually is best handled individually, in the field.

What is called 'field training' is essentially on-the-job training, but it is conducted in the office as well as in the field. The trainee, under supervision, apportions his or her time between a branch, district, or regional office and a marketing territory. Because field training is individualised instruction, it is quite informal. In the field, the trainee learns by watching an experienced marketing-person in action and by practising marketing techniques under that individual's tutelage.

Opinion among marketing executives is divided with respect of the best timing of group versus individual instruction. Most believe that the trainee should receive formal group instruction and indoctrination before meeting the customers and starting to sell. A sizable minority, however, believe in assigning trainees to marketing jobs for individual instruction before sending them on to marketing schools. In support of the minority view, three things can be said: (1) new personnel have a chance to prove that they have what it takes to sell before money is spend on their formal training; (2) new persons are not always, not even usually, hired in groups large enough to justify immediate formal training-people hired between programmes can be put to work until the next school begins; and (3) there is considerable evidence to indicate that prior on-the-job experience not only furnishes needed learning motivation but makes formal instruction more meaningful. The minority position, nevertheless, clearly is inappropriate when highly technical products are sold to sophisticated buyers. In such cases, product training is not only highly important but best provided through formal group instruction at the outset of trainees' marketing careers.

Executing Marketing Training Programmes

A great deal of planning work and attention to detail is prerequisite to successful execution of a marketing-training programme. Important decision must be reached, as we have previously noted, on training aims, programme content, and instructional methods. Organisationally, the executive must make certain that the trainers—whether full time or on special assignment—are themselves trained and fully understand their programme responsibilities. Members of the group selected for training must be notified, necessary travel reservations made, and living accommodations arranged. Location of instructional facilities must be decided, instructional materials prepared, and training facilities must be decided, instructional materials prepared, and training aids assembled. Once these things are done, the stage is set for actual execution of the programme.

Effectiveness of programme execution, of course, depends upon instructional skills as well as skilful coordination of different planning phased and 'housekeeping' details. Successful programme administration is very much an art, but, in essence, it involves doing everything that can be done to produce a training atmosphere as conducive as possible to learning. Discussion in the following centres on (1) the timing of training programmes, (2) their location, and (3) instructional materials and training aids.

Timing Initial Marketing Training Programmes

The number of persons recruited annually directly affects the timing of initial marketing-training programmes. More precisely, timing depends upon the number of new persons who must be trained each year, and this, in turn, depends upon factors such as the size of the marketing force, marketing-personnel turnover, and management's plan for changing the size and composition of the marketing force. When the number is large, comprehensive highly structured programmes may be scheduled several times a year, the exact dates being set after consideration of recruiting quotas and deadlines. When the number is small, formal training programmes, if held at all, necessarily are scheduled more infrequently, perhaps only once each year. Thus, for example, one company with a small marketing force recruiting June college graduates schedules their training to begin in late June or early July.

There is an optimum number of trainees who may be effectively trained during a particular programme. It depends upon such factors as training aims, subject matter content, amount and availability of training talent, and instructional methods. Individualised training may be indicated in some situations, although it is expensive per individual trained, its timing can be highly flexible, depending only upon availability of trainees and trainers. In most situations, however, limitations of training funds and talent dictate that recruits be trained in groups, programmes being scheduled whenever the backlog of untrained people approximates the optimum. No precise answer can be given to the question: How large is an optimum-sized training group? Experience indicates that, for most companies, groups smaller than 12 to 15 involve inordinately high cost, while those larger than 30 to 40 incur losses in training (that is, learning) effectiveness too great to be tolerated.

Training Continuing Marketing Training Programmes

Modern marketing management regards marketing training as a never-ending process. This view recognises that initial marketing-training programmes cannot prepare the marketing-person for indefinitely effective job performance – the beneficial effects of training gradually erode away. This view also stems from modern management's conviction that all training and all learning must be continuous – new information must be assimilated, and older concepts require modification in the light of new developments. New products, new refinements of marketing techniques, new product applications and uses, new customer problems, new types of marketing aids, new marketing suggestions – all these and other developments requires that each marketing-person's training continue as long as he or she is on the job. In many situations, marketing personnel may be kept abreast of new developments informally, perhaps through field distribution of information bulletins. But when new developments accumulate, are unusually important, or imply a need for significant changes in marketing-persons attitudes and behaviour patterns, a formal retraining programme should be scheduled. Many companies integrate a short retraining programme into a series of marketing meetings or even into a single marketing convention.

In some marketing forces some but not all marketing-persons have deficiencies that many correctable through training. If their weaknesses lie in different areas, the most practical and economical solution is to use on-the-job coaching. If several people are weak in the same general area(s), it is both practical and economical to use group instructional methods in an organised formal programme (often scheduled for an off-peak marketing period).

Even, when marketing management has no clear indication of the need, regular scheduling of training programmes seems advisable. A survey of nearly 500 purchasing agents revealed that 60 per cent felt that the majority of marketing-people calling on them either had never learned or had forgotten how to sell. The same survey strongly implied that continuing training should provide marketing personnel with more adequate product information and teach them how to present it in terms of user benefits.

Management's assumption should be that marketing-people will welcome the opportunity for further training. Experience shows that most marketing personnel are eager for help in improving marketing techniques; most feel entitled to explanations of policy changes; most want to learn how to tie in their efforts more closely with advertising programmes; and most are anxious to learn more about new products, model and design improvements, and shifts in market conditions. The majority of marketing people, in other words, want to be kept abreast of current developments and welcome effort to interpret the significance of these developments in terms of their own job performance. If formal retraining programmes are designed and 'sold' as means of helping marketing-people do their jobs more effectively, they should not only be receptive to instruction but should derive benefits from it. Unless marketing personnel are convinced of the future value of continuing training, its results will fall short of what could be reasonably expected. If it can demonstrate that training results in more take-home pay and increased job satisfaction, most marketing-people will demotivated. And when marketing-people believe that these benefits may be obtained through a continuing marketing training programme, the programme's chances of successful execution are greatly enhanced.

Location of Marketing Training Programmes

Some companies hold formal initial marketing-training programmes at the central offices and plant; others conduct separately executed programmes at some or all branch offices. Each plan has advantages and disadvantages. The centralised programme held at a manufacturing plant generally provides better product training, but higher costs are incurred in bringing trainees to the central point and housing them there. In many companies, too, the small number of people to be trained does not justify decentralised formal programmes, and central location is a practical necessity. Many large companies, by way of contrast, do have the option of using decentralised training programmes. They can train new marketing-people in or near the territories to which they are later assigned, and thus can acquaint them early with field marketing problems. However, since decentralised product training often requires the substitution of motion pictures, slides, and working models, it may be less realistic, less interesting and less effective than training given at a factory. But decentralised programmes suffer from even more serious defects. Unless closely supervised by higher management, their execution tends to be poor; and the trainers, who commonly have other responsibilities and regard training as a diversionary sideline, often turn in poor teaching performances. Generally, then, except in the very large company, with its vast pool of administrative and instructional skills and other resources, formal initial marketing-training programmes should be held at central locations.

Retraining programmes for seasoned marketing-people also may be held either at centralised or decentralised points. Because these programme often are short, the decision may hinge almost entirely upon where the needed instructional talent is available and whether it is more convent and economical to transport and house the trainers or the trainees. If retraining programmes are timed to coincide with marketing conventions, they may be held nationally (either at the home office or convention headquarters elsewhere), or regionally, on decentralised basis.

Instructional Materials and Training Aids

Critically important to successful execution of a marketing-training programme are the instructional materials and training aids. The exact nature of these will vary, of course, not only for different companies but for programmes with different aims and content. Discussion in the following sections focuses on pertinent features and uses of the main types of instructional materials and training aids.

Manuals

Often known as 'workbook,' manuals are used in most formal group-type marketing-training programmes. The best manuals generally contain: outlines or summaries of the main presentations, related material, statements of learning objectives for each session, orienting questions or 'thought provokers,' cases and problems for discussion, plus directions for certain sessions, such as those involving role playing or other simulations. Many manuals also include concise statement of marketing, pricing, marketing personnel, and other policies, together with details on company systems and procedures as they apply to the marketing-person's work. A few contain detailed information on the products and their applications. Discretion should be exercised in selecting items for inclusion. It is all, too easy to clutter up a manual with information of little or infrequent value to the trainee. Manuals often are designed with a dual purpose in mind; to serve as study guides during formal training, and as references later, thus, many appear in loose-leaf form that facilitates subsequent additions changes.

Other Printed Materials

Other printed matter includes regular company bulletins, marketing and product handbooks, and industry and general business magazines and journals. Company publications are used chiefly to furnish field marketing personnel with up-to-date and needed information. Keeping field marketing personnel informed is also the main reason that many companies provide their marketing-people with subscriptions to industry and general business magazines and journals. Texts and technical and trade books are used to supplement workbook material, although trainees are rarely required to read them thoroughly during formal training. The usual practice is to assign or merely suggest selected readings, with the exceptions that the books will be used later as references.

Training Aids

A training aid is an auxiliary device capable of contributing to instructional aim through transmission of sight and/or sound stimuli. Probably the most used and indispensable training aid is blackboard—no training facility should be without one on which to illustrate points, summarise discussions, and the like, adding visual to vocal appeal. Modern substitutes for the blackboard (for example, the Vue-Graph projector, transparency roll, and screen) offer such improvement as making it possible for the instructor to face his class even while his or her writing appears on a screen, and conserving instructional time through using professionally prepared diagrams, charts, statistical tables, and so on. But no substitute is as fail-safe as a blackboard, none so free of possible mechanical or power failure. Even, when main reliance is placed upon the Vue-Graph or other mechanically operated device, blackboard and chalk should be available for standby use, and to illustrate and explain points that arise in informal discussion. Although mechanical training aids supplement or support the blackboard as the basic training aid, none supplants it entirely.

The motion-picture projector and film form an appropriate training aid, especially when the instructional aim requires the depicting of motion or description and explanation of complex situations. In conveying technical information concerning installation and operation of new machine-tool models, for example, nothing short of actual demonstration is as effective as a movie. Substantial costs are incurred in producing special training film of high quality, since professional cameramen, actors, a director, and often specially constructed, sets are needed. In deciding whether to produce tailor-made films then, management must seek to appraise their probable instructional effectiveness against the cost. Most marketing-training films seek to convey information on products and their applications, but some aim at the refinement of marketing techniques. One firm, for example, used an amateur-produced (hence, low-cost) 'candid-camera' film of its marketing personnel in action as an aid to improving their job performance. For the firm with limited funds, not wanting to resort to amateur-produced films, marketing-training films of varying quality, most relating to marketing fundamentals, are available commercially. It goes almost without saying that any training film, whether company-produced or commercially produced, should be previewed before it is used for instructional purposes.

Much of the motion picture's effectiveness can be achieved at lower cost with still pictures projected form slides or filmstrips. A sound disc may furnish a commentary together with 'timed' changes in still pictures; or the instructor may make comments, varying the change interval between pictures by using a remote-control device. Many companies produce their own training slides and filmstrips, but a wide variety of commercially produced items also is available for purchase or rental.

Tape-recording and playback equipment is ideally suited for training aimed at improving marketing techniques. Actual or simulated marketing presentations may be taped and played back for individual or group appraisal. Recent advances in miniature (and sometimes concealable) tape-recording devices even make it easy for marketing-persons to tape their own marketing interviews and play them back later. Thus, they gain greater objectivity in appraising their own effectiveness, and in finding ways to improve their performance. Larger records are used in formal programmes to tape group discussions and role-playing sessions, the tapes being played back later with appropriate commentaries and appraisals by participants and the trainer. Increasingly, too, instructions in marketing-training programmes tape their own sessions routinely. Later playbacks are helpful in improving teaching effectiveness and in conserving preparation time for repeat performances.

Closed-circuit television, not ordinarily classified as training aid, is used in place of training films, especially where instructional timing is important. It is particularly appropriate in decentralised programmes, such as those in which new product lines are being introduced to marketing-persons and/or dealer marketing personnel. Other training applications of closed-circuit television include its use in short, decentralised retraining programmes focusing on important policy changes, and as a substitute for national marketing meetings devoted primarily to training.

Evaluating Marketing Training Effectiveness

All marketing training represents investments of time, money, and effort—and marketing management should expect return commensurate with the investment. Evaluating returns from marketing training is not easy, however. Results, such as improved marketing performance, may not show up until long after programme completion. Despite such evaluation problems, it is possible to measure, somewhat roughly, training effectiveness. Management can make certain comparisons, such as the following: the length of time new marketing personnel take to attain the productivity level of the average experienced person; marketing results of trained versus untrained personnel; and the respective training histories of the most and—least effective marketing-people. A few companies plot each marketing-person's marketing records on a 'before and after' training basis, generally converting these records to share-of-the-market comparisons. It must be recognised, however, that any evaluation of training effectiveness based mainly on marketing records can be, at best, only an approximation. Territorial marketing volumes are influenced not only by marketing-people's efforts but by such important factors as competitive activity, economic fluctuation, and advertising pressure. No method yet devised is fully satisfactory for precisely isolating the influence of any one of these factors. It should be noted, too, that any quantitative evaluation of marketing-training effectiveness necessarily fails to take into account many intangible benefits from training (for example, improved marketing-force morale.) In spite of their technical deficiencies, however, comparative studies involving rough quantitative measures should provide management with a basis for evaluating training results.

Management should attempt to measure the effectiveness of individual marketing training programmes both while they are in programme and upon completion. The purpose should be to obtain needed insights for improving the effectiveness of future programmes. Tests and examinations of various kinds are used for measuring trainee retention of materials presented. These are used most appropriately when trainees are expected to memorise information, as in the case of product specification and applications. Most marketing trainers see little value in using tests and examinations for evaluating the effectiveness of training in marketing techniques. Trainees' performance in role-playing assignments may be a better means for appraising whether trainees have learned and, more important, are able to apply what they have learned.

Trainers in some companies are required to rate each trainee's performance in sessions such as in role playing, panels, and other group discussion in which he or she takes an active part. Necessarily, such ratings are subjective, but they do provide trainees with learning trainees to rate each trainer's performance, either in each session or in the total programme, is spreading. This may help in stimulating trainers to improve their instructional effectiveness. More than a few marketing executives, however, argue that trainees are in no position to judge the trainers' effectiveness until they gain additional field experience. Nevertheless, 'comment sheet' similar to that shown in Table-6 are being used in increasing number of marketing-training programmes. Many companies now also ask trainees to evaluate training programmes after they return to their territories and have had a chance to put what they have learned into practice.

Table-6

Form for Trainee Rating of Marketing-Training Session

Session Review

A brief, candid review of this training session will help you to evaluate what you have learned and help us in our efforts to improve the programme.

Please answer all questions. Do not sign your name; the results are anonymous.

Place an X where appropriate to describe your reactions to each of the following:

1. Materials covered	Exciting	☐☐☐☐☐	Dull
2. Instruction	Excellent	☐☐☐☐☐	Poor
3. Worthwhileness of material	Great	☐☐☐☐☐	Little
4. Completeness of coverage	Very Complete	☐☐☐☐☐	Totally Inadequate

5. How might the session have been improved?

____

____

____

❑❑❑

8

Quality Management to Meet Customer Satisfaction

Introduction

Midas stated that the key to actual productivity improvement is understanding the elements that can bring about productivity growth. One of these is the important leverage quality strategy can have in productivity improvement. Danforth pointed out that too many people think that high quality always cost more: this is wrong. Producing more – inefficiently – at the expense of quality is no way to increase productivity. Putting more inspectors on the line to find mistakes is the wrong approach. Doing something over again that was not done right the first time decreases efficiency, wastes money, and lowers productivity. Fiegenbaum estimated that poor quality can represent about 15–40 per cent of the plant's productive capacity. Cole estimated the impact of implementing the 'find and fix' philosophy in the automobile industry by stating: "An estimated one out of every ten workers in automobile assembly plants in the United States is engaged in repairing substandard items, resulting in truly staggering costs for scrap, rework, retest, downtime, yield losses, and disposal of substandard components." Cole further explained that another inefficiency that results from this philosophy is that it increases the number of inspectors required to detect defects.

Cole pointed out that inspection detracts from productivity and that reliance on inspectors causes employees to be less concerned about quality, which in turn leads management to hire even more inspectors. Indeed, problems are passed on to the dealer, who receives larger dealer preparation fees to make adjustments and corrections. The consumer often receives a costlier product of poor quality. This cycle reveals the disadvantages of separating quality assurance from its execution.

Quality and Customer Satisfaction

Case Study A: PCB Manufacturing Company

A manufacturing company that produces Printed Circuit Boards (PCB) to customer order was interested in improving the quality of the PCB. The parts and components used for the assembly of the boards were from different suppliers. The parts and components were assembled in a group machining process at a certain rate of PCB per hour in each machine group cell. The PCB production process operated at a yield of 63 per cent. The proportion of the output that does not conform is 37 per cent. Owing to high demand for reliable PCB, the firm can no longer afford to ship defective PCB to the customer. To resolve the problem, the firm instituted eight inspection and rework processes. The direct and indirect manufacturing cost due to inspection and rework was approximately $288,000 per week. The increased inspection and rework stations created additional problems: increased product cycle time, more work-in-process inventory, decline in labour productivity, increased handling, and additional defects created by the inspection in rework process itself. These problems also affected the overall effective utilisation of such resources as labour and energy. The profit margin of the firm was also affected significantly.

Improvement Methodology and Results

Careful analysis revealed that there was no control in place to monitor the production process. Control charts were developed and implemented in all operations. The statistical process control mechanisms enabled the process performance to be monitored properly. Corrective actions were taken to ensure good quality at the source of production. Data gathering and analysis were collected in real time. The implementation of statistical process control led to significant improvement in both productivity and quality. The tremendous amount of paper work at each station impacted labour productivity, and a work simplification technique was used that reduced twenty-four forms to five. The bottleneck problems between operations were resolved through the analysis of production time, queuing time, arrival time, and waiting time for jobs. This enabled production line balancing. Employee total involvement and commitment to quality improvement at the source of production enabled production errors to be determined and resolved in real time.

This case study demonstrates that productivity and quality are connected. Techniques implemented to improve quality also improved productivity, and *vice versa*. There is a correlation between productivity and quality; it is virtually impossible to have one without the other. However, there has to be a balance between the desire to obtain gains in productivity and the desire to improve quality. The productivity and quality objectives, actions, and resources utilised for improvements must be carefully analysed. Productivity and quality issues are corrected, interrelated, and inseparable. Productivity increases as quality improves.

Case Study B: A Shoe Manufacturing Environment

A medium-sized shoe-manufacturing company had problems in maintaining a balance of production cost, schedule, and quality. Customer complaints revealed dissatisfaction with sport shoes quality and also delays in receiving orders on time. Dress shoes were an average of 30 days behind the delivery schedule. In order to meet customer demand, the company placed emphasis on pushing the schedule. This resulted in a high production cost and decreased quality of the shoes produced. A consultant investigated the root cause of the various problems. It was determined that the production process was imbalanced. The input and output of each operation varied significantly. It was also found that the shoe injection moulding operation was introducing defects into the product. This caused additional rework to be performed. More inspectors were added to the line to inspect quality into the product. The consultant performed a motion and time study of each operation and recommended an approach to balance the production line. The injection moulding operation was redesigned.

Case Study C: A Restaurant

A fast-food restaurant unit was unsure of how to deal with the numbers of complaints received from customers who purchased hamburgers, fish sandwiches, chicken sandwiches, apple pie, french fries, and drinks for quick consumption. Within a period of 3 months there were 506 complaints from customers. The complaints ranged from an improper amount of ketchup on hamburgers to total omission of lettuce and tomatoes on some orders. A total of 216 customers also complained about the amount of time spent waiting on the line to give orders and receive food. A careful analysis of the current mode of operation revealed that the sandwich production process was not streamlined. There were cross motions between work stations, and the arrangement of lettuce, tomatoes, ketchup, salt and pepper, and other cooking ingredients was a scattered process. An attempt was made to understand the number of people expected within a given hour. From records and a random observation of the arrival patterns of customers to the restaurant, it was clear that a new strategy was needed to accommodate peak periods such as lunch from 11:30 a.m. to 1:15 p.m. and dinner from 5:30 to 7:28 p.m. The restaurant implemented two new techniques: cooking ingredients were arranged by sandwich types, and common ingredients were placed in sequence steps that allowed a better flow of work. Cross motion between attendants was eliminated. The chances of making an error were minimised. The queuing technique was used to predict the arrival pattern and total number of customers expected within a given time period. Implementation of these two new ideas resulted in 79 per cent reduction in the total number of customer complaints within an equivalent 3 month period. The average waiting time in the line was reduced from 11 minutes to 4 minutes during the peak demand periods. The fast-food unit was able to attract additional customers.

This case study shows that pressure on productivity or output in one direction without careful attention to quality can be costly. However, the improvement in the quality of services in this case study was found to have a positive impact on productivity and the overall profit posture.

Case Study D: A Bank

A medium-sized bank had received a series of complaints from checking account customers. At the end of a month, 921 customers complained of having not received the correct cancelled cheque, or the wrong transaction number was recorded in their statements. The cheque processing operation was a manual method involving almost thirty operators. The operators utilised serial code devices and organised the reader work area to process each customer batch of cheques from the main input source. A careful analysis of the operation revealed that human error and the volume of cheques processed were major contributors to the customer complaints. It was recommended that the management of the bank implement a cheque processing serialised conveyor.

The machine had the capability of organising cheques by serial number, last name, and address code. After the implementation of the new system, the jobs of thirty operators were eliminated. The number of complaints from the checking account customers was reduced from 921 to 63 per month. Most complaints after the implementation of the new cheque serialised conveyor system were about mechanical damage from the system. These complaints were kept at a minimum through proper overhauling of the system.

As shown in these four case studies, productivity and quality objectives, issues, problems, solutions, and results are interrelated. It is almost impossible to have one without the other. Organisations that put a programme in place to manage productivity and quality together are bound to receive positive results. However, benefit also comes from the application of creativity from employees and management in addressing various day-to-day production or service challenges.

Understanding the Basic Cost of Quality

In this section, an approach is presented on how the basic cost of quality is computed. The costs of conformance are made up of costs associated with prevention and appraisal. The costs of non-conformance are made up of internal and external failure costs.

Let

CA_{ijt} = Appraisal costs incurred in performing task i, in site j, in period t, resulting from inspections and repeated checks.

CP_{ijt} = Prevention costs incurred in performing task i, in site j, in period t, resulting from preventive action taken to avoid defects in design, development, manufacturing, service, and purchasing.

CI_{ijt} = Internal failure costs incurred in performing task i, in site j, in period t, resulting from items that do not conform to requirements or specifications prior to shipment from the activity or site; i = 1, 2, 3, ..., m; j = 1,2, 3, ..., k; and t = 1, 2, ...n.

CE_{ijt} = External failure costs incurred in performing task i, in site j, in period t, resulting from items that do not conform to requirements after shipments from site.

TC_{ijt} = Total cost of quality incurred in performing task i, in site j, in period t.

AV_{ijt} = Accepted units of measure for cost of quality of task i, in site j, in period t.

$$TC_{ijt} = (CA_{ijt} + CP_{ijt} + CI_{ijt} + CE_{ijt})$$

Where TC is expressed in hours of work or monetary terms.

The following steps can be used to obtain TC:

(1) Choose a specific, obervable task.

(2) List each element involved in the task.

(3) Identify the input and output of the task.

(4) Identify the effort spent on all the variables specified in expression. The components are:

CA_{ijt}, CP_{ijt}, CI_{ijt}, and CE_{ijt}

(5) Estimate in quantitative terms the time (hours) spent for each item in step 4, and compute TC_{ijt} in monetary terms by conversion.

Using the values of TC_{ijt} obtained, the analyst should investigate factors contributing to each cost category and interact with both supplier and customer or process owner to provide actions that eliminate or minimise the various cost categories. In performing the analysis, the analyst must always recognise the relationship that exists between supplier, process owner, and customer.

Cost of Inspection per Sample

In a given task, the cost of inspection per sample can be computed by expression:

$$CI_{ijt} = C_f + NC_v + (CI)\,(PI) \quad (3.2)$$

Where:

CI_{ijt} = cost of inspection per sample in task i, in site j, in period t

PI = probability of inferring the process has changed when it has not

C_f = fixed cost of inspection per sample

N = sample size

C_v = variable cost of inspection per unit

CI = cost of inferring that the process has changed when it has not.

The Productivity and Quality Problem

Although several factors contribute to the economic decline and the consequent standard of living, there seems to be general agreement that the productivity level and growth rate and the quality of goods and services can have a major impact on the national economy. For example, during the first half of last century, the United States maintained productivity leadership in the world with a fourfold labour productivity increase. However, since World War II, productivity growth in the United States has declined considerably.

The data compiled by Kendrick and Bowen reveal an awesome decline in the annual productivity growth rate in the U.S. private business sector: from 3.2 per cent to 2.1 per cent and 0.8 per cent. Rahn also presented a similar trend of labour productivity growth in the United States business.

Between January, 1985 and August, 1986, several major corporation cut back the number of workers to reduce their losses and to stay in business. Lying off workers is not the answer to productivity and quality problems. The answer lies in an ongoing improvement process that ultimately requires integration of all the elements of the work organisation to achieve the elimination of waste, reduction of cost, and defect-free product through implementation of better techniques and working conditions. Although the productivity and quality problem in the United States may be unique to its economic climate, a careful look at other countries will reveal that similar problems and trends exist in other countries as well. Kendrick presented a productivity comparison between the United States and the rest of the world. Although the quality of goods and services has received unprecedented attention in recent years, expert opinions indicate there is a lot to be done in improving quality in all industrial sectors. Juran presented his perception of the relative quality of goods and services produced by the West and those produced by Japan. Japan is shown to have a leading edge in quality. In 1980, the American Society for Quality Control conducted a survey using 10,000 questionnaires to determine the opinions of the heads of household on the quality of the goods and services produced in the United

States. The results of this survey indicate that quality deserves significant attention in all industrial sectors. Holusha stated that the quality issue has major implications for the health of the U.S. automobile industry, which reported a combined loss of more than $4 billion in 1980 and laid off more than 200,000 workers.

Productivity and Quality Management Challenges

Edosomwan stated that as the current explosion of technology continues, organisations will be faced with the following productivity and quality management challenges:

(1) **Managing the Dynamic Change in Technology Life-cycle to Improve Productivity and Quality:** As shown in the various types of technology used to improve productivity and quality in the early 1960s had an average life cycle of ten years. From the producer, supplier, and consumer perspective, the ten-year life span for a typical technology was still short before new technologies were introduced into the work environment. By 1986, most technology life cycles have shortened to about two years and six months by the year 2000. This continually shortening life cycle poses a real challenge for all organisations that desire to use technology as a mechanism for productivity and quality improvement. It requires that the change from one product type to another will be done at a much faster pace. Product model development, specification monitoring, prototype testing, product manufacturability and serviceability, and process qualification and improvement will have to be performed within a short time. Just-in-time productivity and quality improvement will require new techniques and tools for managing the dynamic change of the input and output elements in the work environment. It also requires a very close working relationship between the supplier, producer, and consumer of the goods and services.

(2) **Emphasis on Quality at the Source of Production and Service:** For several decades, the emphasis has always been on inspecting quality into a product and service. As a result, almost every process within the work organisation has an inspection station. In addition to the cycle time of a product or service, inspection stations add operations that also create additional rework, which

in turn increases the cost of production of service. By the year 2010, the shortened life cycle of technologies will not allow enough time for work-in-process inspection or inspections after each process. Quality will be needed at the source of production. All the mechanisms needed for a transformation process must perform correctly the first time with high reliability.

(3) **Technical Vitality Requirements for Productivity and Quality Management:** The complexity of the production and service processes will increase with increasingly sophisticated automation. The new technologies will require high-level skills for design, implementation, and maintenance. The productivity and quality management will require advanced interdisciplinary knowledge, with strong demand skills that will act as a systems integrator.

(4) **Motivating Workers to Increase Productivity and Improve Quality in the Work Environment:** Although several motivational techniques exist today, the effectiveness of the existing techniques may not be adequate in this era of technological explosion. New motivational techniques that address the changing values and role of workers will always be needed. More emphasis will have to be placed on task enlargement, task evaluation, psychological evaluation, morale management in real time, and other physiological needs of workers.

(5) **Assessing and Measuring the Impact of Technology on Productivity and Quality:** The rate of return on investment (ROI) and the net present value (NPV) method have been the most widely used approaches for justifying the productivity of new technologies. Defects per unit produced has also been used to justify the quality of new technologies. In the era of expanded technology, the highly capital-intensive work environment requires a comprehensive approach for justifying the productivity and quality of new technologies before and after their introduction into the work environment. Such a comprehensive approach must consider the total cost of doing business.

(6) **Managing the Impact of Group Technology Application:** In recent years, some organisations have realised benefits in productivity and quality

improvements through group technology applications. However, the group technology layout requires ongoing process control and monitoring. It is a challenge to balance the parameters and variables among processes, work cells, and machines. As GT applications receive more emphasis, appropriate productivity and quality management techniques are needed.

(7) **Planning and Analysis of Production and Service Variables:** To properly manage productivity and quality in a dynamic technology-oriented work environment, the input and output components and the factors affecting them must be carefully planned. The total cost of doing business must be analysed periodically to continue to minimise product of service cost overruns. Emphasis should be placed on using comprehensive productivity and quality planning techniques in both manufacturing and service organisations.

(8) **Managing the Loop between the Supplier, Producer, and Consumer:** Dynamic change in work processes and the technology life cycle brings about a shorter response time for all production and service requirements. Real time management of productivity and quality requires the elimination of excessive transportation, repetition of tasks, and delays between the supplier, producer, and consumer. The network of information that is the supplier, producer, and consumer loop must be achieved. Cost minimisation criteria, service turnaround time, error-free product, and service guarantee must be applied to vendor selection. For each process, material and other requirements must be delivered in time to facilitate real time productivity and quality improvement.

(9) **Ongoing Search for Productivity and Quality Management Techniques and Methodologies:** The need exists for additional techniques and methodologies for improving, monitoring, planning, analysing, measuring, and evaluating productivity and quality in a sophisticated high-technology work environment. Useful techniques for productivity and quality improvement are developed as the work organisation changes.

(10) **Managing the Changing Values and Composition of the Workforce:** As more attention is given to productivity and quality improvement through technological development and implementation, the values of the workers

are bound to change with the new technology. How the quality of working life affects productivity and quality improvement will have to be addressed. New, flexible working conditions may have to be adopted to accommodate the changing values of men and women in a technologically advanced society. Technological advancement increasingly makes it possible for many to work at home. However, unless on-line process control linkages are developed for the sophisticated information network, system downtime is bound to have a significant negative impact on the productivity and quality of goods and services.

(11) **Effective Organisation Structure for Productivity and Quality Management:** The hierarchical organisation is the most widespread in the business environment. Hierarchical organisations have stability in their favour. They provide efficient mechanisms for coordinating large numbers of people through simultaneous central direction and specialisation. However, the multi-layers of management within the hierarchical structure can sometimes be an impediment to the quick resolution of problems within a work organisation. The bureaucratic delays and bottlenecks created by the various multi-layers of management are not adequate for an environment with a dynamic need for productivity and quality improvement. By the year 2010, a typical economic entity will experience dynamic change and disturbance primarily driven from the shortened technology life cycle. To quickly respond to productivity and quality management, an alternative organisational structure that utilises fewer levels of management layers will be sought. The new form of organisational structure maybe viewed as a flattened hierarchical structure with minimal levels of management. The main benefit to be derived from such a structure is a quick response rate to people, productivity, and quality issues. It will facilitate clarity and economies of scale, direct the vision of individuals and managerial units toward performance, and improve the day-to-day decision-making process.

(12) **Better Coordination of the Productivity and Quality Management Hierarchy:** For our tools and techniques to improve productivity and quality, the state or level of application within the productivity and quality management hierarchy, must be carefully understood.

Components of the Comprehensive Productivity and Quality Management Model

The comprehensive productivity and quality management model components encompass a management information system and a feedback mechanism that provide the necessary information about production or service process characteristics and variables, process performance through measurement, action on the process inputs, the transformation process, and action on the output. To improve productivity and quality, all production and service parameters must be characterised with complete understanding of repeatability and variability. There must be a system for real time measurement, control, evaluation, planning, and improvement. Correction of problems and defect removal should be done through system-aided root cause analysis. Every step towards quality management should be towards maintenance or upgradation in quality of the product or service to suit to the needs of ultimate user.

❑❑❑

Index

❑❑❑